Aging and the Aged in Medieval Europe

edited by

Michael M. Sheehan, CSB

It is generally known that some of the institutions that support the elderly in modern society developed in Europe during the Middle Ages. The degree, however, to which the medieval world reflected on the meaning and causes of aging, its attitudes towards the elderly, their number in proportion to the general population, and questions touching the ways in which individuals, families, and the society as a whole sought to provide for its aging members are, for the most part, unknown. Given the importance of such questions today, it is not without interest for all of us to be more aware of the roots of this aspect of our society. The essays collected in this volume provide a significant step forward in our knowledge of these matters.

Information on the understanding of aging by physician, philosopher, and theologian, description of the methods of delaying the onset and alleviating the symptoms of old age, reflection on the meaning and value of those last years within the divine plan of creation, and preliminary soundings on attitudes to the aged, as revealed by literature and the history of language, are presented in the first part of the collection. A second series of essays looks to the aged themselves, exploring their number, their condition within local societies, and the various expedients that were developed to provide for them as their powers diminished. The welfare limitations of medieval society are patent, but it is suggested by these studies that some of its attitudes towards the elderly and some of its methods in coping with the problems concomitant with aging were remarkably sophisticated. On occasion, they suggest the necessity of second thoughts about attitudes and solutions that have become sacred in modern social thinking.

An introductory bibliography suggests lines of future research.

PAPERS IN MEDIAEVAL STUDIES

11

AGING AND THE AGED

IN MEDIEVAL EUROPE

Selected Papers from the Annual Conference of the
Centre for Medieval Studies, University of Toronto,
held 25-26 February and 11-12 November 1983

edited by

MICHAEL M. SHEEHAN, CSB

PONTIFICAL INSTITUTE OF MEDIAEVAL STUDIES

CANADIAN CATALOGUING IN PUBLICATION DATA

Main entry under title:
Aging and the aged in medieval Europe

(Papers in mediaeval studies ; 11)
Includes bibliographical references.
ISBN 0-88844-811-2

1. Aged - Europe - History - Congresses.   2. Aging -
Europe - History - Congresses.   3. Social history -
Medieval, 500-1500 - Congresses.   I. Sheehan, Michael
M. (Michael McMahon), 1925-   . II. University of
Toronto.   Centre for Medieval Studies.   Conference
(1983).   III. Pontifical Institute of Mediaeval
Studies.   IV. Series.

HQ1064.E9A344 1990   305.26'094'0902   C89-090761-7

𝐿𝐴 801

© 1990 by

Pontifical Institute of Mediaeval Studies
59 Queen's Park Crescent East
Toronto, Ontario, Canada M5S 2C4

ASHLEY CRANDELL AMOS

PATRICK OSMUND LEWRY

FRANK TALMAGE

friends and colleagues

TO   THEIR   MEMORY

Acknowledgements

The Centre for Medieval Studies of the University of Toronto organized the Conference on Aging and the Aged in Medieval Europe in 1983. The Planning Committee included Sharon Ady, Rosemary Beattie, John Boyle, Bert Hall, William Leckie, Osmund Lewry (†), John McCall, Nancy McElwee, Maureen Riggin, Michael Sheehan, Robert Taylor, Prudence Tracy, and Norman Zacour. They saw the conference through all stages of planning and execution.

The assistance of Professors Jocelyn Hillgarth and Joseph Shatzmiller was crucial in the decision to publish the collection of the papers that had been selected. Dr. Antonette diPaolo Healey, Professor Norman Zacour, and my Basilian confreres Claude Arnold, William Irwin, Armand Maurer, and Joseph Wey helped solve many problems in the preparation of the text.

Publication of this volume was assisted by the Centre for Medieval Studies of the University of Toronto, which made its computer type-setting and printing equipment available, and by a grant from the estate of the late Dr. E. Dawne Jubb. Anna Burko was of invaluable assistance in the edition of the text and in the preparation of photoready copy.

To all, my thanks.

M.M.S.

Contents

Part Two
The Elderly: Numbers, Activity, Support

Foreword

Michael M. Sheehan, CSB

Pontifical Institute of Mediaeval Studies

Saint Benedict considered the "elders" to be the backbone of his monastery. In his *Rule,* these *seniores,* wise in the passage of the years, were expected to oversee manual labour, meals, and the novitiate; they were to listen to the troubles of the monks and, where necessary, to their sins. And they were to be honoured by their younger confreres. Less frequently mentioned are the *senes,* the "old men." They were not equated with the sick, but were discussed with the youngest members of the house, those who, incomplete as they were, required special care. A realistic comment on the fact that the maturity that brought ability for major responsibilities might also bring diminished capacity is provided in the discussion of the monastic porter. This officer was to be a "wise old man" (*senex sapiens*): his wisdom enabled him to make the decisions his office required, but his age kept him at his post, for he was unable to move without difficulty.

Thus centuries ago, in one of the most stable of Western institutions, one that has proved well able to integrate its elderly members exploiting their strength and providing for their weakness, the equivocal quality of old age was stated. In our contemporary world, the policy of defining the limited capacity of those who grow old in chronological terms has brought with it a set of problems not faced in the matter of fact way of the *Rule* but partly hidden in euphemism; the problems remain and on a scale without precedent. The process of aging has become the object of a major enterprise of study and invention and we have observed the adaptation and creation of social supports to provide for the needs of the elderly as these have been identified. Many of these developments are largely or completely new, only made possible by the progress in many fields that is characteristic of our era. But, though much that has been done during the past thirty years is unprecedented, our attitudes towards these matters seem to be derived to a considerable extent from our past. Those attitudes, deeply rooted in history, have important consequences for what is done today, including decisions on the allocation of resources. Thus it seemed appropriate, as part of the scholarly enterprise that is presently given to the examination of problems touching the process of aging and the elderly themselves, to examine the experiences of medieval Europe that have contributed to the formation of contemporary attitudes. Furthermore, as many of the social usages and support institutions of the Middle Ages are the remote ancestors of our own, their history too needs to be known.

As the Conference Committee of the Centre for Medieval Studies began discussions, the ramifications of its theme, "Aging and the Aged in Medieval Europe," unfolded to reveal problems and possibilities of daunting richness. It soon became clear that, while medieval writers often reflected on the aging process and described it in considerable detail, there was little reflection on the elderly as a social group or on the specific assistance that was needed by them. Thus it was evident that it would be possible to design a programme that would discuss aging as conceived by medieval thinkers; but, when it came to an analysis of the position of the aged in that society and the special supports that it provided for them, questions would have to be asked of sources in terms that the creators of those sources never envisioned. In other words, it would be necessary to impose contemporary preoccupations on a society that scarcely thought of them, an enterprise at once a challenge to the historian and a danger.

Thus it was possible to propose papers based on medical treatises that would describe the symptoms of old age and the physiological process of aging, would seek to explain it and propose ways of delaying its onset or assuaging its effect. With the philosophers, exegetes, and theologians of the various medieval traditions, explanations of the aging process from various points of view suggested attitudes to be adopted towards it and its victims; some explanation of the purpose of aging could be expected as well. These attitudes towards aging and the aged were known to be reflected in a more subjective way in literature. Here many lines of approach could be developed. The analysis of the formation of vocabulary touching the old and of the sets of meanings of associated words was one of them. Or again, descriptions of the physical appearance of the elderly by poets and prose writers provided a spectrum of possibility from the objective to social criticism and satire. Furthermore, it was expected that much could be learned along these lines from the graphic and plastic arts. Finally there were the reflections on being old by the elderly themselves. Such projects would have to ransack a vast body of literature in many languages and an iconography of major proportions. The understanding that they might provide could also be refined by comparisons of the perceptions of old age and the elderly in other cultures, comparisons that could at once provide a criticism of and an insight into the one that was being explored in detail.

Then there was the problem of the position of the aged in society. Was there any recognition of them as a group in social, family, or religious ritual? Did custom or law identify the elderly of any class or status and provide for and limit them in any way? Were there roles that they tended or were expected to assume? Furthermore, how did medievals provide for their elderly? Granted that preliminary indications were vindicated and it was the lameness, decrepitude, blindness, more frequent illness, or general inability to perform the task long expected of certain members of society, rather than the fact that they were seen to be old, that led to the provision of special care for them, it is still possible to ask the questions that preoccupy us today. What can be learned of their role and their care within the family, be it the family based on kinship or those elective families based on religious vows? (A similar question might be asked of the diocesan clergy, a numerous group whose way of life sometimes tended to sever them from both forms of social support.) In other cases the family solution and its cognate arrangements are known to have been abandoned in preference for care in the alms houses and hospitals that proliferated at the time and that may already have been moved to distinguish between those elderly who could, with housing and a small supplementary income, provide for themselves and those who were dependent not only on those services but also on the care of others. Finally there was the corody, an arrangement by which the elderly were sometimes associated with a religious community so that, with varying degrees of independence, they could enjoy the kind of support that a prosperous religious house could provide for its members. Much has been written of the corody, often because of the disputes and the criticism it involved, but what was its actual significance in terms of need during the period in question? All of these solutions can, in the end, be examined from the point of view of their provision of basic needs: what can be known of the diet, clothing, and housing provided for the elderly in each of the different arrangements that they made or that were made for them?

It was with this vast field of research in mind that the Conference Committee requested papers on the theme "Aging and the Aged in Medieval Europe." Of the many offered, twenty-six were selected for the sessions held 25-26 February and 11-12 November 1983. A selection of those presentations is offered in the essays that follow.

Abbreviations

ASF	Archivio di Stato di Firenze
BHG	*Bibliotheca hagiographica Graeca*
BL	British Library (London)
BN	Bibliothèque nationale (Paris)
BRO	Berkshire Record Office
BRUO	*Biographical Register of the University of Oxford*
CChR	*Calendar of Charter Rolls*
CPR	*Calendar of Patent Rolls*
CR	*Close Rolls*
CSEL	Corpus scriptorum ecclesiasticorum Latinorum
CUL	Cambridge University Library
EETS	Early English Text Society
ERO	Essex Record Office
GLRO	Greater London Record Office
Gmc.	Germanic
Go.	Gothic
HME	*Historia monachorum in Ægypto*
Lat.	Latin
MGH	Monumenta Germaniae historica
ML	Medieval Latin
ModE	Modern English
MS(S)	manuscript(s)
NLM	National Library of Medicine (Bethesda, Md.)
NRO	Norfolk Record Office
ODEE	*Oxford Dictionary of English Etymology*
OE	Old English
OED	*Oxford English Dictionary*
OFr.	Old Frisian
OHG	Old High German
ON	Old Norse
OS	Old Saxon
P & J	"Pelagius and John" (see below, p. 64, n. 2)
PG	Patrologia Graeca
PL	Patrologia Latina
PRO	Public Record Office
SRO	Suffolk Record Office
T.B.	*Talmud Babli*
VCH	*Victorian County History*

Part One

Understanding of the Aging Process

and Attitudes to the Aged

1

The Care and Extension of Old Age
in Medieval Medicine

Luke Demaitre

Pace University

The rising prominence of geriatrics as a medical specialization is not yet reflected in a comprehensive study of its pre-modern antecedents.[1] The treatment of aging in medieval medicine remains largely unexplored, in contrast with analogous fields such as obstetrics and gynecology.[2] Therefore, and in the interest of time, this paper is intended as a preliminary survey and as an introduction to further exploration rather than as an in-depth discussion of one particular author or aspect, even though the latter proposition often seemed more attractive in the course of my research. An earlier endeavour to survey medieval pediatrics,[3] and the study of medical writings on the whole, have made me conscious of several pitfalls, among which the danger of oversimplification is only one.

---

[1] The most recent general survey from a medical-historical viewpoint is by Joseph T. Freeman, *Aging: Its History and Literature* (New York, 1979). Focused on the pre-industrial era and narrower in scope is Gerald J. Gruman, *A History of Ideas about the Prolongation of Life: The Evolution of Prolongevity Hypotheses to 1800* (Philadelphia, 1966). Gruman has also edited a series of twelve articles by Frederick D. Zeman, "Life's Later Years: Studies in the Medical History of Old Age" (1942-1950), together with reprinted essays of other authors, in *Roots of Modern Gerontology and Geriatrics* (New York, 1979). The most scholarly historiographical introduction is Mirko D. Grmek, *On Ageing and Old Age: Basic Problems and Historic Aspects of Gerontology and Geriatrics,* Monographiae biologicae 5.2 (The Hague, 1958).

[2] In addition to Paul Diepgen, *Frau und Frauenheilkunde in der Kultur des Mittelalters* (Stuttgart, 1963), the literature on this field keeps growing, stimulated both by contemporary interests and by the age-old fascination with Trotula.

[3] Luke Demaitre, "The Idea of Childhood and Child Care in Medical Writings of the Middle Ages," *Journal of Psychohistory* 4 (1977) 461-490. Since more research is needed on medieval pediatrics, it is gratifying to see my findings utilized and expanded by Silvia Nagel, "Puer e pueritia nella letteratura medica del XIII secolo," in *Per una storia del costume educativo (Età classica e medio evo),* Fondazione Giangiacomo Feltrinelli, *Quaderni* 23 (1983) 87-107.

Aging and the Aged in Medieval Europe, ed. Michael M. Sheehan, CSB. Papers in Mediaeval Studies 11 (Toronto: Pontifical Institute of Mediaeval Studies, 1990), pp. 3-22. © P.I.M.S., 1990.

Before the fifteenth century only a handful of works were devoted exclusively to the care of old age – fewer, in fact, than were devoted to childhood – so that the pertinent passages must be traced in a great variety of compendia on pathology and therapeutics. Moreover, the medical treatises that lend themselves most readily to comparative analysis are those on theory: they dovetail with doctrines of natural philosophy and themes of literature, and their examination might overlap too much with other papers in this collection. However, even the medieval writings on "practical medicine" are mostly prescriptive or normative rather than descriptive, and thus they present what ought to be done rather than documenting what really occurred. Clinical observations and, above all, information about actual procedures must be gleaned from didactic *exempla* and casual remarks scattered throughout texts that range from scholastic commentaries to individualized *consilia*. As I will show with a few illustrations, such references deserve to be collated systematically – however time-consuming this process may be – because they promise to yield far more lively and more reliable insights than can be derived from the following synopsis of the major phases.

Medieval geriatric thought drew upon the three major medical traditions. The Greek legacy of the Hippocratic corpus and of Galen's writings may be characterized as primarily diagnostic and dietetic.[4] The Arabic authors of the tenth and eleventh centuries, especially Haly Abbas in his *Liber regalis,* Haly ibn Ridwan in his *Tegni,* and Avicenna in his *Canon,* emphasized formulas and polypharmacy.[5] The European tradition, commonly ignored and indeed quite latent in many academic treatises after the age of monastic and cathedral schools, evinced a concern with the concrete and mundane aspects of aging. During the twelfth century Arabic influences became more dominant than their Greek sources, for example in the Salernitan therapeutics and in the *Regimen of Health* of Moses Maimonides.[6] Two generations later, classical refer-

---

[4] The most pertinent Hippocratic loci are *Aphorismi* 1.13-14; 2.39-40, 44, 54; 3.18, 31; 6.6, 57; and 7.41, 82; *De morbo sacro* 1.22; and *De septimanis.* Galen, *De causis pulsuum* 3.5, *De marcore* 2 and 5, *De sanitate tuenda* 5, and *De temperamentis* 2.2.

[5] Haly Abbas, *Liber regalis* 1.1.21 and 2.1.24; Haly ibn Ridwan, *Tegni* 3.123; Avicenna, *Canon* 1.1.2.3, and *Cantica* 2.99-104; see Trevor H. Howell, "Avicenna and the Care of the Aged," *The Gerontologist* 12 (1972) 424-426.

[6] The *Flos medicinae scholae Salerni* in *Collectio Salernitana* 5, ed. Salvatore de Renzi (Naples, 1859), verses 32, 229, 268, 340, 412, 1820, and 2717-2718. Also Brian Lawn, *The Prose Salernitan Questions Edited from a Bodleian Manuscript (Auct.F.3.10)* (London, 1979), *quaestiones* B186, B242, Ba29, BA47, Ba59, L2, P22, P31-32, P73, P135, C10. Moses Maimonides, *The Preservation of Youth,* trans. (from the original Arabic of the "Essays on Health") Hirsch L. Gordon (New York, 1958). Maimonides, *Über die Lebensdauer: Ein unediertes Responsum herausgegeben,*

ences were totally absent from Roger Bacon's books *On the Delay of the Consequences of Old Age* and *On the Preservation of Youth*.[7] Much of the latter work was appropriated – though also altered more substantially than some historians have suggested –[8] by Arnald de Villanova (1235-1311) around 1300.[9] Arnald, and several of his contemporaries at the universities of Montpellier and Padua, strove to combine the three medical traditions in their geriatric prescriptions and in their discussions of the aging process.[10] I am puzzled, however, by the impression that the growing number of explicit references to Galen is not matched by closer adherence to the sensible chapters on gerontology ("senum curandorum scientia" or "epistēmē gērokomikē") in his *Hygiene* or *De sanitate tuenda*.[11] This may be due to an incomplete translation or to another flaw

---

übersetzt, und erklärt von Gotthold Weil (Basel, 1953). Samuel Kottek, "L'Art de conserver sa santé: Essai de comparaison entre un texte de Maimonide (Hilchot Deot, ch.4) et le *Regimen sanitatis* de Salerne," *Revue d'histoire de la médecine hébraïque* 87 (1970) 5-9.

[7] *De retardatione accidentium senectutis cum aliis opusculis de rebus medicinalibus*, ed. Andrew G. Little and Edward Withington in *Opera hactenus inedita Rogeri Baconi*, Fasc. 9 (Oxford, 1928).

[8] Arnaldus de Villanova, *Epistola de accidentibus senectutis et senii*, in Magninus Mediolanensis, *Regimen sanitatis* (Strasbourg, 1503), fols. 114r-128r; and *De conservanda iuventute et retardanda senectute*, in *Opera omnia* (Lyon, 1509), fols. 86r-90v. Arnald's dependence on Roger Bacon seems overstated by Withington in his introduction to *De retardatione*, pp. xlii-xliii and, even more, by Else Förster, *Roger Bacons De retardandis senectutis accidentibus et de sensibus conservandis und Arnald von Villanovas De conservanda iuventute et retardanda senectute* (Leipzig, 1924). Förster was contradicted, with the charge that she did not see Bacon's *De conservatione iuventutis*, by Johann Steudel, "Zur Geschichte der Lehre von den Greisenkrankheiten," *Sudhoffs Archiv* 35 (1942) 9.

[9] Arnald's *De conservanda iuventute* was translated into English by Dr. Jonas Drummond in 1544, ed. Charles L. Dana, *The Conservation of Youth and Defense of Age* (Woodstock, Vt., 1912). There is also an Italian translation by Clodomiro Mancini and Gino Fravega, *Il libro di Arnaldo da Villanova sul modo di conservare la gioventù e ritardare la vecchiaia* (Genoa, 1963).

[10] Thus, Bernard de Angrarra, *Questiones circa libros amphorismorum et artem commentatam*, in Erfurt, Wissenschaftliche Bibliothek der Stadt, MS. Amplon. F 290, fols. 40r, 56r, 65v, 72v, 115v, 116r. Bernard de Gordon, *De conservatione vite humane*, 4: *Regimen sanitatis*, in Paris, BN, MS. lat. 16189, fols. 156r-170r; *De marasmode*, in Vatican MS. Pal. lat. 1234, fols. 135-139. Magninus Mediolanensis, *Regimen sanitatis* (see n. 8 above), fols. 8-10, 15, 38v. Over a dozen *quaestiones* on senescence and prolongevity raised by Taddeo Alderotti, Dino del Garbo, Turisanus, and Guglielmo de Brixia are listed by Nancy Siraisi, *Taddeo Alderotti and his Pupils* (Princeton, 1981), pp. 319-402.

[11] Book 5, chapters 8-10, in *Galeni Opera omnia*, 20 vols., ed. Carl G. Kuhn (Leipzig, 1821-1833), 6: 345-360. While the early fourteenth-century physicians cite Galen for their biological views on aging (and for many of their therapeutic prescriptions elsewhere), they seem to ignore Book 5 of the *Hygiene*. It is possible that this book was not included in earlier translations such as that by Burgundio of Pisa (12th century), even though the translation by Niccolo da Reggio (fl. 1308-1345), *Libri sanativorum I-V*, was characterized as "translatio nova": see Lynn Thorndike and Pearl Kibre, *A Catalogue of Incipits of Mediaeval Scientific Writings in Latin* (Cambridge, Mass., 1963), 479 and 87.

in the textual transmission, as is the case for the *Texaurus regis Francie* composed by Guido da Vigevano for Philip VI in 1335. Guido's book apparently did not circulate, so that the first part, *On the Preservation of Health of the Old* failed to contribute to the elaboration of this field.[12] The same fate befell a large number of *consilia* and of individualized regimens drawn up by fourteenth-century physicians for their illustrious or well-heeled patients.[13] On the other hand, a rather plain *Treatise on the Regimen of Man,* compiled by Sigismund Albich (1347-1427), physician to the notorious King Wenceslas IV of Bohemia (†1419), seems to have become celebrated under the title *Vetularius.*[14]

From the last quarter of the fifteenth century we have three very different yet equally fascinating works. The strangest is the neoplatonist *Liber de vita producenda sive longa* by Marsilio Ficino (1433-1499), the humanist physician to the Medicis.[15] The first printed monograph on old age is the *Gerontocomia,* written for Innocent VIII by Gabriele Zerbi who, ironically, was assassinated in 1505 by the slaves of a Turkish pasha whose life he had been unable to prolong.[16] The *Gerontocomia* was

---

[12] According to Grmek, *On Ageing,* p. 58, the single MS containing this part, Paris, BN, MS. lat. 11015, was "misplaced" and thus remained unknown. For more detailed information see Bert S. Hall, "Guido da Vigevano's *Texaurus regis Franciae,*" in *Studies on Medieval Fachliteratur,* ed. William Eamon, Scripta: Mediaeval and Renaissance Texts and Studies 6 (Brussels, 1982), pp. 33-44. Hall (p. 36) cites a second MS (A.D. 1375), which also remained obscured until its recent acquisition by the Center for British Art at Yale University, and he suggests (p. 36 n. 1, on the authority of Ernest Wickersheimer) that a third copy of the first part occurs as *Liber de regimine sanitatis* at the end of Chantilly, Musée Condé, MS. 569. Hall further states (p. 37) that Guido's geriatric advice "is culled mainly from the pages of Galen's *De sanitate tuenda,*" a point that merits further investigation.

[13] While several of the treatises cited in this paper were dedicated to distinguished patrons, the custom-made regimens that might yield more information on "actual" geriatrics still need to be retrieved from the MSS. Also the *consilia* await collation and comprehensive study, towards which a first step was taken by Peter Riesenberg, "The *Consilia* Literature: A Prospectus," *Manuscripta* 6 (1962) 3-22.

[14] According to Grmek, *On Ageing,* p. 58, and in the MSS listed in Thorndike and Kibre, *Catalogue of Incipits,* 861. I have consulted National Library of Medicine (formerly Armed Forces Medical Library, Bethesda, Md.) MS. 491, fols. 3r-14r, which may be incomplete since it is simply titled *Regimen sanitatis* and pays no special attention to old age.

[15] See Antonio Costa, "Echi celsiani e spiriti nuovi in un libro quattrocentesco d'igiene dell'età senile (il *De vita producenda sive longa* di Marsilio Ficino)," *Archivio "De vecchi" per l'anatomia patologica* 62 (1977) 223-236. Written and printed in 1489 as the second volume of Ficino's triptych *De triplici vita,* this work owes much to Arnald de Villanova. It also repeats much from Book 1 (*On the Health of Scholars,* 1480) and anticipates the astrological-magical medicine of Book 3 (*On Obtaining Life in Heaven,* 1490). I am indebted for this information to Professor John Clark of Fordham University, who is preparing a critical edition.

[16] *G. Zerbi Veronensis ad Innocentium VIII Pon. Max. Gerontocomia feliciter incipit* (Rome, 1489). See Frederic D. Zeman, "The *Gerontocomia* of Gabriele Zerbi: A Fifteenth-Century Manual of Hygiene for the Aged," *Journal of the Mount Sinai Hospital* [New York] 10 (1944) 710-716. See also Grmek, *On Ageing,* p. 26. The most comprehensive survey of Zerbi's life and writings is in Levi R. Lind, *Studies in Pre-Vesalian Anatomy* (Philadelphia, 1975), pp. 141-156.

published in 1489 but is extant in very few copies.[17] Finally, a work of which only a single manuscript exists but which deserves to be edited because it recapitulates most of the earlier authors (including Ficino and Zerbi), is the treatise *On the Preservation of Old Age,* written around 1500 for Archbishop Lorenz of Würzburg by Burchard Horneck, physician to Emperor Frederick III.[18]

If 1500 is a convenient date to end this quick synopsis, and if a new age began in geriatric medicine with the iconoclasm of Paracelsus (1493-1541)[19] and with the pathological anatomy of Antonio Benivieni (1440-1502) – and of Leonardo da Vinci (1452-1519), who dissected a centenarian –[20], it is important to emphasize the continuity of history. Most of the earlier ideas on aging were adopted by such sixteenth-century physicians as Luigi Cornaro and Girolamo Cardano, David de Pomis and Jean Fernel, Laurent Joubert and André du Laurens.[21] In fact, the

[17] The only copy in North America is at the National Library of Medicine in Bethesda, Maryland. An English translation by Levi R. Lind (Philadelphia, 1988) was published too late and proved too unreliable to be utilized for this paper.

[18] Burchard Horneck or Hornecke, *De senectute conservanda,* in Bethesda, NLM, MS. 500, fols. 24r-94[95]r, *incipit* [Prologue] "Cum mecum ipso duram humani generis sortem revolverem ..." [Text] "Senectus quam Galienus semitam ad mortem appellat ...." I have discovered recently that the treatise, which I have transcribed, was largely plagiarized from Zerbi's *Gerontocomia* with substantial omissions, several rearrangements, and revealing interpolations. This discovery, which does not affect the tenor of the present paper, is discussed in my forthcoming article on "The Care of Health in Old Age: The Development of Gerocomy in the Renaissance," for *Aging and the Life Cycle in the Renaissance,* ed. Adele Seeff and Edward Ansello (University of Delaware Press, in preparation).

[19] Theophrastus Bombastus von Hohenheim, *De vita longa libri IV* (Basel, 1560). See G. Pfohl, "Paracelsus-Geriatrie und Gegenwartsgerontologie," *Medizinische Welt* 29 (1978) 1862-1866. E. F. Scheller, *Langlebigkeit mit Paracelsus-Arzneien: Versuch einer Geriatrie nach Paracelsus* (Heidelberg, 1977). K. Quecke, "Gerontologie und Geriatrie im Schrifttum des Paracelsus," *Medizinische Monatspiegel* 8 (1959) 193-197.

[20] Joshua Leibowitz, "Early Accounts in Geriatric Pathology (Leonardo, Harvey, James Keill)," *Koroth* 7 (1980) 254. See also Elmer Belt, "Leonardo da Vinci's Studies on the Aging Process," *Geriatrics* 7 (1952) 205-210.

[21] Luigi Cornaro (1467-1566) of Venice, who died just weeks before his hundredth birthday, wrote the *Trattato della vita sobria* when he was 83. See William B. Walker, "Luigi Cornaro, a Renaissance Writer on Personal Hygiene," *Bulletin of the History of Medicine* 28 (1954) 525-534. Girolamo Cardano (1501-1576), Milanese physician and mathematician, poignantly described his own aging process in *De propria vita liber* (1575). His voluminous writings also include *De sanitate tuenda* (Book 4: *De senectute*) and *De utilitate ex adversis capienda* (Book 2: *De senectute*). David de Pomis (1525-ca. 1600), a Jewish practitioner in Venice, wrote *Enarratio brevis de senum affectibus praecavendis* (Venice, 1558). See A. Mecchia and L. di Florio, "Cenni di geriatria in un'opera del medico umbro, Davide de Pomis," *Pagine di storia della medicina* 10 (1966) 58-62. Jean Fernel (1497-1558), champion of Galenism in Paris, discussed the aging process in the "Physiologia" (3.5) and "Pathologia" (4.16) of his *Medicina* (Paris, 1554). Laurent Joubert (1529-1583), Montpellier professor, reviewed the traditional question "Whether it is possible to prolong man's life through the use of medicine," in the second chapter of his *Erreurs populaires au fait de la médecine et régime de santé.* The chapter is translated by Frederick M. Gale in *Journal of the History of Medicine and Allied Sciences* 26 (1971) 391-399. André du Laurens (1558-1609), physician to Henri IV, left *A Discourse of the Preservation of the Sight ... and of Old Age ...,* trans. Richard Surphlet (London,

"Scientific Revolution" hardly made a dent in the traditional definitions, pathology, and therapeutics of old age until well into the nineteenth century.[22]

The medical definitions of old age varied widely when it came to chronology, with some medieval authors placing the beginning of senescence as early as at thirty-five and others as late as at seventy.[23] Even between Hippocrates and Galen there was a rather marked difference. Of the Hippocratic seven ages of man, the sixth (from forty-five to fifty-six) was called *presbutēs* or "seniority," and the seventh (from fifty-six on) *gerōn* or "old age": this division may sometimes be found behind the medieval distinction between the *senectus* of *senes* and the *senium* or advanced old age of *seniores*.[24] Galen's fourfold division of life, however, in which old age or *gerōn* began at the end of adulthood around sixty, prevailed as part of the fourfold humoral scheme. This scheme, which may be viewed as a philosophical and physiological forerunner of the scientific and physical DNA principle, attempted to explain all processes of life in qualitative terms as the interaction of warm, cold, dry, and moist; as the result of "innate heat" (*calor naturalis*) and "radical moisture" (*humidum radicale*); and as the changing mixture of the "secondary humours," namely phlegm, blood, choler or yellow bile, and melancholy or black bile. In this humoral scheme, senescence was explained as a progressive cooling and drying of the body, with a rise in the melancholic and ultimately in

---

1599). Several other sixteenth-century medical authors, whose works need to be examined as evidence of continuous traditions – and of expanding interest – in geriatrics, include Diomedes Amicus, Aurelio Anselmo, Jacques Bording, Henry Cuffe, Castore Durante, and Gilbert Fuchs.

[22] See Grmek, *On Ageing,* p. 53, and Steudel, "Zur Geschichte," p. 8. Suffice it to cite a few post-Harvey authors: Benedictus de Bacquere, *Senum medicus* (Cologne, 1673); Harcourt de Longeville, *Histoire des personnes ... qui ont rajeuni, avec le sécret de rajeunissement, tiré d'Arnould de Villeneuve* ... (Paris, 1714); Johann H. Cohausen, *Hermippus redivivus, sive Exercitatio physicomedica curiosa de methodo rara ad CXV annos prorogandae senectutis per anhelitum puellarum ...* (Frankfurt, 1742); Sir John Floyer, *Medicina gerocomica: or, The Galenic Art of Preserving Old Men's Healths ...* (London, 1724).

[23] The earliest *terminus a quo* occurs, for example, in the definition by Bernard de Gordon, "Senectus seu [etas] consistencie durat a xxxv fere usque ad lx annos," *Liber pronosticorum,* in Vatican MS. Pal. 1174, fol. 83v; "secunda etas adolescentie seu iuventutis extendit se usque ad xxxv annos ...; tercia autem etas ... est etas senectutis usque ad extremum vite," *Regimen sanitatis,* ibid., fol. 53r. At least *senium* (see n. 24 below) was thought to begin at seventy, the end of man's normal allotted span in the biblical tradition (Ps. 90 [89]:10). Physicians with a yen for astrology and numerology devoted special attention to the multiples of seven. The background of this chronology is summarized in my review of John A. Burrow, *The Ages of Man: A Study in Medieval Writing and Thought* (Oxford, 1986), in the *Bulletin of the History of Medicine* 62 (1988) 298-299.

[24] This distinction is attributed to Roger Bacon (and contrasted with the synonymy of *senectus* and *senium* in the Latin versions of Greek and Arabic works), with the suggestion of a Christian origin, by Withington in the introduction to *De retardatione,* p. xxxvii.

the phlegmatic humour; hence, the complexion of old age was defined as inherently cold and dry but "accidentally" or secondarily also cold and moist. Furthermore, since life was essentially based on continuous digestion or combustion, in analogy with the flame fed by the burning wick and fueling oil in a lamp, the aging process was also defined as the advanced wasting of the innate heat until it became inadequate to keep up with the remaining radical moisture, however little.[25]

Galen's emphasis on wasting (*marasmos, marcor*), or on the weakening of the metaphorical wick, had two significant corollaries for Galenic practitioners. It would cause skepticism towards the possibility of delaying an intrinsic development in the body, and thus towards claims of prolonging life by external artifice. Second, this emphasis underlay the prescription of a lean diet to prevent premature drowning of the flame. When Arabic authors, on the other hand, stressed the drying out or *desiccatio*, that is, the depletion of the metaphorical oil as the cause of aging and death, they encouraged the belief that it was possible to extend life by diet and special remedies: thanks to these authors, the quest for eternal youth was for centuries to enjoy respectability within medical science, as I will indicate shortly.[26] Still with regard to the aging process itself, I should point out that it was not considered a disease by most medieval physicians who debated this topic in formal *questiones,* their equivalent of the scholastic *quodlibeta.*[27] Hence we may question the assertion of one historian that they adhered to the "doctrine that the process of aging

---

[25] See especially Thomas S. Hall, "Life, Death, and the Radical Moisture: A Study of Thematic Pattern in Medieval Medical Theory," *Clio medica* 6 (1971) 3-23. Also Peter H. Niebyl, "Old Age, Fever, and the Lamp Metaphor," *Journal of the History of Medicine and Allied Sciences* 26 (1971) 351-368; Theoharis Theoharides, "Galen on Marasmus," ibid., pp. 369-390; and Michael McVaugh, "The 'humidum radicale' in Thirteenth-Century Medicine," *Traditio* 30 (1974) 259-283. The humoral scheme permeated from medicine into theology, for example in the thirteenth century when Saint Bonaventure attributed the symptoms of aging (trembling, grey hair, abdominal swelling, and decline of libido) to original sin as the ultimate cause, but to the increase of phlegm and melancholy as immediate cause: see Rainer Jehl, *Melancholie und Acedia: Ein Beitrag zu Anthropologie und Ethik Bonaventuras* (Paderborn, 1984), pp. 87-88.

[26] See, for example, the *disputationes* on prolongevity in seventeenth-century commentaries on Avicenna's *Canon* 1.i by Pedro Garcia Carrero, Ponce Santa Cruz, and Carolus Vallesius, cited by Nancy Siraisi, *Avicenna in Renaissance Italy* (Princeton, 1987), pp. 211-213. Such discussions were still the combined result of scholastic medicine and philosophy, as they had been in the teaching of Albertus Magnus, reflected in *Quaestiones super De animalibus,* Lib. 7, q. 29: "Utrum iuventus possit renovari?" and q. 31: "Utrum aetas possit renovari per assumptionem viperae vel alterius veneni?", ed. Ephrem Filthaut in *Opera omnia,* Vol. 12 (Münster, 1955), pp. 184-185.

[27] For example, Jacques Angeli (ca. 1390-1455), chancellor of the University of Montpellier, argued against the proposition that "senes sunt egri" in his *Puncta medicine,* Vol. 3, 3.16.1, in Seville, Bibl. Colombina, MS. 5-7-18, fol. 88vb.

is wholly pathologic": she based her claim on the title *The Cure of Old Age,* which Richard Browne in the seventeenth century gave to his translation of Roger Bacon's *Epistola de retardatione accidentium senectutis.*[28]

The *accidentia senectutis,* or normal concomitants of old age, as well as abnormal or diseased conditions, became the subject of geriatric pathology in early medical thought. Several ailments were listed specifically, for example in the Hippocratic *Aphorisms* (3.31), as occurring

> to old people: dyspnoea, catarrhs accompanied with coughs, dysuria, pains of the joints, nephritis, vertigo, apoplexy, cachexia, pruritus of the whole body, insomnia, defluxions of the bowels, of the eyes, and of the nose, dimness of sight, catarract (glaucoma), and dullness of hearing.[29]

This list may be compared with Roger Bacon's catalogue of normal concomitants, namely

> grey hair, paleness and wrinkling of the skin, weakness of the faculties and powers, diminution of the blood and spirits, bleariness of the eyes, abundance of mucus, putrid spittle, weakness of breathing, insomnia, anger and mental restlessness, and lesion of the instruments of the senses in which the *virtus animalis* works [i.e. the faculties of the brain].

Bacon adds that these *accidentia* are called diseases when they occur in adolescents.[30] At this point we may also observe that Friar Roger has been credited with the invention of eyeglasses: while this invention may have been made only towards the end of the thirteenth century, it certainly was one of medieval medicine's greatest boons to old age.[31]

A great number of geriatric diseases were mentioned more incidentally and are yet to be collected systematically. A few instances may suffice here. Baldness, while not considered an exclusive problem of aging, was attributed to a cooling and drying complexion, and likened to the falling

---

[28] Sona R. Burstein, "The 'Cure' of Old Age: Codes of Health," *Geriatrics* 10 (1955) 328. See Ernst L. Wynder, "Richard Browne: Translator of Roger Bacon's 'The Cure of Old Age and Preservation of Youth'," *Preventive Medicine* 7 (1978) 28-30.

[29] In the translation by Francis Adams, ed. with introduction by Emerson C. Kelly, *The Theory and Practice of Medicine by Hippocrates* (New York, 1964), p. 302. Compare n. 25 above, for the symptoms mentioned by Saint Bonaventure.

[30] *Epistola de accidentibus senectutis,* Ch. 2, "Accidentia senectutis et senii," in *De retardatione,* ed. Little and Withington, pp. 18-19 (my translation). Compare also Robert Burton's list in the seventeenth century: "the old are full of aches in their bones, cramps and convulsions, earthbent, dull of hearing, weak-sighted, hoary, wrinkled, harsh, so much altered that they cannot know their own face in a glass, a burden to themselves and others ...," *The Anatomy of Melancholy* 1.2.3.10, ed. Floyd Dell and Paul Jordan-Smith (New York, 1938), p. 241.

[31] See Edward Rosen, "Did Roger Bacon Invent Eyeglasses?" *Archives internationales d'histoire des sciences* 7 (1953) 3-15; and "The Invention of Eyeglasses," *Journal of the History of Medicine and Allied Sciences* 11 (1956) 13-46 and 183-218.

of the leaves in autumn.[32] The loss of teeth appears in the prescription of a soft diet, for example by Burchard Horneck, who added a poignant marginal note to the text recorded by his scribe: next to the sentence "if the old man lacks teeth," he entered in his shakily aging hand, "as I do."[33] Elsewhere Horneck recommended a liniment of almond oil against curvature of the spine, "which occurs to older people" – and again he added a personal note, a credit to Bartholomeus Montagnano "my teacher and father who advised me and adopted me as his son."[34] Curvature is mentioned further in an unlikely context by Jacques Angeli (ca. 1390-1455), chancellor of the medical faculty of Montpellier for the last twenty-two years of his life. In his *Puncta angelica,* as he titled his *Questiones,* Angeli determined that, for humans to walk upright, their hearts must generate natural heat in abundance to sustain the *spiritus* of their bodies, and he interjected that "therefore we see old people bend on account of the weakened natural heat."[35] In a similar vein Galen, in a treatise translated by Arnald de Villanova, casually observed that tremor appears in the old because of their weakened *virtus.*[36]

The passing references to specifically geriatric diseases, such as the few cited above, call for several caveats. First, more research is needed to disentangle various clusters of clinical descriptions. For example, prostate problems may lie concealed not only behind the old-age dysuria first mentioned in the Hippocratic *Aphorisms*[37] but also among the numerous cases of calculus or stone reported in Arabic and Latin treatises[38] and in *consilia* for notables, from Pope Gregory VIII and Boniface VIII to

---

[32] Thus, Jacques Angeli, *Puncta medicine,* Vol. 1, 3.30.1 and 6.9.1, in Seville, Bibl. Col., MS. 5-7-16, fols. 84r and 209v.

[33] Burchard Horneck, *De senectute conservanda,* fol. 42r. The loss of teeth was also a subject discussed in natural philosophy, for example "Queritur quare in pueris dentes renascantur, in senibus si cadat, minime?" in Lawn, *Prose Salernitan Questions,* p. 120, cf. p. 251.

[34] *De senectute,* fol. 89r. The same note is repeated on fol. 94v.

[35] "Propter hoc videmus senes incurvari propter debilitatem caloris naturalis," *Puncta,* Vol. 1, 1.1.6, in Seville, Bibl. Col., MS. 5-7-16, fol. 12r.

[36] "Accidit tremor senibus et illis similiter quibus debilitatur et dissolvitur virtus corporum," *Translatio libri Galieni de rigore,* ed. Michael R. McVaugh in *Arnaldi de Villanova Opera medica omnia* (Barcelona, 1981), 16: 49.

[37] See above. The opposite of dysuria, namely incontinence, is the object of a *questio,* "Quidam est qui sexagesimum agens annum contingere [*sic,* continere] non potest urine effusionem; causa queritur et cura .... Non videtur quod ipse possit curari ...," in Lawn, *Prose Salernitan Questions,* pp. 201-202.

[38] Among the Arabic treatises, available to the West in translations, were Rasis' *De preservatione de egritudine lapidis,* Avicenna's *De morbo lapidis,* and Avenzoar's *De curatione lapidis.* Latin treatises, in addition to the chapters on stone in compendia that merit systematic investigation, include the *Experimentum fratris Egidii de ordine Augustini ad frangendum lapidem in vesica sine incisione,* Johannes Jacobi's *De calculo,* Johannes de Matiscone's *Practica ad lapidem,* Gabriele Zerbi's *De preservatione corporum a passione calculosa,* and Antonius Guaynerius' *De artetica et calculosa passione.*

Cardinal Bessarion.[39] One even suspects that prostatic calculus was occasionally the reason for lithotomy or "cutting for the stone," particularly when the Celsan method was followed.[40] Inversely, the modern reader will too easily conflate diverse diseases into one category. It is tempting, for instance, to confuse identifiable descriptions of arthritic and rheumatic ailments with more general allusions to *rheuma* or "flow,"[41] and to *gutta* or "drop" (from which the word "gout" was derived for the "rich man's disease," originally called *podagra*).[42]

Another caveat for the historian of geriatric disease is that the classical physiological schemes of humours and faculties dictated descriptions that cannot be readily interpreted in our current terms. Thus, as Michael McVaugh has recently pointed out, "it would be a mistake to suppose a real identity" between Parkinson's disease and the tremor described by Galen and his commentators.[43] We should further keep in mind that our fragmentary textual evidence is a shaky basis for generalizations, either in the attempt to trace precedents of modern syndromes or in the argument *ex silentio* that a disease was not known as such in the Middle Ages. This caution applies especially when our own pathology is still incomplete, as in the field of neurology. Therefore, it seems wise to resist the temptation to associate with Alzheimer's disease the medieval combination of such symptoms as forgetfulness, irritability, and the inability to perform simple tasks.[44] On the other hand, some historians may go too far in claiming that insanity was not recognized as a disease but accepted in the old, as it was in children, as an inevitable part of "an age of limited rationality."[45] It is probably more accurate to state that the aged insane

---

[39] *Mirabilis cura contra malum calculi quam misit Johannes Hispaliensis Gregorio papae*, in Vienna, Österreichische Nationalbibliothek, MS. 5311, fol. 41v. Arnald de Villanova, *Tractatus contra calculum* (dedicated to Boniface VIII), in London, BL, MS. Harl. 3665, fols. 33-44. Hieronymus Vallensis, *De cura lapidis ad cardinalem Bessarionem*, in Vatican MS. Urb. 1416, fols. 61-67.

[40] The "Celsan Operation" and other methods are described and illustrated in Loren C. MacKinney, *Medical Illustrations in Medieval Manuscripts* (Berkeley, 1965), pp. 80-82 and figs. 82-83.

[41] Thus Grmek, *On Ageing*, p. 58, suggests that Sigismund Albicus devoted special attention to the prophylaxis of "rheumatism," whereas in reality Albicus spoke only of *reumata* or "flows" in the head, caused by sleeping in a draught and so on: *Regimen sanitatis*, in Bethesda, NLM, MS. 491, fol. 13v.

[42] A readable introduction, though typically slighting the Middle Ages, is by William S. C. Copeman, *A Short History of the Gout and the Rheumatic Diseases* (Berkeley, 1964).

[43] McVaugh, introduction to Arnald de Villanova, *Translatio*, pp. 13-14.

[44] While those symptoms need to be examined in medieval texts on old age, their occurrence in younger years would come closer to *senilitas praecox* as a disease category – along the lines of Roger Bacon's suggestion, noted above on p. 10. The phenomenon of a very different but even more precocious "senility," namely *progeria*, may be reflected in the description of young people "with a horrible face, wasted, hairy and so shaggy that the smallest hairs stand, and the whole face looks like that of an ape" (Bernard de Gordon, *De marasmode*, in Vatican MS. Pal. 1234, fol. 138r).

[45] Keith Thomas, *Religion and the Decline of Magic* (New York, 1971), p. 563.

were not considered treatable, but it should also be added that they were granted care as well as indulgence in the home or, if necessary, in the hospital.

The hospital has been called the greatest medieval contribution to geriatrics by a historian who otherwise has few kind words for the period,[46] yet it seems thus far not to have been studied in this light. We know there were almshouses that gave shelter specifically to old people, from the *gerontocomia* mentioned by the *Codex Justiniani*[47] to the Sankt Nicholaus Spital in Kues. The latter, today still a charming landmark along the Mosel, was founded by Cardinal Nicholaus Cusanus, who in 1458 provided that it should house thirty-three needy old men over the age of fifty (together with six religious, six noblemen, and twenty-one burghers).[48] Of the municipal hospitals, only a few excluded the old – and these were primarily pilgrims' hostels such as St. Jacques in Valenciennes in 1434 –[49] but most opened their doors explicitly to "old, sick, and impoverished burghers."[50] Some, including St. Jan's Hospital in Bruges, had rooms for aged but more prosperous *proveniers* or pensioners (*prebendarii*) who bequeathed their possessions to the institution.[51] There can be little doubt that the earliest professional medical attendance to hospitals, itself still inadequately documented, benefited the aging residents and in turn stimulated the development of the clinical observation and therapeutics of senescence.

At the centre of therapeutics, both of old age and of its concomitants, lay the regimen or governance of the so-called six "nonnaturals," the factors that are neither part of our nature (the naturals), nor against nature by causing disease (the contranaturals), but are necessary to life and health.[52] It is to the credit of medieval authors that they frequently reiterated the

---

[46] Erwin H. Ackerknecht, "Geriatriegeschichtliches," *Praxis* 65 (1976) 321.

[47] 1.3.45, ed. Paul Krueger, 9th ed. (Berlin, 1915), p. 31.

[48] Jakob Marx, *Verzeichnis der Handschriften-Sammlung des Hospitals zu Cues* (Trier, 1905), p. iv. See E. Gottfredsen, "Nicolaus Cusanus und die Medizin," *Münchener medizinische Wochenschrift* 84 (1937) 1812-1834.

[49] Valenciennes excluded the aged, paralyzed, "phrenetics," and those with other incurable diseases: Henry H. Beek, *Waanzin in de Middeleeuwen: Beeld van de gestoorde en bemoeienis met de zieke* (Nijkerk, 1969), p. 147.

[50] St. Jacob's Hospital in Leeuwarden was founded in 1478 for "respectable burghers who are old, ill, and impoverished"; the Alkmaar city government decreed in 1465 that St. Elizabeth's Hospital was to remain a hospital for "old, poor, and mad women," Beek, *Waanzin*, p. 268 n. 7 and p. 145.

[51] Jozef Geldhof, *Pelgrims, dulle lieden en vondelingen te Brugge, 1275-1975: Zeven eeuwen geschiedenis van het Sint-Juliaans-gasthuis* (Bruges, 1975), pp. 75-76.

[52] The concept of the nonnaturals goes back to the Galenic "neutral causes," and it has been the subject of several studies, among which one of the most recent is Chester R. Burns, "The Nonnaturals: A Paradox in the Western Concept of Health," *Journal of Medicine and Philosophy* 1 (1976) 202-211.

Hippocratic precept to tailor the regimen to the patient's habits, the importance of which naturally increased with age.[53] The first of the non-natural factors was the ambient air or, in modern terms, the environment. The air surrounding the old should be sufficiently warm and moist as well as free from draughts and noxious fumes.[54] As an *adnexum* to this first factor the bath often appears, as in the following remarkable anecdote reported by Arnald de Villanova:

> A famous physician, an octogenarian of long experience, wanted to use a steambath (*stupha*) or a tub bath, on account of the need of his body [for warmth and moisture]. So, one day he entered and, because he was old and quite low in natural warmth, he did not find the air of the stew or bath sufficiently warm; therefore, he had burning charcoal (*carbones*) added. Soon after this, one of the servants fainted, and another, about to pass out, pulled the first one outside. When the master saw this happen, he left the bath, and thus his treatment was prevented that day. Wishing to return the following day, he did not want to bring the servant who had fainted, but he called a young physician who was very dear to him, and he asked him to investigate the matter.

The young physician, having found out but obviously dismissed the fact that the servants had not eaten that day and also that they had blown on the charcoal, solemnly reported to his older colleague that,

> as the master well knows, man cannot live in a place unless the [inhaled] air is colder than the heart. Hence the youths, whose hearts abound in intense heat, fainted sooner than the master, who, however, would also have fainted in the end if he had stayed longer.[55]

The second nonnatural factor, which usually occupies the largest part of regimens in general as well as of those for the old, comprised food and drink, even though most physicians insisted that the old should eat and drink with greater moderation than the young.[56] It would lead us too far

---

[53] For example, "magnam vim habet consuetudo ... quoniam natura gaudet in consueto," Bernard de Gordon, *Lilium medicine*, in London, BL, MS. Harl. 3698, fol. 66v. Habit also plays a decisive role in the *questio* "utrum senes debeant regi per similia aut per contraria," in Erfurt, Wissenschaftliche Bibliothek der Stadt, MS. Amplon. Q 174, fols. 118-119.

[54] Burchard, *De senectute*, fol. 31r. A stranger "environmental hazard," derived from Avenzoar and perhaps related to allergy, was the proximity of cats, whose breath causes putrefaction of the lungs and "phthisis" in the elderly, according to Arnald de Villanova, *De conservanda iuventute*, fol. 87r.

[55] Arnald de Villanova, *De circumspectione medici*, in Munich, Bayerische Staatsbibliothek, Clm. 18444, fol. 305r. On baths, see also Roger Bacon, *De balneis senum et seniorum*, ed. Little and Withington with *De retardatione*, pp. 96-97.

[56] Burchard, *De senectute*, fols. 36v-38v. Compare the Hippocratic *Aphorisms* 1.14; commenting on *Aphorisms* 1.13, many *questiones* are extant, such as "quare senes facilius ferant ieiunia quam pueri" in Lawn, *Prose Salernitan Questions*, p. 101. See also Taddeo Alderotti, "Utrum senes multum cibum sustinere possint," in Siraisi, *Taddeo*, p. 372.

here to pursue the details of the geriatric diet. Let me, rather, select a few representative vignettes from Burchard Horneck. Because the stomach weakens with advanced age, Burchard recommended bread that is "baked twice" or the even more digestible sea toast (*panis nauticus*), even though he warned that it might cause constipation.[57] Like most of his colleagues he considered light meat and poultry most healthful, but he thought that certain kinds of venison could increase the natural warmth, and he added in his own hand that he had "observed this in Graz while treating a cold fever of the emperor" (who was then presumably in his late sixties).[58] Since fish were of a moist and cold complexion, they were not an old man's best food; nevertheless, Burchard devoted over ten pages to various river and sea species, favouring the latter as less filling: these pages were dedicated to the dean of the Würzburg cathedral, Thomas de Lapide, who was evidently a gourmand as well as a gourmet. The dean fancied sweet-water "lobsters" (*locuste*) which, "though hard to digest, one may like to eat for pleasure, when they are seasoned in wine with some water and after adding salt, mint, parsley, and spices – but after one has first removed the *intestino fecem deferente* through the centre of the tail."[59] Cheese, on which "Zoroaster survived in the desert for twenty years," was excellent for the aging stomach, particularly "the young, soft, unsalted kind, which people here call green cheese."[60] And so we could continue, but let us leave this section by a too brief reference to wine, which, as Burchard summed up in agreement with more than just the medical profession, not only is both food and drink but also "works like medicine" by warming and moistening, cheering up, restoring the blood, aiding sleep and digestion, purging, and provoking perspiration.[61]

The third nonnatural factor, emptiness and fullness or *inanitio et repletio,* dealt primarily with the excretions, which could be assisted by various purges.[62] We will discreetly skip these, though not without an equally discreet word about their surprising *adnexum,* namely coitus. The treatment of sex by medieval physicians in general awaits further study,

[57] *De senectute,* fol. 54r. Arnald de Villanova also warned that the aged should not eat freshly baked bread, *De conservanda iuventute,* fol. 90r.

[58] Burchard, *De senectute,* fol. 59r. Burchard served Frederick III (1415-1493) towards the end of the emperor's life.

[59] *De senectute,* fol. 67v.

[60] Ibid., fols. 70v-71r.

[61] Ibid., fols. 42v-43r. "Vinum subtile facit in sene cor iuvenile, sed vinum vile reddit iuvenile senile," *Flos medicinae scholae Salerni,* vv. 412-413.

[62] Purges ranged from laxatives, diuretics, and emetics to clysters or enemas, and to cupping and bleeding. The prescriptions and proscriptions of each of these for aged patients would provide the substance for a separate study.

and its bearing on the geriatric regimen is rather limited, so that the following observations are preliminary.[63] While coitus in old age was considered beneficial to emotional health, which more appropriately falls under the sixth nonnatural, it was frowned upon in the traditions of medicine and of natural philosophy as hastening the waste of warmth and the consumption of vital moisture. In fact, Albertus Magnus related that a "grizzled monk" who had been sexually quite active to his last days, was in autopsy found to have a shriveled brain.[64] One of the few objections, however, that might be viewed as having vague moral implications, is voiced in the assertion of Gabriele Zerbi, on the authority of Galen, that "venery is proper only to adolescence because the earlier and the later ages emit no sperm, or it is infertile or poorly fertile."[65] Lest we infer too much from this objection, I should add Zerbi's endorsement of a widespread recommendation that an old man at night keep "in constant embrace a girl who is close to menarche (*pollutioni proximam*)" because her youthful natural warmth will cure both his indigestion and his insomnia.[66]

---

[63] An excellent recent introduction is Danielle Jacquart and Claude Thomasset, *Sexuality and Medicine in the Middle Ages*, trans. Matthew Adamson (Princeton, 1988). Avenues for further research may be indicated by the following statements: "Prolongat vitam coitus moderamine factus / Quibus sit licitus; e contra valde nocivus" (*Flos medicinae scholae Salerni*, vv. 268-269); "Defectus autem appetitus generationis et minutio est de signis pronosticantibus senectutem, et iuvantur proprie cum hiis cum quibus augentur et confortantur calor et spiritus et humores, et ex quibusdam aliis quorum taceo rememorationem propter pudicitiam" (Arnald de Villanova, *De conservanda iuventute*, fol. 87r); "Coytus temperatus corpus humanum in sanitate preservare facit" (Johannes Phisicus, *De conservatione sanitatis usque ad annum 120*, in Munich, Bayer. Staatsbib., Clm. 8184, fol. 184r) where many specific benefits of sex and negative effects of abstinence (as well as of excess) are listed; "Coitus immoderatus cito adducit senium et finaliter mortem" (anon. *Regimen sanitatis*, in Vienna, Öster. Nationalbib., MS. 4173, fol. 231r). Coitus destroys the body's powers and thus "parum competit senibus," according to Magninus Mediolanensis, *Regimen sanitatis* (Strasbourg, 1503), fol. 38v.

[64] "Narravit mihi magister Clemens de Bohemia quod quidam monachus griseus accessit ad quandam dominam pulchram et sicut famelicus homo eam ante pulsum matutinarum expetivit sexaginta sex vicibus, in crastino decubuit et mortuus est eadem die. Et quia fuit nobilis, apertum fuit corpus eius, et repertum est cerebrum totum evacuatum, ita quod nihil de ipso mansit nisi ad quantitatem pomi granati, et oculi similiter annihilati," *Quaestiones*, Lib. 15, q. 14, ed. Filthaut, *Opera* 12: 268.

[65] In the version of Burchard, *De senectute*, fol. 81r. Michele Savonarola (1384-1462) attributed a decline in longevity in his era to precocious marriages, which led to weakened generations issued from immature sperm, *Il trattato ginecologico-pediatrico in volgare*, ed. Luigi Belloni (Milan, 1952), pp. 194-196. Albertus Magnus suggested that deficiently mobile semen in advanced age might result in defective offspring, an idea supported by modern findings on Down's syndrome: see Luke Demaitre and Anthony A. Travill, "Human Embryology and Development in the Works of Albertus Magnus," in *Albertus Magnus and the Sciences: Commemorative Essays 1980*, ed. James A. Weisheipl, Studies and Texts 49 (Toronto, 1980), pp. 438-439.

[66] In Burchard, *De senectute*, fols. 41v and 79v. This recommendation reaches from the pseudo-Aristotelian *Secretum secretorum* and Roger Bacon to Thomas Sydenham (1624-1689) and

Wakefulness and sleep, and rest and exercise, the fourth and fifth non-naturals, received proportionately little coverage in the geriatric regimen – and, interestingly enough, less where Arabic influences were stronger.[67] Most Latin authors believed that the old needed less sleep, and several encouraged intermittent naps, but some did adopt the Arabic insistence on longer sleep.[68] Idleness was to be shunned most of all and, as Arnald de Villanova wrote, "the best kind of exercise is frequent walking, rhythmic bending (*vicissitudinaria incurvatio*) ... and climbing towards higher places."[69] Fitness would be enhanced by gentle massages and even more by morning rubs with oil, which are recommended in virtually every regimen for the old.[70] Various exercises were also prescribed for the mental faculties of reason, imagination, and memory.[71] Zerbi stressed that "the geriatrician (*gerentocomus* [*sic*]) should help not only the body of the aging patient but also his mind and soul, as Cicero says. For the mind, too, is extinguished unless it is fueled as the light is by oil. The bodies of the aged are burdened by the fatigue of exertion, but their minds rise by exercising."[72] Even a little anger could provide good mental stimulation.[73] It was preferable, however, according to Zerbi, that the mind be kept active "by conversations and also by some pleasant and solvable riddles, sometimes from *physica* or from theology, but mostly from rhetoric" and, in those with the right complexion, by the study of dogma

---

into the eighteenth century (see n. 22 above). For its basis in the misinterpretation of Galen's advice, see Bacon, *De retardatione*, ed. Little and Withington, pp. xl, 211 n., and 215 n.

[67] Thus, Roger Bacon paid far less attention to exercise than Arnald de Villanova. Magninus Mediolanensis states that the aged, while they can exercise their strong limbs but not the weak ones "lest they incur greater weakness," are not capable of vigorous exercise "such as jousts, tournaments, warfare, long journeys, races, and wrestling matches." He concludes that "this age group should devote itself to what they can sustain without strength, for example councils, government, and judgments, which are wont to become better in the old," *Regimen*, fol. 10r. See also Walter Artelt, "Arzt und Leibesübungen in Mittelalter und Renaissance," *Medizinhistorisches Journal* 3 (1968) 222-242.

[68] "Sex horis dormire sat est iuvenique senique," *Flos medicinae scholae Salerni*, v. 229. Bacon, however, claims that *senes* should sleep more than youths, *De retardatione*, p. 93. Burchard suggests that insomnia, chronic in old age, be overcome with soporifics ("cum hymnoticis [*sic*]"), *De senectute*, fol. 79v. On insomnia as an "illness" in old age, see Jacques Angeli, *Puncta*, Vol. 3, 5.8.3, fols. 171v-172r.

[69] *De conservanda iuventute*, fol. 88r.

[70] "All the sages who treated of the regimen of health do not cease to say that the old and very old should be anointed with oil when they rise in the morning," Bacon, *De retardatione*, p. 68.

[71] The effects of senescence on these faculties, their respective location in the central, anterior, and posterior parts of the brain, the "physiology" of the aging brain, and particularly the *topos* and treatment of senile amnesia are the subject of a separate study on which I am working.

[72] Zerbi, *Gerontocomia*, p. 115v.

[73] Bacon, *De retardatione*, p. 71; Burchard, *De senectute*, fol. 82v.

(*doctrinalibus studiis*) and of mathematics.[74] These distractions would, furthermore, promote emotional well-being.

The emotions or *accidentia animae* constituted the last, and for us perhaps the most interesting, category of the nonnaturals. Depression and lethargy were the dangers most commonly feared for an age that had been called "a path to death" by Galen as well as by nonmedical authors.[75] According to the natural philosophers, the heart and brain were growing colder with advancing age, and melancholy and phlegm exceeded the humoral balance.[76] The dangers of melancholic depression and phlegmatic lethargy were to be resisted by two medical methods, which – then as now – often seesawed for priority, namely psychotherapy and pharmacotherapy. The former was preferred by authors such as Zerbi, who emphasized the value of conversations (*confabulationes*). He observed that seniors liked to be flattered, that their tastes ranged from serious topics to exciting stories such as those "whose tellers or singers are called bards in French," and that they delighted more in talking than in listening.[77] Further psychological remedies included entertainment by music and games, wearing colourful clothes, and living in brightly decorated rooms.[78] Roger Bacon suggested that "among the best is to sit and talk with beautiful, suitably dressed young girls, and to obtain victory over one's enemies."[79] Bacon, however, like other authors who borrowed heavily from Arabic sources and who have commonly caught the attention of later generations, placed far greater faith in pharmacotherapy.

With the applications of medicines we cross from the regimen of the six nonnaturals, or the maintenance of daily life, into the area of therapeutics proper – even though the medieval distinctions between diet and pharmacy, or between foods, spices, perfumes, and medicines do not quite coincide with our own. More pertinent classifications distinguished between singles and compounds, and between "rational" and "empirical"

---

[74] Zerbi, *Gerontocomia*, p. 118r.

[75] See the *incipit* of Burchard's *De senectute*, n. 18 above. Also, "senectus est via ad mortem," Jacques Angeli, *Puncta*, Vol. 3, 5.22, fol. 217r. References to Galen are provided by Bernard de Gordon, *De conservatione vite humane*, 4: *Regimen sanitatis*, in Vatican MS. Pal. 1174, fol. 54r.

[76] Burchard, *De senectute*, fols. 85v-87v; Bacon, *De conservatione iuventutis*, with *De retardatione*, pp. 126-127. See Heinrich Schipperges, "Melancolia als ein mittelalterlicher Sammelbegriff für Wahnvorstellungen," *Studia generalia* 20 (1967) 723-736. The cooling and drying of the brain were also held responsible for the loss of short-term memory in old age.

[77] Zerbi, *Gerontocomia*, p. 118r. The qualifications of a good storyteller are enumerated on p. 118v.

[78] Bacon, *De conservatione iuventutis*, with *De retardatione*, pp. 137-138.

[79] Ibid., p. 138. Bacon also cited the *Secretum secretorum*, "the book that Aristotle wrote in his old age at the request of Alexander," for the view that "laughter accelerates old age," *De retardatione*, p. 48.

drugs. The latter classification roughly coincides with the distinction between substances that worked by a supposedly known quality, and those whose efficacy was "occult" and based on their entire substance.[80] It would be tedious to run through the medicines that were prescribed in geriatrics because of their qualities such as warming, moistening, strengthening the stomach, purging melancholy, and so on.[81] One, however, the *mirobalanum* or *mirabolanus,* I find particularly fascinating because it was believed to possess all these qualities and it is omnipresent in the materia medica for old age.[82] Its identity is something of a puzzle, as it ranges from the behen-nut in Pliny to the "Indian pear" or the *halilaj* in Arabic and to the modern mirabelle plum.[83] Since most recipes called for myrobalans, especially the *chebuli* or Kabul variety, to be pickled or preserved (*conditi*), one is tempted to think of a forerunner of "stewed prunes."[84] Four or five species of myrobalans were combined in the *trifera* or *triphera saracenica,* one of the special compounds among which theriac or treacle was the most famous and whose power exceeded the sum of their simples.[85]

With regard to medicines with occult efficacy, it is worth noting that recipes for such empirical compounds were occasionally credited by

[80] For the distinction in Bacon, see Withington's comments, *De retardatione,* pp. xxxviii-xli. The distinction is applied by Bernard de Gordon, *De marasmode,* fol. 139r.

[81] For example, Arnald de Villanova (elaborating on Roger Bacon) recommended chewing on rhubarb, which "clears up the face and invigorates the soul and the five senses with its odour, strengthens the principal organs and the entire body, opens the passageways of the brain, and expels winds," *De conservanda iuventute,* fol. 89r.

[82] Arnald de Villanova includes *mirabolani* in several of his recipes, and he adds an "electuarium de quinque mirabolanis secundum receptam paucis notam in viam conservationis sanitatis et prolongationis vite et reiuvenescentie, est res probata et perfecta et donum electum vite, nam stomachum confortat et adaptat et aque superfluitatem a nutrimento ... purgat, et usus eius caniciem retardat, et ad decrepitam etatem venire facit nutu Dei," ibid., fols. 86v-87r. An *electuarium vite de mirabolanis* is described on fol. 89r.

[83] The word is derived from the Greek *muron* (unguent) and *bálanos* (acorn, date), and it originally referred to the astringent fruit of species of *terminalia* (*combretaceae*). "Myrabolanorum species sunt quinque bonorum: citrinus, kebullus, bellericus, emblicus, indus," *Flos medicinae scholae Salerni,* p. 29. The black chebule or Kabul variety (*ihlilaj* or *halilaj*) or "Indian pear" is the most prominent, although belleric myrobalan (*balilaj*) is still used today, for example in Egypt, as both a styptic and a purgative: Joseph S. Graziani, *Arabic Medicine in the Eleventh Century as Represented in the Works of Ibn Jazlah* (Karachi, 1980), p. 196.

[84] *Mirabolani conditi* recur in Roger Bacon ("nothing in this world can take their place," *De conservatione iuventutis,* with *De retardatione,* p. 128), Arnald de Villanova, Bernard de Gordon, Jacques Angeli, Magninus Mediolanensis, Gabriele Zerbi, and so on.

[85] "According to Haly *super Tegni* (3.123) [*trifera*] was an Indian medicine, more effective for the prolongation of life than anything known to the Greeks," Withington, glossary to Bacon, *De retardatione,* p. 220. Arnald de Villanova includes a *sermo super triferia* [*sic*] and a recipe in *De conservanda iuventute,* fol. 88v. *Triphera* is also recommended for gynecology in Salernitan writings, including the *Flos medicinae* and Trotula.

academic physicians to "old women" or *vetulae,* a group more often associated with malignant magic.[86] There was a large group of vegetable and
animal ingredients that supposedly worked by sympathetic magic. For
example, agaric, a white fungus, would purge phlegm because it was of
the same colour;[87] since a cuckoo had total recall, its brains were thought
to cure amnesia.[88] Sympathy or harmony with the universe further
required that a compound be prepared under the right constellation.[89] A
few occult medicines were singled out as *secreta* that surpassed all common remedies. Roger Bacon listed rosemary and aloewood, viper's flesh
(the principal ingredient in theriac) and "bone of stag's heart," ambergris
and pearls, gold, and the mysterious "warmth from the noble animal" –
which could mean either distilled human blood or, less unappetizing, the
nocturnal embrace mentioned earlier.[90] To this list Arnald de Villanova
added *aqua vite,* the distillate of wine that was clearly a novelty in the
late thirteenth century: Arnald explained, "I have seen it" and it is "so
sublimely effective that some of the moderns would say that it is water of
gold and water of eternity (*aqua perennis*)."[91]

---

[86] "Didici a vetulis magis per viam experimenti quam racionis quod malve ... solvunt dolorem
in pleuresi," Bernard de Gordon, *De regimine acutorum,* in Vatican MS. Pal. 1083, fol. 280v. A
more common theme is that, "according to the advice of physicians, it is imperative to stay away
from old women," who become infected and infectious after the poisonous matter of the menstrua is
retained rather than expelled: Johannes de Ketham, *Fasciculus medicinae,* trans. Luke Demaitre
(facsimile ed., Birmingham, Ala., 1988), p. 52. This gynephobic theme, shared by two spurious but
influential compendia (the *Problemata Aristotelis* and the *Secreta mulierum* attributed to Albertus
Magnus), led Johannes Phisicus to warn "a conversatione vetularum" because they are dangerously
venomous: *De conservatione,* fol. 183v.

[87] As greenish rhubarb purged choler and dark Indian *mirabolani* purged black bile: *questiones*
B 162 B and Ba 113 in Lawn, *Prose Salernitan Questions,* pp. 80 and 194. On the same ground,
mother's milk was prescribed against cataract by Burchard, *De senectute,* fol. 29r.

[88] Bernard de Gordon, *Lilium medicine,* fol. 28r. An alternative was the hoopoe, e.g. in
Nicolaus Falcutius, *Sermones medicinales, Sermo 3* (Venice, 1490), 2.5.5, fol. 69v.

[89] Burchard, *De senectute,* fol. 32v. Bernard de Gordon prescribed a "five-water elixir" that
should stand outside from May to September in order to ferment and to "receive strength and power
from the sun and stars," *De marasmode,* fol. 139v.

[90] See n. 66 above. Bacon's list and interpretation of *secreta* are discussed by Withington, *De
retardatione,* pp. xxxix-xli. Bernard de Gordon's occult ingredients include dew, thrice-distilled
human blood, the purest gold (he prescribes a method of purifying florins), flowers of bugloss, and
ambergris: the last three are to be added "in as great a quantity as the wealth of the recipient will
allow," *De marasmode,* fol. 139v. Gold is also given serious consideration by Burchard, *De senectute,* fol. 90r-v.

[91] "Quidam appellant eam aquam vite et certe et vidi ... ita quod dixerint aliqui de modernis
quod est aqua perennis et aqua auri propter sublimitatem operationis ... sincerat corpus et membra et
prolongat vitam, et ex eius operatione dici meruit aqua vite," Arnald de Villanova, *De conservanda
iuventute,* fol. 89v, following a critique of the magical formula or interpretation of *aqua auri* that
was given by Bacon, for whose prescription of gold as *sol mineralis* Arnald also substituted *sal de
minera* or salt, fol. 87v. See also Paul and Rose Jaulmes, "La Rectification de l'alcool, invention
languedocienne," *Monspeliensis Hippocrates* 46 (1969) 17-29.

It will be noticed that we have now descended to the level of "marvelous waters," *electuaria* or elixirs, and the quest for eternal youth. A first aspect of this quest concerned the delay of the appearances of old age, especially grey hair and wrinkled skin.[92] While magical cures for these appearances were indeed proffered by several medieval physicians, they will not be discussed here for the following reasons: the "superstitious" side of medieval medicine has often enough obscured its more sensible insights; such cures are still in demand today; and, above all, they seem quite frivolous when compared with the second aspect of the quest, namely the delay of old age itself. This aspect dovetailed with the question, raised not only by physicians but also by theologians, "whether human life can be prolonged by artificial means *(per artem)*."[93] The most optimistic answers virtually promised immortality through miracle drugs, advertised with unequalled flair by the alchemist Theophrastus Bombastus Paracelsus.[94] More modest claims were made, for example by Bernard de Gordon (ca. 1258-ca. 1318), for an electuary of his "own invention" that would, "if accompanied by a good regimen, make man insenescible insofar as that is possible by nature, because it strengthens the heart and intestines, expels all superfluities, and increases the natural heat."[95] The general assumption, however, was that medicine could, at best, extend life to its furthest natural term – that is, to the inevitable extinction of the innate heat – and improve the quality of that advanced age.[96]

Quite a few medieval physicians apparently were living testimony to this more realistic hope, not only by remaining active in their old age, but even by surviving well beyond the average life expectancy. In a recent study, Danielle Jacquart has suggested, though with careful reservations,

[92] Emphasized by Bacon, *De retardatione,* pp. 46-57 and 69-72.

[93] Bernard de Angrarra, *Questiones,* fol. 40r-v. The theological theme, the *Adjal,* was "the subject of heated debate" in Islam, more than in Judaism, according to Gotthold Weil, ed., *Moses Maimonides, Über die Lebensdauer* (Basel, 1953), p. 29. The theological aspect is reflected in the query of an anonymous physician around 1400, "Utrum mors possit retardari," *Questiones,* in Wiesbaden, Landesbibliothek, MS. 56, fol. 334r-v. The medical interpretation dominates in the *questiones* cited here in nn. 6, 10, 26, 94, 95, and 96.

[94] See n. 19 above. Other optimists were the fifteenth-century Johannes Phisicus (see n. 54); Laurent Joubert, who, in the sixteenth century, explicitly contradicted Galen and Avicenna and claimed that, by the medical art, life can be prolonged "even further than is ordered by Nature," *Erreurs populaires,* trans. Gale, p. 399; and the eighteenth-century Johann Cohausen (see n. 22).

[95] Bernard de Gordon, *De marasmode,* fol. 139v. On fols. 137v-138r, Bernard discusses at some length the question to what extent life can be prolonged by medicine.

[96] Thus, "Vitam prolongat sed non medicina perennat," *Flos medicinae,* v. 32. "Est valde lamentabile sed verbum angelicum [i.e. Angeli's own thesis] dicit quod vita naturalis non potest prolongari quin quocumque modo impediatur calor naturalis a corrupcione humidi .... Ego tamen noto hic quod calidum superfluum assuescendo ducit ad perfectionem et non plus. Item senium non impeditur nisi apparenter," Jacques Angeli, *Puncta,* Vol. 3, 5.22, fol. 217v.

that physicians may have lived longer than their contemporaries between 1350 and 1500 (as they more clearly did in the sixteenth and seventeenth centuries).[97] In fact, for the authors from 1200 to 1600 cited in this paper, the average lifespan was an astonishing sixty-seven years – and one of those to die the youngest, at forty-eight, was Paracelsus, the purveyor of panaceas against old age. Aged doctors may have curtailed their bedside practice, as I infer from my lack of direct evidence at this moment, but they remained professionally productive with their expert advice, as their writings demonstrate. A good example is the *Preservation of Old Age,* which Burchard Horneck wrote in his late sixties,[98] and whose prologue offers a fitting conclusion for this paper.

> Contemplating the hard fate of the human race, among the various vexations that the mortal kind suffers I also considered laborious old age, which brings a thousand ills and often heavy hardship. I am now experiencing all these myself, even though I refused to believe those who had experienced them for the longest time. However, so that this heavy and hardly bearable burden of old age may not completely depress and crush me, I am collecting from the physicians and also from philosophy whereby I may relieve man, if not from all – for this cannot be done by nature – then at least from some discomforts and grave miseries of old age, or somehow to revive him; or, if I cannot even accomplish this, that I may at least soften those vexations that attack old people ....

Burchard hoped, indeed, that his book would "not only lift the troubles of old age, but also render old age sweet and even pleasant."[99] By this aspiration, evidently shared by many of Burchard's colleagues, medieval medicine is a source of inspiration to modern geriatrics.

---

[97] Danielle Jacquart, *Le Milieu médical en France du XII᷄ au XV᷄ siècle* (Geneva, 1981), pp. 146-148. Another comparative and, indirectly at least, medical aspect of longevity is discussed by Vern Bullough and Cameron Campbell, "Female Longevity and Diet in the Middle Ages," *Speculum* 55 (1980) 317-325.

[98] In fact, to be a good *gerontocomus,* the physician himself should be of advanced age, according to several authors such as Gabriele Zerbi: Zeman, "The *Gerontocomia*," p. 712.

[99] Burchard, *De senectute,* fol. 24r.

2

Study of Aging in the Arts Faculty
of the Universities of Paris and Oxford

P. Osmund Lewry, OP †

Pontifical Institute of Mediaeval Studies

The study of aging has received some attention in the history of medieval medicine,[1] but hardly any has been given to the studies pursued by students in arts at Paris and Oxford. The interest there was philosophical rather than medical but, since university education was primarily, and for the majority, in arts and only a few followed the study of medicine in the higher faculty, the educated man's views were for the most part shaped by notions acquired in philosophy even if he acquired some popular knowledge of medical teaching. The philosophers produced a small and neglected literature discussing a set of short treatises grouped together amongst Aristotle's *Parva naturalia:* "On the Long Duration and Brevity of Life" (*De longitudine et brevitate vitae*), "On Youth and Old Age" (*De iuventute et senectute*), "On Death and Life" (*De morte et vita*). Altogether some forty ascribed commentaries have been identified from the thirteenth to the fifteenth century, poorly distinguished because of overlapping interests and confusion of titles; more survive without ascription.[2] The works of Peter of Spain and Albert the Great are accessible in

---

[1] This study is not concerned with the history of medicine as such, for which the reader is referred to Luke Demaitre, "The Care and Extension of Old Age in Medieval Medicine" above, pp. 3-22.

[2] The ascribed commentaries are listed according to author by Charles H. Lohr, "Medieval Latin Aristotle Commentaries," *Traditio* 23 (1967) 313-413; 24 (1968) 149-245; 26 (1970) 135-216; 27 (1971) 251-351; 28 (1972) 281-396; 29 (1973) 93-197; 30 (1974) 119-144. Care must be exercised in distinguishing the texts commented, because the text now known as *De longitudine et brevitate vitae* first circulated as *De morte et vita* and the material headed *De iuventute et senectute* includes a section *De respiratione* as well as the *De morte et vita.*

Aging and the Aged in Medieval Europe, ed. Michael M. Sheehan, CSB. Papers in Mediaeval Studies 11 (Toronto: Pontifical Institute of Mediaeval Studies, 1990), pp. 23-38. © P.I.M.S., 1990.

printed edition, but for the other masters it has been necessary to go to manuscripts. Circumstances – including the brevity of life – largely restrict this survey to the thirteenth-century beginnings and to manuscripts in Oxford.

By the 1240s the ban on the teaching of Aristotle's natural philosophy at Paris began to be disregarded. The *libri naturales* had been read earlier and by the 1240s Roger Bacon was teaching them, although we have no surviving teaching on the texts of present interest. The *De anima* was put on the curriculum of the English nation in 1252,[3] and after the decent hesitation that marks the adoption of a new academic programme, the *Parva naturalia* were prescribed by the faculty in 1255.[4] What is widely read today will be taught tomorrow and required for examination the next day.

In fact, one of the earliest witnesses to the place these texts were carving out for themselves in the curriculum is the remarkable Parisian examination compendium, probably from the 1240s, preserved in the Barcelona MS. Ripoll 109.[5] At a time when they were not yet required reading and so merited no revision questions, unlike the massive collections thought appropriate for grammar and logic, the contents of the *libri naturales* were reviewed in an ordered summary of the divisions of natural philosophy. The *De anima* appears here as a study of life at the rational level, and medicine is mentioned as the counterpart of human psychology, a study of the make-up of the living body.[6] Subordinate to the *De anima* are the texts dealing with the different ways the soul is affected or is active within the body. "The soul is affected by the tiredness of the body and such like ... and not only by its movement but also through heat continuously consuming the natural humidity that is the source of life."[7]

---

[3] See Heinrich Denifle and Emile Chatelain, eds., *Chartularium universitatis Parisiensis*, Vol. 1 (Paris, 1889), p. 228, no. 201.

[4] Ibid., p. 278, no. 246.

[5] See P. Osmund Lewry, "Thirteenth-Century Examination Compendia from the Faculty of Arts," in *Les Genres littéraires dans les sources théologiques et philosophiques médiévales, définition, critique, et exploitation, Actes du Colloque international de Louvain-la-Neuve, 25-27 mai 1981*, Université catholique de Louvain, Publications de l'Institut d'études médiévales, 2ᵉ série: Textes, études, congrès, vol. 5 (Louvain-la-Neuve, 1982), pp. 101-116.

[6] Barcelona, Archivo de la Corona de Aragón, MS. Ripoll 109, fol. 135va: "Est aliud corpus compositum ex materia et forma, que est substancia et motor. Hec autem substancia est anima, cuius sunt tres species .... Tertia species est anima racionalis, de qua et suis operacionibus agitur in libro *De anima*. Vnde si de aliarum operacionibus ibidem agitur, hoc est inquantum sunt principia operacionum anime racionalis. De complexione vero illius corporis, in quo est anima racionalis, agit proprie medicina."

[7] Ibid.: "Sunt autem alii libri particulares et subalternati, in quibus agitur de diuersis passionibus uel operacionibus anime cum corpore secundum diuersas proprietates quas recipit anima a corpore in mouendo uel econuerso. Suscipit enim anima in mouendo corporis fatigacionem et

This, the compiler says, is dealt with in *De morte et vita* in regard to the vegetative soul; the interior recall of natural heat in sleep is dealt with in *De somno et vigilia* in regard to the sensitive soul.[8]

In 1255, when the Parisian studies were reorganized to include natural philosophy, masters had to allot one week in June, at the end of the academic year, to the teaching of *De morte et vita*, the last text to be named.[9] The earliest Oxford statute stipulating set books for those determining in arts, that of 1268, only mentions three required texts in natural philosophy, *Physica*, *De anima*, and *De generatione et corruptione*.[10] With the reorganization of the curriculum in 1340 there is the first mention of the shorter texts, *De minutis naturalibus*, as an option for inceptors.[11] Surely *De morte et vita* was included here, and silence of the statutes is poor ground for supposing that it was not taught earlier. It is likely that British curiosity about the natural world, already manifest in the twelfth century, and freedom from the Parisian restriction on their teaching favoured the early introduction of the texts on aging at Oxford.

These texts had been translated by James of Venice before 1150. Their assimilation owed much to Arabic expositions. From the early thirteenth century the masters were familiar through the Latin version of Avicenna's *De anima*, a digest of Aristotle's psychology, with the fundamental polarities of dry and moist, cold and hot, that underlie his account of aging. In Avicenna they would have met, for example, the thought that

> ... boys, although they are wet, are yet strongly retentive ... youths, however, on account of their heat and agile movements, although their make-up is dry, yet their memory is not like that of infants and boys; but it happens that old people, on account of the humour that prevails in them, do not remember those things that they see.[12]

---

huiusmodi, et eciam totum compositum, et non solum a motu duo sed eciam a calore consumente continue humidum naturale quod est uite principium."

[8] Ibid.: "Et hoc modo liber *De morte et vita;* et ille sumitur proprie a parte anime vegetatiue. Item anima fatigatur propter motum suum in corpore et ideo necesse est quiescere et dormire propter suam vexacionem. In sompno eciam reuocatur calor naturalis ad interiora et sic fit materialiter. Et secundum hoc est liber *De sompno et vigilia*, qui continet duos libros parciales. Et iste sumitur proprie a uirtute anime sensitiue quantum ad communem particulam que dicitur 'sensus communis'."

[9] *Chart. univ. Paris.*, 1: 278, no. 246: " ... librum *de morte et vita* in una septimana."

[10] Strickland Gibson, ed., *Statuta antiqua universitatis Oxoniensis* (Oxford, 1931), p. 26 (8-10).

[11] Ibid., p. 32 (12-13).

[12] Avicenna, *Liber de anima* 4.3, ed. S. van Riet, *Avicenna Latinus* (Louvain, 1968), p. 43 (6-12): "Unde pueri quamvis sint humidi, tamen firmiter retinent ... iuvenum autem propter calorem suum et propter motus suos agiles, quamvis complexio sit sicca, tamen memoria eorum non est sicut memoria infantium et puerorum; senibus vero accidit propter humorem qui praevalet in eis non memorare ea quae vident."

Michael Scot's Latin version of Averroes' epitome of the *Parva naturalia* was probably circulating in Paris by 1230, providing material with a more direct bearing on the texts.

Book 3 of the epitome was devoted to a summary of *De longitudine*. Here one finds a distinction between the longevity of genera, species, regional groups, and individuals. Passing away is explained by the predominance of the passive qualities of moisture and dryness over the active, heat and cold. If natural heat is too weak to digest the humours or too intense, natural proportion is lost and decay sets in. Where the elements water and fire predominate over earth and air, the active qualities will be in a more favourable ratio and the organism will be more resistant to external change and disease. Moisture is the nourishment of heat; without it there will be desiccation, and, natural heat consuming natural moisture, coldness and dryness will prevail. These are the qualities of old age, while warmth and moisture belong to youth. Sexual abstinence, abundance of flesh, being a woman, a warm and moist maritime climate, all contribute to a long life. Diet, fresh air, sleep, exercise are part of a regimen for protracting life. But all these are of little avail without that intrinsic balance, the *complexio media,* which Galen talks about but which eludes precise medical knowledge.[13]

Adam of Buckfield, an M.A. of Oxford by 1243,[14] was an early and prolific commentator of the *libri naturales,* able to profit by Averroes' summary. One exposition of *De longitudine* is found unascribed, under the old title *De morte et vita,* in the Vatican MS. Vat. lat. 5988, fols. 22ra-24rb.[15] Adam situates his text in relation to *De somno et vigilia* and the *Meteora,* where the qualities are treated. He also distinguishes the general treatment of the causes of health and sickness that pertains to the philosopher from the particularities of the physician.[16] He relates

---

[13] *Averrois Cordubensis Compendia librorum Aristotelis qui Parva naturalia vocantur,* ed. Emily Ledyard Shields and Harry Blumberg, Corpus commentariorum Averrois in Aristotelem, versionum latinarum vol. 7 (Cambridge, Mass., 1949), pp. 129-149. English translation by Harry Blumberg: Averroes, *Epitome of Parva naturalia,* Corpus ... versio anglica vol. 7 (Cambridge, Mass., 1961), pp. 54-61.

[14] See Alfred B. Emden, *A Biographical Register of the University of Oxford to A.D. 1500* [henceforth *BRUO*], 3 vols. (Oxford, 1957-1959), 1: 297, "Buckfield, Adam de."

[15] Two commentaries are described by Lohr, "ML Aristotle Commentaries," *Traditio* 23, pp. 322-323, nos. 19 and 20, of which this is the second, no. 20.

[16] Città del Vaticano, Biblioteca Apostolica Vaticana, MS. Vat. lat. 5988, fol. 22ra-rb: "Deinde dat ordinem huius libri ad quosdam libros precedentes, dicens quod prius determinatum est de sompno et uigilia, sicut in precedenti determinatum est eciam de causis egritudinis et sanitatis quantum pertinet ad phisicum, scilicet de causis uniuersalibus (naturalibus *MS.*) eorum et non de causis particularibus parcium egritudinum et sanitatum, que pertinent ad medicum, sicut in quarto *Metheorum.* Nunc autem determinandum est de propriis causis longitudinis uite et bre/uitatis, et sic ordinat auctor istum librum (des *canc. MS.*) ad librum *De sompno et vigilia* et ad 4 *Metheorum.*"

Aristotle's talk of a greater flame consuming a lesser (ch. 3, 465b23-26; ch. 5, 466b28-33) to superfluous heat rapidly consuming its food and finally, lacking food, the very matter of the organism itself.[17] With Adam's exposition are logical works of Peter of Ireland,[18] and, in view of the fact that Peter is reputed to have been the teacher of Aquinas in natural philosophy at Naples from around 1239 to 1244, it is of interest to see that MS. Vat. lat. 825, fols. 92va-102rb, contains a commentary on the same text ascribed to Peter, a lengthy and detailed work with some references to Avicenna and about a dozen to Averroes.[19] Peter is overshadowed by his pupil, who left no commentary on this text.

Often Adam's commentaries are little more than literal exposition drawing extensively on Averroes, but marginal glosses in the Oxford MS. Corpus Christi College 114, fols. 235r-237r, include questions too. Seeking to understand the role of the dry and cold in aging, Adam makes the precision that, although dryness has a firm and stable character in itself, in the aged it is inimical to the harmony of a balanced constitution.[20] Similarly, superfluous and unnatural heat is a cause of decay, while natural and well-proportioned heat is a cause of long life. The ideal combination for longevity is a fiery, rather than an airy, heat and an airy, rather than a watery, moisture. Proportion is all important, the balance of qualities.[21]

Bodleian MS. Digby 55, fols. 25va-27rb, contains a short literal commentary under the headline *De morte et vita,* corrected to *De longitudine et brevitate vitae.* This material, with much from Averroes, appears to be

---

[17] Ibid., fol. 22vb: "... calidum siue alimentum flamme parue tarde consumit suam materiam, set magna flamma consumit eam uelociter propter caliditatis excellenciam et ita in quantum contraria est, quia magis calidum minus calido contrariatur et non superfluum in quantum huiusmodi ..."; fol. 23vb-24ra: "Sicut enim magna flamma corrumpit minorem in consumendo materiam siue alimentum parue flamme, et ita per accidens, eodem modo calor naturalis in animali, qui de sui natura digestiuus est, semper digerit. Si non (enim *MS.*) habeat alimentum in quod agit, consumit propriam materiam in qua est, scilicet humorem naturalem in quo iudicatur, et ita ex consequenti destruit seipsum et ipsum animal."

[18] See Michael Bertram Crowe, "Peter of Ireland: Aquinas's Teacher of the *Artes liberales,*" in *Arts libéraux et philosophie au moyen âge, Actes du quatrième Congrès international de philosophie médiévale, Université de Montréal, Montréal, Canada, 27 août – 2 septembre 1967* (Montreal, 1969), pp. 617-626.

[19] Ibid., pp. 622-623.

[20] Fol. 237rb: "Dicendum quod non quelibet stabilitas siue firmitudo est causa uite uel permanencie iuuentutis set solum illa que facit armoniam et complexionem temperatam stare que est subiectum uite. Set firmitas huic armonie repugnat magis."

[21] Ibid.: "Dicendum quod calidum superfluum est causa corrupcionis non temperatum .... Modo queratur cuiusmodi calidum sit magis causa longe uite, vtrum scilicet aereum uel igneum. Et quod aereum uidetur, quia calidum quod est causa longe uite debet esse proporcionale humido aereo; set huiusmodi est calidum aereum et non igneum: quare, etc. .... Dicendum, ut iam conclusum est, quod calidum igneum principaliter est magis causa longe uite."

an abridgement of Adam with some additions. It resembles a work in the
Vienna MS. Nat. bibl. lat. 2330, fols. 48ra-49vb, sometimes thought to be
by Siger of Brabant,[22] but here it is transmitted with commentaries of
Geoffrey of Aspall. Geoffrey, an M.A. of Oxford by 1264,[23] is better
known for question commentaries, and an unascribed fragment of one on
De longitudine in MS. Merton College 272, fols. 282rb-294vb, may be
linked with a complete ascribed text in the Cambridge MS. Gonville and
Caius College 509, fols. 287ra-302rb,[24] which might offer insights into
Oxford teaching around 1260.

The transmission of *De longitudine* under the title *De morte et vita* has
obscured the attention given to the proper material on death and life in
the first two books of a treatise by Peter of Spain.[25] Peter, of Portuguese
origin, is better known for his handbook of logic, a medieval best-seller.[26]
Dealing with the causes of death in book 1 of his treatise, he talks of
death ensuing when the radical moisture on which natural heat feeds is
exhausted[27] and heat wins the victory over moisture.[28] This conception
of radical moisture (*humidum radicale*), as recent studies have shown,[29]
had its origin in the medical literature of antiquity. Isaac Israeli's work in

---

[22] See Antoine Dondaine and L. J. Bataillon, "Le Manuscrit Vindob. lat. 2330 et Siger de Bra-
bant," *Archivum Fratrum praedicatorum* 36 (1966), pp. 170, 186-188. The works attributed to Siger
on *De longitudine et brevitate vitae* and *De iuventute et senectute* are listed by Lohr, "ML Aristotle
Commentaries," *Traditio* 29, pp. 136-137, nos. 23 and 25. The content of the latter is described by
Fernand van Steenberghen, *Siger de Brabant d'après ses œuvres inédites* 1, *Les Œuvres inédites,*
Les Philosophes belges, Textes et études 12 (Louvain, 1931), pp. 263-267, from the München
Staatsbibliothek MS. Clm. lat. 9559, fols. 71vb-73vb. The authenticity of these works is discussed
by van Steenberghen, *Maître Siger de Brabant,* Philosophes médiévaux 21 (Louvain, 1977), pp.
196, 203.

[23] See *BRUO*, 1: 60-61.

[24] See Enya Macrae, "Geoffrey of Aspall's Commentaries on Aristotle," *Mediaeval and
Renaissance Studies* 6 (1968) 108-109.

[25] The work is preceded by the title *Tractatus bonus de longitudine et brevitate vite* in the edition by P. Manuel Alonso, *Pedro Hispano, Obras filosóficas*, Vol. 3, Consejo superior de investigaciones científicas, Instituto de filosofia "Luis Vives", Ser. A, núm. 4 (Madrid, 1952), pp. 413-490,
and accompanied only by the text of the *translatio vetus* of the *De longitudine*, which first circulated
under the title *De morte et vita*, ibid., pp. 405-411. The distinction has been noted by Lohr, "ML
Aristotle Commentaries," *Traditio* 28, pp. 360-361, no. 6.

[26] Peter of Spain (Petrus Hispanus Portugalensis), *Tractatus called afterwards Summule logicales*, ed. Lambert M. de Rijk (Assen, 1972).

[27] *Liber de morte et vita et de causis longitudinis ac brevitatis vite* 1.2; ed. Alonso, 3: 424
(16-21).

[28] Ibid., p. 426 (13-19).

[29] See Michael McVaugh, "The '*humidum radicale*' in Thirteenth-Century Medicine," *Traditio*
30 (1974) 259-283, with the bibliography given there, particularly Thomas S. Hall, "Life, Death, and
the Radical Moisture," *Clio medica* 6 (1971) 3-23.

Arabic on fevers systematized Galen's diagnostic. In the Latin version of Constantinus Africanus, the *Liber febrium*,[30] which circulated early in the twelfth century, the West had an account of hectic fever in which *pthysis* is described as an unnatural consumption of body moisture, something occurring naturally in aging. Similar teaching was to be found in his translation, the *Pantegni,* and his paraphrase, the *Megategni*.[31] But it is Avicenna who in his pharmaceutical work, *Liber canonis,* characterizes the moisture inherent in the members since birth as "radical".[32]

Peter of Spain develops his account of three moistures with an elaborate example designed to show that when the moisture derived from nourishment is exhausted the material of the organism itself will be consumed, much as the wick of a lamp will be charred, drawing on its inherent moisture, when the oil fails.[33] A comparison of the heart afflicted by fever to a charred wick is found in Burgundio's version of Galen,[34] but again it is Avicenna who transmits it in his *Canon,* employing it not only for the final stage of hectic fever but also for the wasting that occurs naturally in old age.[35] Time, Peter says, is only indirectly a cause of perishing:[36] the ages of childhood, adolescence, and youth conserve life, but those of the elderly and very old hasten death, for in them

---

[30] *Opera omnia Ysaac,* 2 vols. (Lyons, 1515), 1: fols. 203v-226v.

[31] Ibid., 2: fols. 37vb, 261va-vb.

[32] Avicenna, *Liber canonis,* bk. 4, fen. 1, tract. 3 (Venice, 1507; repr. Hildesheim, 1964), fol. 413vb: "... sicut incipit flamma adurere corpus lichinii et humiditates eius radicales ...."

[33] *Liber de morte et vita* 1.2, pp. 427 (7)-428 (12); ibid., p. 428 (1-12): "... deficiente utraque humiditate oleagina, lucerna totam consumit lichini humiditatem et ipsa in fine propter sui subiecti ac pabuli devastationem extinguitur, similiter et accidit in recessu caloris; nam deficiente nutrimentali humiditate inducit resolutionem in substantialem, cuius ultimata resolutione caloris extinctionem consequi necesse est. Sicut autem lucerna primo agit in humiditatem circumstantem, demum in imbibentem, quibus consumptis radicalem devastat, similiter calor naturalis humiditates primas nutrimentales primo consumptioni tradit et ad ultimum radicalem resolvit per cuius resolutionem extinctus perit et mors adest."

[34] *De differentiis febrium* 1.7, in *Galieni opera* (Venice, 1490), fols. 439v-440r.

[35] *Liber canonis,* bk. 1, fen. 3, doctr. 3, fol. 53ra: "Calor igitur innatus est causa extinguendi seipsum accidentaliter propterea quod sit causa sui ipsius materiam consumendi sicut lampadis flamma que extinguitur propterea quod suam consumit materiam et quanto plus siccitas secundum augmentum procedit: calor innatus secundum diminutionem incedit. Ergo accidit defectus nunquam cessans vsque ad vltimum quod est defectus restaurandi humiditatem loco eius quod resolutum fuit: defectus igitur semper augetur." See too bk. 4, fen. 1, tract. 3, fol. 413vb, and Peter H. Niebyl, "Old Age, Fever, and the Lamp Metaphor," *Journal of the History of Medicine and Allied Sciences* 26 (1971) 351-368.

[36] *Liber de morte et vita* 2.1, p. 442 (6-12): "Tempus autem cum motum sequatur, est per accidens causa corruptionis quia per motum qui est causa eius per se; est autem causa generationis per accidens accidentis, quia motum per accidens est eius causa. Tempus igitur causa corruptionis dicitur, quia rerum corruptio sub tempore accidit, omnes enim res quecumque sunt in tempore, cum tempore labefiunt et corrumpuntur."

heat is weak and they are like an oil lamp about to be extinguished.[37] Aristotle is rightly questioned for saying that a hot climate favours a long life: hot air dries up the organism and accelerates aging. Constantinus is right to say that animals live longer in temperate regions.[38] Some hold the view that there are things that arrest the aging process and induce a state of youth through a rejuvenation of the flesh, but Peter's sober opinion is that whatever delays natural old age by conserving moisture and warmth conserves youth and delays natural death.[39] His last word, following Aristotle, is on the longevity of vegetables: the olive has a robust warmth and an unctuous airy moisture, not readily dried up.[40] What we lack is unction!

Peter may have been a student in arts at Paris before the strike of 1229, but around 1246-1249 he was teaching medicine in Siena. Meanwhile he had written his *Summulae logicales* and perhaps studied medicine at Montpellier. His treatise on death and life was probably written in the 1240s or 1250s,[41] but its form and the medical knowledge may argue against it being arts teaching. However, one of the two surviving copies, now in the Oxford MS. Corpus Christi College B 243, fols. 15va-28va, was made by a Dutch scribe working at Oxford in 1423 and was owned at various times by Duke Humfrey of Gloucester and the astrologer John Dee. Peter became court physician to Pope Gregory X in 1272. Four years later, when he became pope himself as John XXI, apparently trusting in his medical skill, he promised himself a long pontificate, although perhaps already in his seventies.[42] These hopes were not fulfilled, and eight

---

[37] Ibid., 3.2, p. 466 (21-23): "Etas pueritie, adolescentie, et iuventutis conservant; sed senectus et maxime senium mortem accelerat. Nam in ipso calor est debilis et est sicut lucerna extinctioni apparata."

[38] Ibid., p. 468 (13-16): "Veritas autem secundum Constantinum asserit animalia in regione temperata diutius conservari, cum in regione calida per resolutionem caloris et humiditatis consumptionem brevitatem vite incurrunt. In frigida per caloris diminutionem."

[39] Ibid., 5, pp. 482 (27)-483 (9): "Aliquorum autem sententiis comprobatur quod quedam res palliantes senectutem videntur inducere statum iuventutis, quamvis etatis processu irremeabili in vite spatio currere certum sit. Iste autem sunt que carnem permutant sicut virorum carnes, et natura novam regenerat ut ad iuventutis decorem reditus fieri videatur, sicut in medicamentis Medee fingitur.

Sed, cum mors naturalis per etatum cursum procedat et in senectute adveniat, iste res videntur ipsam retardare; sed vere omnes res que senectutem naturalem, humidum et calidum conservando, retardare dicuntur ac iuventutem conservare, mortem naturalem rationabiliter retardare iudicantur."

[40] Ibid., 6, p. 489 (27-30): "Plante igitur calide et humide habentes humidum aereum unctuosum longioris vite sunt, sicut oliva et relique oleagine, nam habent caloris fortitudinem et humidum ei proportionale, non leviter siccabile, neque congelabile, quemadmodum in animalibus longe vite."

[41] See the discussion of his career and works in De Rijk's edition of the *Tractatus*, pp. xli-xliii.

[42] Ibid., p. xxviii.

months later, in May 1277, he died of injuries sustained in the collapse of the roof of his newly constructed apartment in the papal palace at Viterbo. As he had once said himself, the causes of death with regard to external injury by chance accidents, like being hit, are unlimited, without certain number, and escape scientific understanding.[43]

A little before 1258 Albert the Great wrote on the *Parva naturalia*.[44] Working not as a university master but in his Dominican studium at Cologne, Albert, like Peter, treated *De morte et vita* and *De longitudine et brevitate vitae* together in one treatise. Albert quickly identifies himself as a man of the North who trusts in a cold and dry climate for long life – he was already around sixty and had more than twenty years to live. If concessions are to be made to Aristotle, it is a temperate warmth, such as that of spring, rather than torrid summer, or glacial winter, congealing the humours, that favours longevity.[45] In regard to the two moistures, nutrimental and radical, Albert extends Avicenna's example of the oil lamp: the wick can be flooded with excess of nutriment as well as being charred when it consumes its own material.[46] There is an inevitable loss of the radical moisture towards old age and an irreversible passage through the stages of life from the hot and moist through the hot and dry to the cold and dry of old age, where death is not bitter, since there is no piercing heat and the members have less feeling.[47]

Later in this work there is a little for those who are curious about the life span of shellfish, crocodiles, and whales,[48] but for Albert's own

---

[43] *Liber de morte et vita* 2.3, p. 454 (9-12).

[44] For a brief account of the *De iuventute et senectute* (*De aetate*) and *De morte et vita* (*De causis longioris et brevioris vitae*) in the chronological sequence of Albert's writings on the *Parva naturalia* see James A. Weisheipl, ed., *Albertus Magnus and the Sciences: Commemorative Essays, 1980*, Studies and Texts 49 (Toronto, 1980), Appendix 1, p. 571 (h) and (i).

[45] *Liber de morte et vita*, tract. 2, ch. 1, ed. Auguste Borgnet, *B. Alberti Magni Opera omnia*, Vol. 9 (Paris, 1890), pp. 351b-352a: "... locus frigidus et siccus sanior est: et longioris vitae sunt in eo homines quam in loco calido, sive sit humidus, sive sit siccus. Sed si debet salvari quod dictum est, tunc oportet quod locus calidus intelligatur temperatus, sicut medium tempus veris inter hyemem et aestatem dicitur calidum et humidum. Tale autem calidum est calidum fovens, et non calidum educens calorem naturalem. Frigida autem regio dicitur, quae respectu hujus medii est frigida, et haec habet frigiditatem glacialem et congelantem humores, et exstinguentem calorem naturalem, sicut hyems dicitur frigida ...."

[46] Ibid., ch. 6, pp. 360a-361b.

[47] Ibid., ch. 7, p. 363a: "Haec autem quae dicta sunt probant, quod primum humidum radicale numquam accipit restaurum per omnia simile, et praecipue in senibus. Et ideo succedunt sibi aetates in his qui vivunt et sic post calidum humidum, calidum siccum, et post hoc frigidum siccum, et tandem intus siccum et extra alienam humiditatem in senio putrescente. Haec autem est causa, quare non amara est mors senum, cum calidum pungens in eis sit quasi nullum; et quod est, est ab alieno humido suffocatum, et ideo impotens ad pungendum, et membra sunt jam quasi putrida et insensibilia."

[48] Ibid., ch. 9, pp. 365a-366b.

thoughts on the ages of human life one must go to his slightly earlier work *De aetate*. Although it has the subtitle *De iuventute et senectute*, this is more an original treatise than a paraphrase of the unrewarding text of Aristotle with that title. The underlying notion here is that each living thing has a life span in which the power of life accomplishes its measure in all its forms unless it is accidentally impeded.[49] Instead of the six ages of Augustine, there is an initial division, following the physiologists, into four ages: one in which the substance and power are being gathered; a second in which they are achieved; a third in which power diminishes without loss of substance; and a fourth in which both wane. After boyhood and virile manhood, old age (*senectus*) is characterized by the absence of any qualitative or quantitative loss in the substance of the organism apart from that of natural moisture: the nerves have not yet shrunk, the skin is unfurrowed, and the back unbowed.[50] There is a time in the burning of the lamp when oil seems to evaporate from the wick yet no loss is noticed in the lamp.[51] There is a midway state in life with the onset of a dry temper making for reliability, a keen grasp of what is perceived and wise judgment, less playfulness and sexual activity.[52] Extreme old age (*senium*), by contrast, is said to be cold and moist, but not with an intrinsic and natural moisture promoting growth, since the organism has dried out radically, affecting the nerves, skin, and bonestructure, hearing, sight, and memory, but with an extrinsic and unnatural moisture related to poor digestion, making the very old susceptible to coughs and wheezy.[53]

Albert's only indications of years are in regard to the age of growth, extending through infancy, teething, puberty, and youth to twenty-four, thirty, or thirty-five according to individual development.[54] We know that

---

[49] *De aetate sive De juventute et senectute liber*, ed. Borgnet in *B. Alberti Magni Opera omnia*, Vol. 9. Tract 1, ch. 1, p. 306a: "... aetas est spatium temporis in vivente relictum, in quo virtus vitae omnem perficit suae mensurae modum, nisi per accidens impediebatur."

[50] Ibid., tract. 1, ch. 2, pp. 306b-307a; ch. 5, p. 313.

[51] Ibid., ch. 5, p. 313b: "... oleum in lampade et imbibitum in licinio, et videtur evaporare de licinio: non tamen sentitur defectus ejus in lampade, sed tunc primum sentitur, cum multum fuerit evaporatum per ignem."

[52] Ibid., p. 313b: "... et in illo medio directe est frigida et sicca propter humiditatis, ut diximus, evaporationem: et ideo talibus attribuitur constantia et fortis apprehensio et sapientia: constantia quidem ex hoc quod est frigidum, bene retinet et siccum: apprehensio autem propter defectum calidi commiscentis operationes rationis: sapientia autem propter multam experientiam et multorum memoriam, quae ex frigido et sicco confortatur. In talibus enim cessant dissolutio jocorum et venereorum propter immobilitatem frigidi abscindentis motum, et sicci quod non de facili movetur extra seipsum."

[53] Ibid., ch. 6, pp. 314-315.

[54] Ibid., ch. 3, p. 310b.

for his pupil, Aquinas, however, following the scheme of six ages, boy-hood and adolescence, reckoned as one age in the fourfold scheme, ended at twenty-five, young manhood at fifty, old age at seventy, and extreme old age continued thereafter.[55] Albert's fourfold division, compared to the sequence of the four seasons, is that found early in the fourteenth century in Dante's *Convivio*. At Florence, as at Naples, *adolescenza*'s spring ends at twenty-five, but the summer of *gioventute* only continues until forty-five, when the autumn of *senettute* begins, though the approach of winter, *senio*, is still at seventy.[56] Roger Bacon in his treatise *De retardatione accidentium senectutis*, drawing on Avicenna and medical sources for a regimen to protract life, says that natural warmth generally begins to diminish after forty-five or fifty years.[57] The philosophers do not usually set a term to human life, though Dante thinks that extreme old age is not normally more than ten years: Plato died in his eighty-first year, so if Christ had not died at the peak of his manhood in his thirty-fourth year, he would have ascended to heaven in his eighty-first year.[58]

Albert's works, though not composed in a university setting, deserved mention here because of their extensive circulation: each survives in thirty manuscripts.[59] Of later thirteenth-century works those of Peter of

---

[55] *In 4 Sent.*, dist. 40, expos. text., *D. Thomae Aquinatis Opera omnia* 11 (Paris, 1874), p. 240b: "... prima aetas dicitur infantia usque ad septimum annum; secunda pueritia usque ad quartum-decimum; tertia adolescentia usque ad vigesimum quintum; quae tres aetates computantur quando-que pro una; quarta est juventus usque ad quinquaginta annos; quinta vero aetas est senectus usque ad septuaginta; sexta senium usque in finem." On the terminology and various reckonings of the ages by medieval authors see Joseph de Ghellinck, "Iuventus, gravitas, senectus," in *Studia mediae-valia in honorem admodum reverendi patris Raymundi Josephi Martin* (Bruges, 1948), pp. 39-59.

[56] *Il Convivio* 4.24.1-4, ed. Maria Simonelli, Testi e saggi di letterature moderne: Testi 2 (Bologna, 1966), pp. 200-201.

[57] *De retardatione accidentium senectutis*, ch. 1, ed. Andrew G. Little and Edward Withington, *Opera hactenus inedita Rogeri Baconi*, Fasc. 9 (Oxford, 1928), p. 10: "... caliditas naturalis minui incipit necessario, et tempus illud incipit post 45 annos vel 50 generaliter."

[58] *Convivio* 4.23.10 (p. 199): "... Cristo, lo quale volle morire nel trentaquattresimo ano de la sua etade; ché non era convenevole la divinitade stare in così discrescione, né da credere è ch'elli non volesse dimorare in questa nostra vita al sommo, poi che stato c'era nel basso stato de la puerizia"; 4.24.6 (p. 202): "Onde avemo di Platone, del quale ottimamente si può dire che fosse naturato, e per la sua perfezione e per la fisionomia che di lui prese Socrate quando prima lo vide, che esso vivette ottantuno anno, secondo che testimonia Tullio in quello De Senectute. E io credo che se Cristo fosse stato non crucifisso, e fosse vivuto lo spazio che la sua vita poteva secondo natura trapassare, elli sarebbe a li ottantuno anno di mortale corpo in etternale transmutato." The reference is to Cicero, *De senectute* 5.14.

[59] See Winfried Fauser, *Die Werke des Albertus Magnus in ihrer handschriftlichen Überliefe-rung*, 1: *Die echten Werke*, Alberti Magni Opera omnia, tomus subsidiarius 1 (Münster i.W., 1982), pp. 126-133.

Auvergne are preserved in MS. Merton College 274, fols. 263ra-283vb.[60]
Peter was appointed rector of the University of Paris in 1275 after the
upheavals in the arts faculty, and ironically his works are transmitted with
that ascribed to Siger in the Vienna manuscript.[61] Peter's discussion of
the balance of cold and heat in regard to aging is enlivened by memorable
illustrations for the student, the tremors of the drunkard, shivering in winter, and heat stroke, and the technique of slaking coals with cinders, used
by charcoal-burners to conserve their fires: either heat is driven in or
overcome by its contrary, cold, or a superabundance rapidly dissolves
natural moisture.[62] He treats at length the material on respiration, and the
high incidence of death from small upsets in old age is related to the low
level of natural heat and the inability of the elderly to support a sud-
den access of heat associated with emotion, because their breathing, the
cooling mechanism of the body, is defective. Less susceptibility to violent emotion makes, however, for an easy death.[63] Unlike Albert, Peter

---

[60] See Lohr, "ML Aristotle Commentaries," *Traditio* 28, pp. 341-342, nos. 15-18. The headlines
indicating the sequence of the material in the Merton MS. are somewhat misleading: fols. 263r-269r,
"De iuuentute et senectute"; 269v-278v, "De respiratione"; 279r-283v, "De morte et vita."

[61] See above p. 28, n. 22, for the writings attributed to Siger.

[62] Oxford, MS. Merton College 274, fol. 269rb: "Dictum est in libro *De problematibus*, in quo
non manifeste inuenitur assignasse causam istius set aliquo modo potest haberi ex hiis que dicit par-
ticula tercia, problemate quinto, vbi querit propter quid ebrii tremunt et magis quando intemperate
vinum bibunt: est autem vinum calidum; tremor autem fit a frigido maxime. Et soluit dicens quod
tremor uniuersaliter causatur propter infrigidacionem. Fit autem infrigidacio aut propter repercus-
sionem calidi ad interius propter frigus, sicut in hyeme accidit, aut propter extinccionem calidi
naturalis. Extinctio autem fit a contrario uel propter longitudinem temporis, sicut in senescentibus
contingit, aut superhabundanciam extranei calidi, sicut accidit in estuatis a sole uel actenuatis ex
labore inmoderato. Hec autem accidit bibentibus intemperatum vinum. Vinum enim intemperatum
bibitum, cum sit calidum uirtute, superhabundanciam caliditatis extranee inducit in corpore.
Superhabundans autem calidum cicius dissoluit humidum naturale, et ideo debilitatur calidum
naturale. Debilitato calido, inducitur frigidum, quod inducit tremorem. Ex quo habetur quod
superhabundancia calidi inproporcionalis corumpit calidum proporcionale et naturale. Et hoc eciam
potest haberi causa propter quam apposito suffocario marcescit ignis; non autem si occultetur cinere
uel si uicissim apponatur et admoueatur, quia coaperato (coapertura ?) apposito reflectitur calidum in
se ipsum et fortificatur. Fortificatum enim, consumit humidum; humido consumpto, corrumpitur
calidum. Et sic manifestum est causa quod suffocario apposito continue, cito corrumpitur; cum
autem vicissim apponitur et admouetur, fit aliqua refrigeracio; qua facta, debilitatur calidum; quo
debilitato, humidum diu saluatur, et per consequens calidum saluatur. Et ista arte utuntur illi qui faci-
unt carbones." The *Problemata* ascribed to Aristotle had been translated by Bartholomew of Mes-
sina between 1258 and 1266. Peter's reference is to *Problemata* 3.5 (871a27-871b31), a chapter in
which there is also an illustration of aging by an oil-lamp (871b6-13). Similar material is found in
chapter 26 of the same book (874b22-875a28), with more on aging, with the same illustration
(875a4-8).

[63] Ibid., fol. 281ra: "... dicit quod, quia mors accidit propter defectum calidi naturalis, contingit
quod in senectute, parvis existentibus passionibus, moriuntur. Et ideo racio huius est quia in senectute uiuencia modicum habent calidum. Calidum enim continue agit in humidum ipsum consumendo; et quanto plus consumitur humidum, tanto calidum magis debilitatur: et quia in senectute

effectively divides the stages of life into three: youth, the time of growth to completion; an intermediate stage of static achievement; and old age (*senectus*), a time of failing power.[64] Natural death occurs through a wasting (*marcefactio*) of natural heat, debilitated over time by the consumption of natural moisture.[65] When heat can no longer break down the food, the motion of the heart is affected, the pulse is weaker, and there is more difficulty in breathing.[66]

If Peter of Auvergne represents the 1270s, Simon of Faversham may stand for Paris around 1280.[67] MS. Merton College 292, fols. 396vb-401va, contain questions by Simon that show a dependence on Albert.[68] In his second question Simon argues that perpetual life is impossible because old age is the consumption of radical moisture: the substance of the wick cannot be restored by extrinsic nourishment.[69] Coming from

---

propter longitudinem temporis humidum consumptum est, ideo calidum est paucum. Si igitur fiat aliqua parua molestia particule que est instrumentum refrigeracionis, statim moriuntur .... Infert correlarium et dicit quod in senectute, modico facto motu contrario, faciliter moriuntur, et propter hoc mors que est in senectute est sine tristicia; dolor enim accidit ex concursu contrarii passionem violentam inferens et contra inclinacionem: et ideo sine dolore moriuntur et omnino separacio anime est insensibilis."

[64] Ibid., fol. 281va: "... est intelligendum quod omnia uiuencia generantur sub imperfecta quantitate, similiter sub imperfectis aliis disposicionibus, et ideo recipiunt alimentum et digerunt illud et conuertunt in substanciam suam et augmentantur. Omne autem quod uadit de imperfecto ad perfectum habet tempus in quo mouetur ad perfeccionem et tempus in quo mouetur ad non esse et corrupcionem. Et cum inter duos motus contrarios cadat quies media, sicut probatur *VIII° Phisicorum,* oportet quod sit tempus medium in quo non deficit, nec perficit, set stat. In tempore perfectus perficiuntur uirtutes et disposiciones; in tempore defectus deficiunt; in tempore status sunt sub sensibili perfectum et defectum status. Et ipse profectus nutritum in ordine ad tempus dicitur 'iuuentus', defectus autem dicitur 'senectus', status autem in quo nec stat, nec deficit, dicitur 'status' absolute."

[65] Ibid., fol. 281vb: "... mors naturalis est marcefaccio calidi naturalis propter longitudinem temporis facta et perfectissima. Calidum enim continue agit in humidum naturale consumendo ipsum. Consumendo autem humidum, debilitat se ipsum, et hoc fit pa⟨u⟩latiue. Sicut autem paulatiue consumit humidum, sic paulatiue debilitat se ipsum. Per longitudinem autem temporis accidit quod totum consumat et resoluat, et tu⟨n⟩c marcessit calidum, et ac⟨ci⟩dit marcefaccio propter temporis longitudinem .... Mortis autem animalis illa que accidit in senectute est marcefaccio calidi in parte refrigeratiua propter inpotenciam refrigerandi que accidit in senectute propter longitudinem temporis."

[66] Ibid., fol. 283ra: "... calidum subtilians alimentum causa est motus cordis, propter hoc maior et forcior est motus pulsus in iunioribus quam in senioribus. Et causa huius est quia in iunioribus calidum maius est quam in senibus; et quia maius est, plus eleuatur de spiritu siue exalacione que sunt causa motus: et ideo forcior est motus pulsus in iuuentibus quam in senibus, et ideo bene medici per pulsum iudicant de calido et de disposicionibus cordis."

[67] See *BRUO,* 2: 672, "Faversham, Simon de"; Lohr, "ML Aristotle Commentaries," *Traditio* 29, p. 145, nos. 14-16.

[68] Albert is named on fols. 397r, 398v, and 399ra.

[69] Oxford, MS. Merton College 292, fol. 397rb-va: "... senectus est paulatim consumpcio humidi radicalis per accionem calidi naturalis. Ista autem corupcio, que dicitur 'mors' in senibus, est quasi sine tristicia, quia humidum radicale et calor naturalis quasi peni/tus consumptum: et ideo,

Kent, "the Garden of England", Simon's reply to the third question sets aside Aristotle, Ptolemy, Avicenna, and Constantinus, as he rhapsodizes over temperate climes where warmth and moisture find their ideal balance.[70] Like Peter of Auvergne Simon adopts the scheme of three ages, *perfectus, status,* and *defectus*.[71] For those who are not dieting, his sixth question, whether abstinence shortens life, receives the reassuring answer that as the lamp wick is conserved by oil, so nutrimental moisture restores lost radical moisture.[72] His six questions on *De iuventute et senectute* have a more biological interest. Students attending these disputes, as with Albert's disquisitions on the gerontology of snakes and oysters, may have felt some of the disappointment of today's psychology students, dreaming of clinical couches in old Vienna while they spur reticent rats through mazes.

A fragment of Henry of Germany's questions on the same text in MS. Merton College 275, fols. 233ra-234vb, shows an interest in the heart as the seat of sensation at the turn of the century.[73] More substantial is the commentary on *De longitudine* in MS. Magdalen College 80, fols.

---

quia paruum remanet ibi de calido, parua est ibi accio, et ideo dicitur in senibus dulcis separacio anime a corpore .... Dicendum, ut predictum est, quod ignis nutritur in lichino et per tempus continuatur, et hoc per lichinum; tamen nichilominus deperdit aliquid de lichino, cum ex eo continue nutritur ignis; tamen ignis calidum naturale saluetur in humido radicali ...."

[70] Ibid., fol. 397vb: "Set habitantes in regionibus temperatis sunt longe vite quia calidum non ebetatur, nec humidum ultra modum exsiccatur, ad quam exsiccacionem sequitur mors in animali. Set ista que dicta sunt videntur esse contra intencionem Philosophi libro *De problematibus*. Ostendit enim ibi quod habitantes in regionibus calidis sunt longioris vite quam habitantes in regionibus frigidis, et assignat causam: quia habitantes in regionibus calidis sunt sicciores et minoris putrefaccionis; set mors causatur ex putrefaccione." The position rejected by Simon is that in *Problemata* 14.9 (909b25-36).

[71] Ibid., fol. 398ra: "Nota quod etas viuencium distinguitur in tria tempora, scilicet in tempus perfectus, defectus, et status ... est tempus defectus quando, scilicet, virtutes viuencium tendunt ad declinacionem, ita quod virtutes insite a generantibus vadunt ad corrupcionem."

[72] Ibid., fol. 399ra: "Sicut enim oleum restaurat consumpcionem lichini et inpediret ne cito deuastetur, consimili medio humidum nutribile restaurat deperditum humidi radicalis et inpedit ne cito deuastetur a calido naturali." Arnald de Villanova, a Montpellier master of the late thirteenth century, writing from a medical perspective in his treatise *De humido radicali*, says (tract. 2, ch. 1, *Arnaldi Villanovani philosophi et medici summi Opera omnia* [Basel, 1585], cols. 303-304): "Dicentes hoc fieri recte, sicut in lampade, ibi enim proprium et immediatum subiectum calidi est humiditas elychnii, quam de facili consumeret calor igneus, nisi hoc impediret humiditas olei, que tamen humiditas olei non restaurat secundum veritatem humiditatem elychnii, sed solum impedit citam eius consumptionem distrahendo calorem virtutis ignei ad alienam materiam." Arnald is referring to the opinion of those who hold that the restoration of radical humidity by nourishment is apparent rather than real.

[73] See Lohr, "ML Aristotle Commentaries," *Traditio* 24, p. 216, no. 1. The commentary that may be by Siger of Brabant, in the Munich MS., displays a similar interest in q. 4, "Utrum sensitivum commune sit in corde" (see van Steenberghen, *Les Œuvres inédites*, p. 265).

180va-184vb, by Walter Burley, a Merton master of the first decade of the fourteenth century,[74] who combines literal exposition with questions. Walter says, against Aristotle, that in hot climates there is a greater drying up and dispersal of natural moisture, because opening of the pores leads to evaporation; in temperate climates there is adequate moisture, because the heat is not so excessive as to open the pores and the warmth is airy and unctuous.[75] Aristotle also says that work induces old age, but Walter is not averse to work in moderation, particularly if one has congealed phlegmatic humours,[76] a common condition in Oxford down by the Isis. What militates against perpetual life is a wasting (*marcedo*) in which excess of heat destroys moisture, either, as Aristotle says, because of abstinence from food, or, as Avicenna says, from too little or too much sleep. In any case, continuous evaporation would lead to the easy death of old age.[77] It is the familiar story of the irreparable decay of the wick, which even nourishment cannot restore, or, to change the image, if you go on adding water, eventually wine will be diluted to the point where it is no longer wine.[78] Our life cycle is like that of a candle: when first lit it

[74] See *BRUO*, 1: 312-314; Lohr, "ML Aristotle Commentaries," *Traditio* 24, p. 184, no. 34.

[75] Oxford, MS. Magdalen College 80, fol. 181va-vb: "... in calidis regionibus est maior exsiccacio et resolucio humidi naturalis quam in frigidis, quia in regionibus calidis aer calidus aperit poros corporum, quibus apertis euaporat humidum cum calido naturali .... Item, animalia in regione temperata sufficienciam habent de humido, quia calidum regionis temperate non est ita excellens vt aperiat poros corporis educendo humidum naturale. Nam humidum eorum remanet interius: propter quod non sunt / faciliter exsiccabilia. Item, habent sufficienciam de calido, quia humidum in animali est aereum vnctuosum, bene compaciens secum calidum: et ideo cum habuerit sufficienciam de humido, et habent sufficienciam de calido."

[76] Ibid., fol. 182vb: "Postea dicit Philosophus quod labor inducit senium, quia labor dessicat (466b14); senectus autem est sicca, vt dictum est. Et istud est verum de labore inmoderato, non de labore temperato. Ideo, si quis habeat humores fleumaticos cogelatos, tali prodest labor temperatus, quia ex motu fortificaretur calor qui degraderat illos humores."

[77] Ibid., fol. 184rb-va: "... corrupcio calidi naturalis potest contingere uel a frigido extrinseco congelante et mortificante, et istam corrupcionem vocat Philosophus 'extinccionem', que proprie est in uiuentibus; alia corrupcio, inquantum scilicet calidum naturale multum habundans propter defectum frigidi conuertit se super proprium humidum ipsum destruendo, et istam corrupcionem vocat Philosophus 'marcedinem'. Et ista corrupcio aliquando est in quibusdam propter nimiam abstinenciam a nutrimento, sicut dicit Philosophus; et in quibusdam propter vigiliam, secundum Auicennam; in quibusdam vero propter nimium sompnum. 3 est corrupcio calidi naturalis que fit per continuam euaporacionem humidi naturalis per calidum naturale conplantatum a natura. Et Auicenna loquens de ista corrupcione, eo quod calidum continue depascit humidum, quocumque deueniat mors que vnicuique destinata est per naturam. Ista autem euaporacio continue facta inducit somnum et tandem mortem, que mors est sine tristicia et sine labore. Nam per longitudinem vite multa fit euaporacio humidi, et ita in fine non potest calidum / agere, et ita mors redditur quasi insensibilis. Vnde mors senum est quasi sine tristicia et sine labore, et talis mors est dulcis, sicut dicit Philosophus."

[78] Ibid., fol. 184va: "... si aliquid modicam aquam infundat doleo repleto vino, augtetur, set tamen debilitatur, et in tantum poterit apponi de aqua quod corrumpitur natura vini. Sic ex parte ista, humidum nutrimentale debilitat humidum naturale ita quod tandem humidum naturale corrumpitur totale. Vnde, sicut ignis nutritur in lichino et tamen continue corrumpit aliquid de lichino, ita quod

gives little light but has the potentiality to give greater warmth and light;[79] finally, however, there is an inevitable decline as the interior reserves of life are consumed in old age.

These stray leaves from early teaching at Paris and Oxford have been used to sketch a history of beginnings between about 1240 and 1310 – within a lifetime of seventy years. Stimulated by the recently translated texts of Aristotle and the epitome of Averroes, these early masters developed an account of aging that met the needs of a natural philosophy course, first in literal expositions and then, with more freedom, in disputed questions. The leaven came from Galen's diagnostic of fevers, transmitted in Arabic, the terminology of radical moisture from Avicenna's pharmacology, and the ubiquitous image of the lamp from the same source. Only the generality of treatment preserved the claim of these studies to be philosophy. Often a biological interest predominated, but the human interest was there too, particularly in the discussions of climate and the regime of life.

---

quantumcumque de oleo apponatur tandem corrumpit totus lichinus, ita calidum naturale nutritur humido radicali ita quod quantumcumque apponatur de humido nutrimentali tandem oportet humidum radicale totaliter corrumpi."

[79] Ibid., fol. 184vb: "... puer est minoris virtutis et potencie quo ⟨ad⟩ operacionem quam homo xxx annorum, tamen est maioris potencie in tempore, quia potest diucius durare. Huius simile potest poni. Contingit aliquando quod candela cum primo illuminatur modicam virtutem habet ad illuminandum medium; postea tamen magis ignitur et magis inflammatur, habet maiorem virtutem calefaciendi et illuminandi medium. Candela igitur in principio sue ignicionis est minoris virtutis quo ad operacionem quam est postea, et tamen in principio est maioris potencie tempore, quia potest diucius durare quam postea."

3

Honour the Hoary Head
The Aged in the Medieval European Jewish Community*

Michael A. Signer

Hebrew Union College-Jewish Institute of Religion
Los Angeles, California

The ninth through fifteenth centuries witnessed the establishment and growth of Jewish communities over most of northern Europe and the Iberian peninsula. These communities were urban and their members were protected by privilegia issued by various ranks of nobility. The legal status of these communities varied with the ruler, the geographic area, and the century. However, Jewish communities in Europe all shared a legal autonomy to conduct their internal community affairs according to the laws of their ancestors. Jews brought a sophisticated legal system based on Scripture and the Talmud into their European settlements. They continued to develop and adapt their legal traditions through exegesis of Scripture and Talmud as well as through a literature of Responsa or decisions of local rabbis on questions sent to them.[1]

Our investigation of the aged in the medieval Jewish community begins with this legal literature. It is our point of departure for two

---

* This paper is lovingly dedicated to Professor Jacob Rader Marcus in honour of his seven decades of teaching Jewish History at the Hebrew Union College-Jewish Institute of Religion. His intellectual rigour remains an inspiration for me, and his book, *Communal Sick Care in the German Ghetto*, set me on the path to a scientific understanding of the Jewish past.

[1] On the autonomous legal status of the Jews in Europe during the period from 800 to 1500 one should consult Yitzhak Baer, *History of the Jews in Christian Spain*, 2 vols. (Philadelphia, 1961); Guido Kisch, *The Jews in Medieval Germany* (Chicago, 1949; repr. New York, 1970); Robert Chazan, *Medieval Jewry in Northern France* (Baltimore, 1973). For the Jewish self-understanding of their legal autonomy one should consult H. H. Ben-Sasson, ed., *A History of the Jewish People* (Cambridge, Mass., 1976), pp. 385-726.

Aging and the Aged in Medieval Europe, ed. Michael M. Sheehan, CSB. Papers in Mediaeval Studies 11 (Toronto: Pontifical Institute of Mediaeval Studies, 1990), pp. 39-48. © P.I.M.S., 1990.

reasons. First, it is accessible. Second, these legal sources formed the basis for religious and social practices whose influence has extended beyond the chronological boundaries of our study.[2] Historians of European Jewry who have utilized these legal sources have given considerable attention to the family. Moritz Güdemann and others have described the early stages of childhood with particular focus on the education of males.[3] Irving Agus has done extensive research on the legal and fiscal status of the family and marriage in France and Germany.[4] Most recently, S. D. Goitein has provided an intimate portrait of family life of Mediterranean Jewry from Arabic sources.[5] These historians have not concerned themselves in a systematic manner with the later stages of life or old age.

In this sense we have almost a *tabula rasa* with respect to the question of the aged in the medieval Jewish community. Therefore the most simple, almost naive, questions mark the outlines of this paper. We begin with an attempt to describe the vocabulary that is utilized to define "old age." Once we have established the basic terms for age and aging we may ask about the awareness of the biology of aging in this literature. How have these biological processes been evaluated? We shall then consider some examples of legal cases emerging from rabbinic Responsa that appear to be associated with the aged. We shall try to consider, throughout the paper, the diversity of our sources and the apparent disparity

---

[2] The impact of social reality on the body of Jewish law is a matter of scholarly debate among contemporary Jewish historians. Haym Soloveitchik, "Can Halakhic Texts Talk History?" *AJS Review* 3 (1978) 153-196, argues in the affirmative yet would minimize the "temporal" factors that influence an authority's legal decision, and gives greater weight to the personal characteristics of the authority. Jacob Katz, *Exclusiveness and Tolerance: Studies in Jewish-Gentile Relations in Medieval and Modern Times* (New York, 1962), implies a balance between social ambiance and the personal characteristics of the Rabbi who offered the commentary or legal decision. Since rabbinic law is still completely authoritative for Orthodox Jews in the contemporary world, there is a reluctance to ascribe a causal status to social reality upon a Rabbi who is called to render a legal decision. My colleague, David Ellenson, describes this theological and sociological problem in two articles, "The Role of Reform in Selected German-Jewish Orthodox Responsa: A Sociological Analysis," *Hebrew Union College Annual* 53 (1982) 357-380; and "Accommodation, Resistance, and the Halakhic Process," in *Jewish Civilization: Essays and Studies,* ed. Ronald A. Brauner, 2 vols. (Philadelphia, 1979, 1981), 2: 83-100.

[3] Moritz Güdemann, *Geschichte des Erziehungswesens und der Cultur der abendländischen Juden während des Mittelalters und der neueren Zeit,* Vol. 1: *Geschichte ... der Juden in Frankreich und Deutschland* (Vienna, 1880); *Quellenschriften zur Geschichte des Unterrichts und der Erziehung bei den deutschen Juden* (Berlin, 1891); *Das jüdische Unterrichtswesen während der spanisch-arabischen Periode* (Vienna, 1873). Israel Abrahams, *Jewish Life in the Middle Ages* (1896), 2nd ed. rev. Cecil Roth (London, 1932), summarizes much of the material in Güdemann.

[4] Irving A. Agus, *Urban Civilization in Pre-Crusade Europe,* 2 vols. (New York, 1965); *The Heroic Age of Franco-German Jewry* (New York, 1969); *Rabbi Meir of Rothenburg,* 2 vols. (Philadelphia, 1947).

[5] Solomon D. Goitein, *A Mediterranean Society: The Jewish Communities of the Arab World as Portrayed in the Documents of the Cairo Geniza,* Vol. 3: *The Family* (Berkeley, California, 1978).

between their evaluation of old age and the treatment of the aged by the community.

The word most commonly associated with "old age" or "aging" is the Hebrew root *ZQN*. These three root letters are associated both with the word for "beard" and the word for "aged." It appears frequently in Scripture as a designation of an individual of advanced age. There appears to be no indication in Scripture, however, of the chronological onset of "old age." The plural form of the noun, *ZeQeNim*, moreover, refers to people of advanced age, but frequently appears to refer to a special class or group of people associated with leadership, just as the word "elder" in English does. An abstract noun *ZeQuNim* appears several times in Scripture and is applied to Sarah and Abraham at the time of the birth of Isaac, and to Jacob at the time of Joseph's birth. *ZeQuNim* would appear to refer to a state of advanced age.[6]

The rabbinic masters between the second and fourth centuries indicated their awareness of the semantic range of the biblical term *ZaQeN* in their discussion of the biblical injunction to rise up before the hoary head (Lev. 19:32). They questioned whether the word *ZaQeN* in that context referred to a scholar of any age or exclusively to an aged person who might or might not be a scholar.[7] In his commentary on the Talmud Rabbi Solomon ben Isaac of Troyes (†1105) claimed that the word *ZaQeN* in the scriptural passage referred to any older person.[8] Rabbi Isaac of Dampierre, in a twelfth-century commentary to the Talmud, interpreted the passage to refer to a scholar as the *ZaQeN* and that chronological age was not a meaningful criterion.[9] We shall return to this talmudic passage, for it has implications for individual behaviour of respect for scholars or the aged. It is clear that the rabbinic discussions about a *ZaQeN* understood the term as indicating more than a biological or chronological stage of life.

Let us turn from the vocabulary of age to the awareness of the biological processes of aging. It is the nature of rabbinic sources to describe the stages of life when they are linked to some ritual demand. This would be the reason that most non-Jews in the contemporary world know that thirteen is the age of religious majority or *Bar Mitzvah* for Jewish males.

---

[6] On *ZQN* and its various forms in biblical Hebrew, one should consult L. Koehler, ed., *Lexicon in Veteris Testamenti libros* (Leiden, 1958), p. 264, cols. a-b.

[7] *Talmud Babli* (henceforth *T.B.*), *Kiddushin* 32b-33a. For English translation see *The Babylonian Talmud*, ed. Isidore Epstein, *Seder Nashim*, Vol. 4, tractate *Kiddushin*, trans. Harry Freedman (London, 1936), pp. 159-164.

[8] Rabbi Solomon ben Isaac of Troyes, *Commentary on the T.B. Kiddushin* 32b.

[9] Rabbi Isaac of Dampierre, *Tosafot* to *T.B. Kiddushin* 32b.

Classical rabbinic literature has nothing at all to say about the biological significance of a male becoming thirteen years old.

Because of the link to laws of purity regarding marital status the female menstrual cycle receives extended treatment in rabbinic literature.[10] While the issue in this context is the menstrual cycle, menarche and menopause are also given consideration. The rabbis linked menopause with the term *ZeQeNaH* or old woman. *Mishnah Niddah* set the question, "Who is regarded as a *ZeQeNaH?* Any woman over whom three regularly set cycles of menstruation have passed near the time of her old age."[11] The sages in the Babylonian Talmud further delineate the issue and ask, "What is to be understood as the 'time of her old age'?" One scholar held that it was the age when her friends speak of her as an old woman. Another scholar held that it begins when people call her "mother" in her presence and she does not mind.[12]

Medieval authorities adopted the latter position in their legal codifications: she no longer minded when people called her an old woman or mother.[13] The northern French scholastic commentary on the Talmud called *Tosafot* raised a most pertinent question about the nature of the aging process described in the talmudic passage. Does the definition of an old woman depend entirely upon the judgment of the woman in question? Is she the one who, because she does not mind, determines that she is aged? The commentary points out that the passage should be interpreted as being applicable to any person who is appropriate to call her "mother."[14]

The commentary by the Tosafists indicates that they perceived a social determination for the term "aged woman." She alone could determine that she did not mind being called an old woman. However, this was modified by a sense that she was called aged by "worthy" peers. In this example one can observe that, for the biology of a woman's aging, both natural and social definitions intersect in Jewish law.

There seems to be no single biological ceremony that marked the onset of old age in a male. However, the exegesis of two talmudic passages indicates certain physiological hallmarks of the aging process. When a

---

[10] On the problem of female purity in the Jewish legal tradition see Jacob Neusner, *The Idea of Purity in Ancient Judaism* (Leiden, 1973).

[11] *Mishnah Niddah* 1:5, in *The Mishnah*, trans. Herbert Danby (Oxford, 1933), pp. 745-746.

[12] *T.B. Niddah* 9a-b. For English translation see *Babylonian Talmud*, ed. Epstein, *Seder Tohoroth*, Vol. 1, tractate *Niddah*, trans. Israel W. Slotki (London, 1948), pp. 59-63.

[13] Moses Maimonides, *Mishnah Torah, Seder Nashim, Hilkhot 'Issure Bi'ah*, ch. 9, par. 5; Jacob ben Asher, *'Arba Turim, Yoreh De'ah*, par. 189, sec. 29.

[14] The Tosafists and their work have been examined in great detail by Efraim E. Urbach, *Ba'ale HaTosafot*, 2nd ed., 2 vols. (Jerusalem, 1980). The Tosafists to *T.B. Niddah* 9b raise the question on the basis of the Jerusalem Talmud. Utilizing the Jerusalem Talmud in order to raise the question on the text of the Babylonian Talmud reflects the customary exegetical method of the Tosafists.

sage is asked why he did not appear in a public place of enjoyment, he responded, "The mountain is snowy." Rabbi Solomon ben Isaac explains the sage's answer, "His beard and moustache have turned white." In the same talmudic discussion there are two statements whose explication evoke further descriptions of the physical attributes of aging. One sage states, "That which I have not lost, I seek." This is explicated as follows: "That which has not been lost to me from old age, I walk bent over and tottering and appear as one who looks for a coin which is missing." Another medieval interpretation of the same passage states, "The old man who does not see what is in front of him fears that he will strike his head on a rock and therefore probes with his hand as if he were looking for a lost object." The final statement in the talmudic passage is "Two are better than three," which means, according to Rabbi Solomon ben Isaac, "The two legs of the days of youth are superior to the three of old age which require a cane for support in addition to the legs."[15] Old age for males is thus pictured as a time of physical infirmity: the walk is unsteady, one is bent over and incapable of walking without support, and one has poor eyesight.

These physical indications are supplemented in medieval Hebrew literature with a description of another aspect of the aging process – forgetfulness. "Therefore, my son, make great effort in the days of your youth and adolescence since you now complain of forgetfulness. What will you do in the days of old age which is the mother of forgetfulness," is the admonition of Judah ibn Tibbon, in twelfth-century Provence, to his son Samuel.[16] In a thirteenth-century text we find a similar theme: "Learn while you are young when you eat what others provide, while your mind is still free and unencumbered with cares, before memory loses its vigor. For the time will come when you will want to learn but will be unable. Even if you do not fail entirely you will labor to little effect; for your mind will lag behind your lips, and when it does keep pace, the memory will not hold fast what the mind attains."[17]

The evaluation of the aging process in these medieval Jewish texts appears to be one of diminishing mental and physical capacity. Women reach old age when they no longer have the power of procreation; men display age through a loss of physical agility and mental acumen. These attributes of the aged are summarized in a commentary on the *Mishnah Aboth* contained in the *Maḥzor Vitry*, a liturgical customary of the twelfth

---

[15] *T.B. Shabbat* 152a with the commentary of Rabbi Solomon ben Isaac of Troyes and the commentary of Rabbenu Ḥananel ben Hushiel of Kairwan, North Africa (†1050) *ad loc.*

[16] Judah ibn Tibbon, "A Father's Admonition," in *Hebrew Ethical Wills*, ed. Israel Abrahams (Philadelphia, 1926), p. 62.

[17] Pseudo-Maimonides, "The Gate of Instruction," in *Hebrew Ethical Wills*, ed. Abrahams, p. 107.

century written by Rabbi Simḥa of Vitry. The Mishna passage under discussion in the commentary is

> At five years old one is fit for the study of Scripture; at ten years, the
> *Mishnah;* at thirteen for fulfilling the commandments; at fifteen for the
> Talmud; at eighteen for marriage; at twenty for pursuing a career; at thirty
> for authority; at forty for discernment; at fifty for counsel; at sixty for old
> age; at seventy for grey hairs; at eighty for strength; at ninety for bowed
> back; and at one hundred he is as one who has already died and passed
> away from the world.[18]

If we pass over the youthful stages of this rabbinic *aetates hominum* to
the commentary on the later stages of life, the same negative evaluation
of old age appears. "*At sixty for old age,* as it is stated in Job 5:26, 'You
will come to the grave in ripe old age (*bakelah*)'." This word, *bakelah,*
has the numerical value of sixty in Hebrew. We may infer from this that
the author of the commentary considered sixty a time of ripe old age
when one was ready for the grave. The association of old age with death
is also asserted in the comment on *at seventy for grey hair,* "David's age
was thirty when he began to reign and he died after forty years on the
throne." The book of Chronicles states that David died *beseyvah tovah,* at
a ripe old age or grey. *At eighty for strength* is explained in the commentary that the individual is given strength (*gevurah*) to live longer than the
time alloted, or that *gevurah* is understood to mean that by the time he
reaches the age of eighty he no longer has strength of his own to eat and
drink, so he lives by the strength of God. *At ninety for bowed back* is
explained, "for he is bent over and ready for burial." *At one hundred he is
like dead,* "for his eyes are clouded over and his face has changed and the
fount of wisdom has ceased from him and he becomes progressively
more demented."[19]

The exegetical literature on biblical and talmudic texts regards the
individual after fifty in a state of diminished mental and physical capacity. All ages after fifty suggest physiological deterioration. No positive
attributes are ascribed to the aged individual in any of these treatises or
commentaries. To become old meant to become dependent upon physical
support and the strength of others. It is not possible to determine whether
the medieval Jewish authors employed these negative attributions as a
result of their own observations of old age or because the context of the
talmudic passage and earlier interpreters guided them.

It is possible to elicit from the rabbinic legal codes and Responsa literature some aspects of the treatment of the aged within the medieval Jewish community. My research has not led me to a particular aspect of the

---

[18] *Mishnah Aboth* 5:21 (my translation); cf. *Mishnah,* trans. Danby, p. 458.
[19] *Maḥzor Vitry,* ed. with notes by S. H. Horowitz (Jerusalem, 1963), pp. 549-552.

legal tradition that focused on the problems of the aged. Examples of these problems do appear within categories of Jewish law that treat the infirm or dying, the acts of honour due to parents, and in the provision for support of disadvantaged individuals.

There is one responsum that treats the case of a man who had become infirm due to age. His eyesight had failed him and he could no longer reckon his accounts. He appointed a guardian to read his account books for him and to settle his affairs. The local court protested this action, claiming that they should have been acting on his behalf rather than a privately appointed guardian.[20]

The aged receive extended consideration in the legal category of acts of honour that are demanded through the biblical command "to rise up before the aged and to act honourably before the hoary head." As we stated earlier in this paper, the term *ZaQeN* meant both an aged individual and one who was a scholar albeit not of advanced years. The legal codes of the thirteenth and fourteenth centuries conclude that age is not the exclusive category demanding that an individual rise in the presence of the *ZaQeN*.[21] One who is young but a sage may also be considered a *ZaQeN*, based on the etymology of *ZaQeN* being an acronym for *Zeh sheQaNah Hokhmah* (one who has acquired wisdom). Some medieval legal authorities, however, indicate that for the young man to be accorded the honour of others rising in his presence he must truly be outstanding in wisdom.[22] The thirteenth-century legal codifier Jacob ben Asher required that whenever an individual seventy-year-old was present even a young sage must rise to his full height to honour him.[23]

The ambivalence about according the honour of rising before the elder as a matter of honouring wisdom or chronological age within social settings is also attested in Jacob ben Asher's code, *'Arba Turim*.

> In a case where there is a very outstanding young scholar and a very old person who is wise but not as wise as the young man – the community seats the young man at the head of the table in a legal academy and they permit him to speak first; but at a wedding feast they seat the old man at

---

[20] Joel Müller, *Responsen der Lehrer des Ostens und Westens* [Hebrew] (Berlin, 1888), 2b-3a, sec. 5. According to Müller's annotations this responsum comes from the period of Rav Hai Gaon (†1038) of Baghdad. It was preserved in the writings of Rabbi Isaac al-Fasi (†1103), who wrote the first epitome of the talmudic text and legal decisions in the Iberian peninsula.

[21] Maimonides, *Mishnah Torah, Hilkhot Talmud Torah*, ch. 9; Moses of Coucy, *Sefer Mitzvot HaGadol*, Positive commandment #13; Jacob ben Asher, *'Arba Turim, Yoreh De'ah*, par. 244.

[22] This position is explicated in great detail by Rabbi Isaac in the *Tosafot* to T.B. *Kiddushin* 32b. Rabbi Solomon ben Isaac of Troyes in his commentary on the same text argues that the commandment refers only to a person of advanced years. Authorities such as Maimonides, Rabbenu Asher, and Jacob ben Asher decide that one rises in the presence of the young scholar. These authorities are cited in the *'Arba Turim*, par. 244.

[23] Jacob ben Asher, *'Arba Turim* 244.

the head of the table and permit him to speak first. In a case where the young man is a sage of outstanding wisdom and the older man is not very elderly – in some places they use old age as the criterion for seating and speaking first even if the young man is outstanding. If neither is outstanding in wisdom or age, then the older person is preferred.[24]

The later section is explained in a sixteenth-century gloss as follows: "One does not embarrass the older man and the young sage is not embarrassed because the older man knows the honour is bestowed upon him because of his age."[25] These passages indicate that although the young sage may be considered a *ZaQeN*, the person of advanced years is given higher honour in those social situations where it is appropriate, except in the talmudic academy (*Yeshivah*) where superior wisdom would be the only criterion for honour.

In the legal discussions about rising before the elder as a sign of honour I discovered the only description of conduct towards non-Jewish elders. The code of Jacob ben Asher indicates that one should honour the elders of the gentiles by rising up slightly and extending one's hand.[26] The northern French commentary of the Tosafists, while not contradicting this practice, asserts that rising before the elders of the gentiles is not rooted in revealed Scripture, for "Nowhere do we find that the Torah makes honouring them equivalent to honouring the elders of Israel."[27] The Tosafists claim that the talmudic passage which is the precedent for honouring the elders of the gentiles is based upon the personal experience of the Rabbi in the Talmud who did so, and not upon the injunction in Leviticus to rise up before the elder. The particular concern for the distinction of honouring gentile and Jewish elders is consistent with the northern French talmudic tradition of interpreting behaviour towards non-Jews as rooted in personal experience, or "keeping the public peace," rather than making divine commandments apply to gentiles as well as to Jews.[28]

The laws regarding the treatment of father and mother are also a significant source of information about the aged in the Jewish communities of Europe. The Rabbis of the Talmud had extended the meaning of the Fifth Commandment of honouring father and mother to mean providing them with material support such as food and clothing. While one

---

[24]   Jacob ben Asher, *'Arba Turim* 244.

[25]   Joseph Caro of Safed (16th cent.), *Bet Yosef* to *'Arba Turim* 244.

[26]   Jacob ben Asher, *'Arba Turim* 244.

[27]   The Tosafists are quoted here from the text of Joseph Caro, *Bet Yosef* to *'Arba Turim* 244.

[28]   On Jewish-Christian social relations in northern France and Germany during the thirteenth century see Katz, *Exclusiveness and Tolerance*, pp. 1-128, and Ivan G. Marcus, *Piety and Society: The Jewish Pietists of Medieval Germany* (Leiden, 1981).

might assume that in the tightly knit communities of Europe such support was freely given by children to their parents, the Responsa literature indicates that it proved troublesome – and that material support for parents by children was a problem in the medieval Jewish community.

There were questions asked of the Rabbis about the utilization of a son's income for the support of his father. If the father had no money to support himself, and the son was a man of means, the community might coerce the son to support the father. Authorities disagreed about whether the son who was begging to make a living must support his father. Most of the authorities indicate that the child should not impoverish himself to support the parent.[29]

In thirteenth-century Germany, Rabbi Meir of Rothenburg indicated that an aged mother had three sons in different economic circumstances, from very wealthy to making a living through teaching (the least wealthy). She had come to the court of her community to demand the sons provide her with support. The court then turned to Rabbi Meir of Rothenburg, who ruled that each son must contribute to the support of the mother proportionate to his means.[30]

When the question was raised about the utilization of charitable contributions to support elderly parents, Meir of Rothenburg replied that he did not consider such contributions acceptable for parental support. To provide for one's parents out of a general charity fund contribution was not considered to be "honouring" one's parents. The only exception he permitted was in cities where there was no local ordinance to collect for a general charitable fund. In that case the child could provide for his parents through charitable contribution. Meir's decision is quoted by later authorities to indicate that parental support and support of general charitable funds were to be two separate gifts.[31]

Another category of the aged population in European Jewish communities was the widow. When a woman's husband died she received her marriage dowry in addition to other sums that had been promised to her in her marriage contract. She was considered competent to act on her own behalf before local courts. However, the length of time between the marriage and the death of her husband often meant that the sums in the marriage contract in both moveable and immoveable goods had changed or become encumbered in other ways. Widows, therefore, appear in the

---

[29] Jacob ben Asher, *'Arba Turim, Yoreh De'ah*, par. 240-241. The conflicting authorities are also cited in a responsum from northern Europe in E. Kupfer, ed., *Teshuvot u'Pesaqim me'et Hokhme 'Ashkenaz veTsarfat metokh Ms. Bodl. 692* (Jerusalem, 1973), pp. 145-146, sec. 87.

[30] Rabbi Meir ben Barukh (Maharam) of Rottenberg, *Responsa, Rulings, and Customs* [Hebrew], ed. Isak Z. Cahana, 4 vols. (Jerusalem, 1957-1977), 2: 118-119, sec. 127.

[31] Ibid., 2: 122, sec. 133; 256, sec. 195.

Responsa literature as a class both dependent and independent, such as the widow who wanted to present a gift to one of her grandsons after her husband and one of her sons had died. Another surviving relative, a grandson, attempted to limit the widow's power to make a gift. The court and the Rabbi who wrote the responsum indicated that she had full rights to deed property.[32]

The widow status, however, did not always provide sufficient cause for favourable judgment. In another case an independent elderly woman claimed that her son-in-law had taken over property by presumptive right that should have been part of her marriage contract. Her claim was that when her husband had made a gift of the property to her daughter and son-in-law she had remained silent to please her husband. Now that her husband was dead she wanted to reclaim the property as her own. The Rabbi decided against her claim. She had remained silent for too many years to remove her son-in-law's presumptive right to the property. Silence in order to please her husband *ab initio* was insufficient grounds for restoring the property to her.[33]

These are only a few examples of the experiences of the aged in the legal system of the European Jewish community. It should be noted that, in the few cases we have adduced, it is not the chronological age that constitutes the legal problem but the social situation. The infirm man, the destitute father, and the widow were judged on the basis of their claims, not on the basis of their age. Further investigations of the legal problems raised by the existence of an aged population will have to take this social framework into consideration.

Our investigation of the legal literature on the aged population of the Jewish community would seem to present us with a divided picture. Growing old or aging was viewed in a most negative manner. It meant the failure to function physically or mentally. We have no evidence that this negative evaluation of aging affected the treatment of the elderly within the community in a negative manner. The contrary appears to be the case. Wherever possible the older person was accorded honour. The Jewish courts protected the rights of the aged not because of their biological make-up, but because the problem they brought to the courts demanded justice. On the basis of the evidence we have adduced, we may conclude that though the medieval Jew might not have welcomed the prospect of growing old, he would not have feared that his community would abandon him.

---

[32] Müller, *Responsen* 54b-55a, sec. 203.
[33] Ibid. 53b, sec. 202.

4

So Teach Us to Number Our Days
A Theology of Longevity in Jewish
Exegetical Literature*

Frank Talmage †

University of Toronto

The mishnaic tractate *Ethics of the Fathers* (5:22) records the statement of Ben Bag Bag: "Turn it [i.e. the Torah] through and through, for everything is in it." For the medieval Jew there was, by and large, no subject or topic that did not have its point of reference in the sacred texts of Judaism, the Bible and rabbinic literature, and that could not be expanded upon by expounding on those texts directly – through exegesis – or indirectly – through eisegesis. In the spirit of recent studies relating to attitudes towards aging in Christian biblical exegesis,[1] I propose to address the treatment of this subject in southern European Hebrew exegetical works.

It must be recalled first that the world of the medieval Mediterranean Jewish intellectual – as opposed to his northern European co-religionists – was in one way or another influenced by the study of philosophy, from the thirteenth century on through the Renaissance Maimonidean philosophy in particular. Whether one espoused it or opposed it (for not all were

---

* My thanks to Moshe Idel and Barry Walfish for bibliographical references. This paper was written in connection with a project supported by the Social Sciences and Humanities Research Council of Canada.

[1] Rolf Sprandel, *Altersschicksal und Altersmoral: Die Geschichte der Einstellungen zum Altern nach der Pariser Bibelexegese des 12.-16. Jahrhunderts* (Stuttgart, 1981), and "Alter und Todesfurcht nach der spätmittelalterlichen Bibelexegese," in *Death in the Middle Ages,* ed. Herman Braet and Werner Verbeke, Mediaevalia Lovaniensia, Ser. 1, Studia 9 (Louvain, 1983), pp. 107-116. On attitudes to aging in the Bible itself, see Avraham Malamat, "Longevity: Biblical Concepts and Some Ancient Near Eastern Parallels," *Archiv für Orientforschung* 19 (1982) 215-224 (Hebrew version: "Li-tefisat 'arikhut ha-yamim ba-miqra u-va-mizrah ha-qadum," *'Eres Yisra'el* 16 [1981-1982] 146-151).

Aging and the Aged in Medieval Europe, ed. Michael M. Sheehan, CSB. Papers in Mediaeval Studies 11 (Toronto: Pontifical Institute of Mediaeval Studies, 1990), pp. 49-62. © P.I.M.S., 1990.

equally enthusiastic), one was affected by it. And whether one espoused
it or opposed it, one knew it well and one's own thinking was coloured
by it. That being the case, how long, according to our thinkers, is the life
spent in the study of (or battling of) philosophical rationalism?

According to Jewish tradition, one cannot live longer than did Moses,
who attained the age of one hundred twenty. But Moses himself in Psalm
90:10[2] gave a more realistic life span: "The days of our years are threescore years and ten, or even by reason of strength fourscore years," numbers that were accepted in rabbinic tradition in the listing in *Ethics of the
Fathers* 5:21 "seventy – the time of old age; eighty the time of strength."
There was some ambivalence about this, however. David Kimhi, the
Narbonese exegete of the turn of the thirteenth century, expressed some
surprise that King David had fallen ill, for, after all, "he was only
seventy" (*Comm.* to 1 Kings 1:1). For it was Kimhi himself who at the
age of seventy-two undertook his campaign to travel across Languedoc,
Aragon, and Castile in defence of Moses Maimonides.[3] Such a journey in
those days, with horse and cart as one's conveyance, was at best no mean
enterprise. Add to this the dangers of travel. "Omnis iniquitas et omnis
fraus abundat in sanctorum itineribus," warns the *Liber Sancti Jacobi,*[4]
while Judah ibn Tibbon at Lunel counsels his son Samuel, Kimhi's
friend, "Do not risk your life by taking the road and leaving the city, in
times of disquiet and changes."[5] One can see, then, the vigour of a man,
who by his own admission was not physically well, at the age of "only"
seventy-two. Yet even if one were to live longer – and Kimhi survived
only another three years or so – it would not be for much. No, one could
not reasonably expect to merit being more than an octogenarian or nona-
genarian at most.

In 2 Samuel 19, it is related that Barzillai the Gileadite, who had aided
King David in Mahanaim, was invited to join the king in Jerusalem. Barzillai replied movingly: "I am this day fourscore years old; can I discern
between good and bad? Can your servant taste what I eat or what I drink?
Can I hear any more the voice of singing men and singing women?
Wherefore then should your servant be a burden unto my lord the king?"
(v. 36). Whereas certain authorities in the Talmud take this as a cue to
explain the nature of the decrepitude of old age, others, for homiletical

---

[2] My numbering throughout is that of the Masoretic text.

[3] See Frank Talmage, *David Kimhi: The Man and the Commentaries* (Cambridge, Mass.,
1975), pp. 27-39.

[4] Cited from Vera Hell and Hellmut Hell, *The Great Pilgrimage of the Middle Ages: The Road
to St. James of Compostela* (London, 1966), p. 22.

[5] *Hebrew Ethical Wills,* ed. Israel Abrahams, 2 vols. in one (Philadelphia, 1926; repr. 1976),
p. 65.

purposes, raise objections: He was a liar, for they knew of a ninety-two-year-old maidservant with a rather robust appetite! He was lewd and lustful, and old age overtakes such people prematurely (*T.B. Shabbat* 152a)! Here was a perfect opportunity for Kimhi and later the illustrious Don Isaac Abravanel, polymath, intellectual leader of Spanish Jewry, and courtier to the Catholic monarchs until 1492, to deny the decrepitude of eighty as they did that of seventy, and, for Abravanel at least, for the same reason. For according to him, David's "premature" physical failure was due to his youthful promiscuity, exceeded only by that of his son Solomon, who succumbed at an even earlier age.[6] Yet Kimhi says nothing regarding Barzillai in this matter, while Abravanel cites the rabbinic midrash as an aside without comment.

Thus virtually all of our writers were much occupied with the question of why the former generations, especially those mentioned in Genesis 5, attained such remarkable longevity. Virtually all, for the Provençal maverick of the turn of the fourteenth century, Joseph ibn Kaspi, was unique in not being terribly enthused by this question. He summarily refers the reader to Maimonides (*Guide for the Perplexed* 2:47), who said it was due to their salubrious diet or lifestyle or perhaps a special dispensation. As for himself, he advises that he

> shall refrain from discussing these questions of the generations of Adam through Noah, for they died thousands of years ago. We have already been solaced [with regard to their demise] and it is a long time since the period of weeping for them has passed. I shall thus let them be and speak rather of those deadheads (*ha-metim*) who lie before us [today]![7]

By far the most comprehensive discussion of this subject was that of Abravanel, who begins by citing the view of certain "gentile scholars," a view mentioned by Thomas, that the years mentioned are not really solar years (*shanah*) but months of twenty-eight days when the moon returns again (*shenit*) to its starting place. Abravanel's rejection of this view is similar to Augustine's refutation of the theory that the years cited in these chapters were one-tenth the length of our years.[8] If this were indeed the case, Enoch would have been five and a half years old when his son Methusaleh was born, and Moses would have accomplished his life's work in ten years. There is surely a limit to juvenile precocity or the reader's credulity! He then cites the aforementioned explanation of Maimonides along with the critique of that explanation by the Geronese

---

[6] Isaac Abravanel, *Perush ʿal ha-torah* (Warsaw, 1861-1862), p. 26b.

[7] Joseph ibn Kaspi, *Mishneh kesef*, ed. Isaac Last, 2 vols. (Pressburg, 1904-1905), 1: 57.

[8] Thomas Aquinas, *Exp. in Gen.* 5, in *Opera omnia*, 34 vols. (Paris, 1871-1880), 31: 46; Augustine, *De civitate Dei* 15.12. My thanks to my student Idit Dobbs-Weinstein for locating the reference in Thomas.

talmudist and kabbalist of the thirteenth century, Moses ben Nahman (Nahmanides), who insisted that it was really the deterioration of the atmosphere in connection with the flood that was responsible for the shortening of the human life span (*Comm.* to Gen. 5:4). Now Abravanel has little truck for those, except himself, who were brazen enough to criticize Maimonides, and no one is allowed to do so with impunity. He is thus quick to point out that, measure for measure, Nahmanides got what he deserved, for his fourteenth-century townsman Nissim ben Reuben Gerondi criticized him, saying that the flood should rather have cleansed and purified the air than pollute it.[9] Despite this, however, on this particular point Abravanel still has to side with Nahmanides. The flood brought an increase of humidity and with it a general rotting and mouldering of natural growth, which had an adverse effect on the human diet. On the other hand, Maimonides was correct as well. There *was* a special dispensation for those generations, not, however, as a favour to them but to benefit the future of mankind. There was a special plan in keeping them alive for so long. Basing himself on his predecessors,[10] he states that, essentially, humankind needed a certain amount of knowledge in order to get civilization started. The acquisition of scientific and especially astronomical knowledge requires a great deal of time-consuming experimentation and observation. The Creator thereby

> demonstrated His providence over the human species by enabling those particular people to live exceptionally long, so that they could perfect their knowledge by their experimentation and investigation to achieve perfection for them and their descendants, so that the Creator's efforts in creating man would not come to naught. However, after knowledge was perfected ..., life spans became shorter because people could depend for their knowledge on what the antecedent generations had attained. It is for this reason that books of astronomy ascribe many things to the ancients[11] ....

---

[9]   See Nissim ben Reuben Gerondi, *Perush ʿal ha-torah*, ed. Leon A. Feldman (Jerusalem, 1968), p. 72 (on Gen. 5:4).

[10]   Although Abravanel mentions only the fourteenth-century Provençal exegete and philosopher Levi ben Gerson (Gersonides) (*Perush ʿal ha-torah* [Venice, 1546-1547], p. 18a-b), his explanation has roots in the midrash, Gen. R. 26:5 ("'The Sons of God saw the daughters of men' [Gen. 6:2]. Why are they called 'the Sons of God'? R. Hanina and R. Simeon ben Levi both said that they lived long lives without suffering and anguish. R. Yose in the name of R. Hunci said: In order to fathom equinoxes and [astronomical] calculations"), and is essentially that of Kimhi (*Perush RaDaQ ʿal ha-torah*, ed. Moses Kamelhar [Jerusalem, 1970] on Gen. 5:4, p. 49) and Nissim ben Reuben Gerondi (*Perush*, ed. Feldman, p. 73), to whose wording Abravanel is in fact much closer. Cf. also Simeon ben Zemah Duran, *Magen 'avot ʿal massekhet 'avot* (Jerusalem, 1960-1961), pp. 212-213.

[11]   Abravanel, *Perush*, p. 26b.

The conclusion of this prolix discussion, then, is that longevity is a gift granted in order to obtain knowledge. But the knowledge of which we have been speaking is of the sort that needed to be acquired only at one point in human history. Would it indeed be desirable for the later generations to attain such extreme longevity – especially for certain of our commentators, namely those of a distinctly Maimonidean bent, who maintain that the afterlife is a greater good than existence in this world? For David Kimhi, it is only after death that the soul "delights in the supreme glory" (*Comm.* to Ps. 1:5) and attains the beatific vision (*Comm.* to Ps. 17:15; cf. ibid. to Ps. 25:5, 30:10).

> "They are abundantly satisfied with the fatness of Your house" (Psalm 36:8). All this refers to the world to come, which is the world of the souls and angels ... "the house of God, the Temple of God, His holy mountain, the mountain of the Lord, and the pleasantness of the Lord." The fatness and pleasure is the attainment of the knowledge of God .... This is the good after which there is no evil, and the satiety after which there is no hunger or thirst, the life after which there is no death, the light after which there is no darkness. (*Comm.* to Ps. 36:9-10)

The theme of attaining true knowledge only after liberation from matter is reiterated in the Psalms commentary of Abraham Rimoch, written after his emotionally shattering experience at the Disputation of Tortosa of 1413-1414.[12] The concept of matter as a restrictive barrier (*masakh mone^c a*) that prevents ultimate apprehension recurs in his interpretation of such verses as "Precious in the sight of the Lord is the death of his saints" (Ps. 116:14; Oxford, Bodl. MS. Hunt. 485, fol. 202r-v), "My soul pines for your salvation, in Your word do I hope" (Ps. 119:81; ibid., fol. 211v), and "When shall I come [and appear before God]?" (Ps. 42:2):

> When shall I enter the realm of the Intelligences, for my soul longs to apprehend these things while it is still in the body. But since matter is a restrictive barrier, it longs fervently and says: "When shall I be separated from matter and appear before Him so that the effulgence bestowed by Him on the Intelligences will be bestowed on me?" (Ibid., fol. 23v)

This world with its vanities is too full of pitfalls.

---

[12] See Frank Talmage, "Trauma at Tortosa: The Testimony of Abraham Rimoch," *Mediaeval Studies* 47 (1985) 379-415. Whereas true intellectual apprehension can take place only in the afterlife, moral perfection through observance of the commandments can only be accomplished in this life. Therefore Rimoch interprets (Oxford, Bodl. MS. Hunt. 485, fol. 207r):
"I am a sojourner in the earth" (Ps. 119:19), therefore I need you to open my eyes (cf. v. 18). Since my days are short, I will not acquire moral perfection during my life [and] it is impossible to acquire it after death. If so, may it be Your will that You not hide Your commandments from me, that is to say, the vicissitudes of fate, enemies, or obstacles would not disturb me from keeping the commandments, which would result in not attaining human perfection.

If a man could live forever absorbed in ratiocination and theological con-
templation, I would be silent. But "what man is he that lives!" (Ps. 89:48).
Will a man overcome (*gever gover*) his [evil] inclination and prevail (*mit-
gabber*) with all his might to cleave to his God? Even so, he will not
deliver his animal soul from the power of the grave (cf. ibid.). And the
psalmist said "Selah" (ibid.) because it is possible to live a long time by
proper conduct but it is impossible to save one's soul forever.

It seems to me that "For what vanity have You created" means: Why
have You created them lusting after their passions, which are vanity and
the cause of dissolution, for it is impossible that there will be found a man
who will live and not see death and will save his rational soul from the
grave, for the vast majority of them are inclined after worldly vanities.
(Ibid., fol. 160r)

No, true spiritual fulfilment would not be possible in this life, even if it
were extended indefinitely.

To be sure, at times the voice of the intellectual as Jew was heard over
that of Jew as intellectual. The theme of the exile resounds throughout the
commentaries of both Kimhi and Rimoch, and both express the despair of
not living long enough to see the redemption. Kimhi interprets:

Israel has been in exile so long that it is as if they say "our bones are dried
up and our hope is lost; we are clean cut off" (Ezek. 37:11) and, we will
not see the redemption of Israel. How shall we live to [the age of] a thousand or more? We ourselves are cut off. (*Comm.* ad loc.; cf. *Comm.* to Ps.
106:4)

For Kimhi, Moses' designation of the human life span as threescore
and ten or fourscore is a plaint of every generation in exile over the brevity of life, "for our days are all too short and we cannot hope to see salvation if the redemption does not approach" (*Comm.* to Ps. 90:10); while
Rimoch in his turn renders:

"O remember [how short my time is; for what vanity have You created all
the children of men!]" (Ps. 89:47) ... I remember how short my time is
and therefore I am angered over the length of the exile.

My complaint is too: "For what vanity have You created all the children of men!" (Ps. 89:47). That is to say, you have created them all for
vanity and nothingness, for [they] have no permanent endurance. If I
could endure forever, I would have hope of seeing goodness. (Oxford,
Bodl. MS. Hunt. 485, fol. 160r)

But our writers are not chiliasts and know that any hope to live to see
the redemption probably remains a bit of pious wishful thinking. No,
until the redemption of Israel is a reality, the only realistic redemption
is that of the soul from its material entrapment. Yet if that is the case
for such scholars as Rimoch and Kimhi, one may ask why the latter
does a seeming about-face when, in his description of the wonders of the

messianic era, he includes extraordinary longevity (*Comm.* to Isa. 65:17, 22). Three-to-five-hundred-year life spans would not be exceptional (*Comm.* to Isa. 65:20; cf. *Comm.* to Ezek. 37:14, Ps. 92:14), and people will live so long that it would not be felt necessary to weep for the dead (*Comm.* to Isa. 65:19).[13] If, then, true bliss is attained only in the afterlife, what is to be gained by prolonging life to five hundred years?

The answer becomes clear when we recall that that which attains the afterlife is the acquired intellect. It is man's task in this world to develop this by "considering [God] in his heart, to understand through philosophical proof as science instructs him" (*Comm.* to Ps. 91:16; cf. *Comm.* to Ps. 25:5). But the road to perfect knowledge is so long that man can traverse only a small portion of it in his seventy or eighty years. Enoch struggled so hard to attain ultimate knowledge that his body was shattered and God took him (*Comm.* to Gen. 5:24; cf. *Comm.* to Gen. 49:12). How long, then, is the journey? This, according to Kimhi, was communicated in a midrashic parable.

> "The tree of life extends over an area of five hundred years' journey, and it is from beneath it that all the waters of the creation sprang forth," and they added the explanation that this measure referred to the thickness of its trunk, and not to the extent of its branches, for they continue thus, "Not the extent of the branches thereof, but the stem thereof has a thickness of five hundred years' journey" ... (Gen. R. 15:6). That is to say, the distance from the earth to heaven is [a] five hundred years' journey as the rabbis said and as the scientists have said. It is the intent of the parable in this passage to say that the trunk refers to the attainment of natural science, which is terrestrial, by the human mind. The foliage refers to what is above the heavens, including a knowledge of astronomy and of the intelligences. (*Comm.* to Gen. 2:9; cf. *Guide* 2:30)

Thus the need for five hundred years; but under the present dispensation, *faute de mieux,* one must exploit to the full the years that one has. How then should one's life be ordered for this purpose? Medieval Jewish writers developed a variety of classifications of stages of the human life; the most common being the threefold (youth, manhood, and old age) and the fourfold (youth, manhood, maturity, and old age; or childhood, youth, manhood, and old age).[14]

---

[13] Longevity in the messianic era would no doubt be promoted by the fact that the Jews would be in the land of Israel with its beneficial climate. Cf. Abraham Rimoch on Ps. 61:7: " 'May You add days unto the king's days!' David said this referring to himself or the king that rules in the land of Israel, because the pure air induces long life" (ibid., fol. 110r).

[14] Leopold Löw, *Die Lebensalter in der jüdischen Literatur* (Szegedin, 1875), pp. 26-36. The terminology varies from writer to writer as does the sense given to particular Hebrew words. I have avoided the archaic term "hoariness" for *sevah* and preferred "advanced old age."

An ideal disposition of this life is described by Jacob Anatoli, a Provençal savant active in the Naples of Frederick II and friend of Michael Scotus, in his collection of homilies, the *Scholars' Goad*. Anatoli takes the three days' wandering of the Israelites in the desert until they found water (Exod. 15:22) to allude to three stages of life, youth (*na'arut*), manhood (*baharut*), and old age (*ziqnah*), each of which is appropriate to the three disciplines of study, the mathematical sciences (*limmudiyyot*), natural sciences (*tiv'iyyot*), and metaphysics or theology ('*elohiyyot*). That water was found on the third day indicates that "old age is the time reserved for the elite for the study of theology, which is the true waters which flow from the place of the living waters .... It is thus proper for intellectuals to devote time to mathematics first, then to natural sciences, and afterwards to theology."[15]

A similar lesson is taught, according to the fifteenth-century Catalonian thinker, Abraham Shalom, in an allegorization of a halakhic text. He expounds on the passage "One who has not said [the prayer beginning with the words] 'true and firm' in the morning and [the prayer beginning with the words] 'true ('*emet*) and faithful ('*emunah*)' has not fulfilled his obligation, as it is said, 'To tell Your loving kindness in the morning, and Your faithfulness ('*emunatekha*) at night' (Ps. 92:2)" (*T.B. Ber.* 12a).

> .... The day is divided into four parts – morning, noon, evening, and night – and man's life is divided into four parts, youth (*na'arut*), manhood (*baharut*), old age (*ziqnah*), and advanced old age (*sevah*). He who wishes to perfect his soul must make an effort to attain truth in his youth in order to attain the ultimate in the truth ('*emet*) and faith ('*emunah*) of the Torah, which is [philosophical] speculation and kabbalah, which are called truth and faith ... in the evening, which is the time likened to advanced old age .... [This is proved from the verse], "To tell (*le-haggid*) Your loving kindness in the morning": that is to say, the divine loving kindness which God showed to man in endowing him with the rational soul, for the telling (*haggadah*) is ratiocination (*haskalah*); "and Your faithfulness at night," for faith is that which survives when one departs from this world and bestows a blessing on his soul that he may merit eternal life.[16]

And again, with a slightly more pietistic flavour, Abravanel broaches this theme in commenting on the passage from *Ethics of the Fathers* (5:22),[17] with which this paper began: "Ben Bag Bag says: 'Turn it [i.e.

---

[15] Jacob Anatoli, *Malmad ha-talmidim* (Lyck, 1866), p. 57b.

[16] Abraham Shalom, *Nevey Shalom* 10.3 (Venice, 1574-1575; repr. Jerusalem, 1966-1967), p. 174b.

[17] The numbering here of these passages, 5:21-22, which were not part of the original tractate and which vary in numbering and ordering in various versions, follows that of Chanokh Albeck, *Shishah sidrei mishnah, Seder Neziqin* (Jerusalem, 1959). On the various traditions, see ibid., p. 351;

the Torah] through and through, for everything is in it; scrutinize it and grow old in it; do not move from it, for there is no greater standard (*middah*) than this.'"

> In this statement, he refers to three categories of study, the first is that of youth and manhood: "Turn it through and through" – that [people should] occupy themselves with careful study of Torah from their youth; the second refers to the aged: "Grow old and frail in it" – let one age in studying it, for in old age one attains theological knowledge, physics, and metaphysics (*ma῾aseh bereshit, ma῾aseh merkavah*) and this is "You shall scrutinize it." The third refers to philosophical quandaries: "You shall not turn from it because there is no greater standard than this." He called the Torah a standard (*middah*) because by it one measures (*yimdedu*) all other sciences.[18]

Thus, as is appropriate to an ethical treatise, read widely by the Jewish public, especially as is still the practice, on the Sabbaths between Passover and Pentecost, Abravanel stresses the role of revelation as a safeguard in the study of philosophy. The effect, however, is the same: the latter part of one's life is the period to be devoted to the study of metaphysics.

Yet when does this period begin? Because of the dangers inherent in the study of metaphysics, it was a commonplace that such study should not be undertaken until one has reached the age of forty – the age, according to the *Ethics of the Fathers* 5:21, of wisdom – or for the more avid rationalists, thirty. Thus, although old age (*ziqnah*) does not begin properly, according to one mishnah, until sixty, preparation for old age should begin considerably earlier.

On this assumption, Anatoli likens the decades of man's life to the days of the week, so that the study of philosophy begins for the exemplary at thirty, for the majority at forty, and for such sinful indolent as, he touchingly confesses, himself (though to be sure he grossly exaggerates his alleged neglect of philosophical study), at fifty. Expounding on Psalm 90:10, he notes that

> the days of our years are threescore and ten and we must be conscious of the final day and prepare for it on the preceding day just as one who is alacritous will begin taking care of his Sabbath needs starting from the fourth day of the week ....

> This is thus proper for the prudent person who has reached the age of forty, the age of wisdom, and whose [physical] vigour is now diminishing.

---

and on Abravanel's text, in which 5:22 precedes 5:21, see Isaac Abravanel, *Naḥalat 'avot* (Jerusalem, 1969-1970), p. 369.

[18] Abravanel, *Naḥalat 'avot*, p. 370.

For before this, the passionate turmoil (*rahav*) of his youth and early man-hood will prevent him [from doing so] and his labour (*ʿamalo*) during that time is travail (*ʿamal*) and vanity (*'aven*). Therefore, on the fifth day the majority of our people prepare their Sabbath needs. Thus one who is fifty who is a counsellor [according to *Ethics of the Fathers* – fifty for counsel] must counsel himself concerning himself.

But who will be so indolent who does not prepare on the sixth day, and whither shall this disgrace lead the one who does not ready his provisions *when he is fifty-five as I am today?* And what will one who has not cooked on the eve of the Sabbath eat on the Sabbath, which is from the age of sixty to seventy when it is proper to maintain a state of sanctity? Then righteousness will go before him and the glory of the Lord will gather him to a world which is entirely a Sabbath ....[19]

The theme of decades is not an infrequent one in the literature.[20] Abravanel's allegorization of the six workdays and the Sabbath is strik-ingly similar to if less elegant than that of Anatoli,[21] and the motif is developed by Abraham Rimoch on the basis of a time-honoured exegeti-cal principle, namely that apparently superfluous letters in the Masoretic text have, for homiletical purposes, special significance. In Psalm 103:3-6 the archaizing second person feminine singular possessive suffixes -*ekhi* and -*aikhi* (as opposed to the usual -*ekh* or -*ayikh*), which are written with an additional *yod,* appear five times. Since the letter *yod* has the numeri-cal value of ten, these verses are taken to refer to the five decades between the ages of twenty and seventy. We find, then, that "Who heals all your diseases (*taḥlu'aikhi*)" (v. 3) refers to the decade from thirty to forty, when one begins "to fix one's attention on and apply oneself to science," while "Who redeems your life (*ḥayyaikhi*) from the pit" (v. 4) speaks of the decade from forty to fifty, "for one who dies during that time dies a death of *karet*," a death roughly analogous to dying without salvation (*Comm.* ad loc., Oxford, Bodl. MS. Hunt. 485, fols. 174v-175r). Implicit in this is the notion that one has not had the opportunity to actualize the acquired intellect, which is all that survives after death, as he explains at

---

[19] Anatoli, *Malmad*, p. 186a. Anatoli modifies these rabbinic Sabbath=World to Come allusions for his own purposes. Cf. *T.B.* ʿ*A.Z.* 3a and Rashi ad loc., San. 97a.

[20] Cf. the interesting allegorization of the seven decades of human life as the seven millenia of world history in Isaac ben Yedaiah's commentary to the aggadot (Marc Saperstein, *Decoding the Rabbis: A Thirteenth-Century Commentary on the Aggadah* [Cambridge, Mass., 1980], pp. 114-116). The "days of the Messiah" (*T.B. Rosh hashanah* 31a) are the years after the age of forty when the intellect is to be perfected.

[21] Abravanel, *Comm.* to Exod. 12:15, p. 21a; cf. the sixteenth-century Palestinian kabbalist Moses Alsheikh's allegorization of the eating of unleavened bread during the seven days of Pass-over (Exod. 13:6) as referring to the imperative of man's enjoying his seventy years free of the cor-ruption of the evil inclination (*Torat Mosheh*, 5 vols. in 2 [Israel, 1921-1922], 2: 24a).

Psalm 7:5-6: "'Let the enemy pursue my soul ... let him lay my glory in the dust.' If I die before my time, my rational soul will not attain its intended perfection, and it will follow that the enemy will lay my glory, which is my soul, [in the dust] forever" (ibid., fol. 12r).

Thus the decades pass, but with them, as we have seen, come increased physical frailty and loss of vigour. And although the mishnah we have been citing continues by saying "eighty for strength" this does not mean that one reaches greater strength, but only that one survives by reason of greater strength. And if some would prefer to read the next phrase "ninety for decrepitude" (literally "for being bent over" [la-shuaḥ]) as "ninety for meditation" (la-suaḥ),[22] (i.e. speaking of Torah),[23] it is so because the time of death is surely approaching. And indeed, the conclusion of the mishnah leaves no doubt: "At one hundred it is as though he were dead and had passed and faded from the world."

Now some could be quite sanguine about this. Shem Tob (Santob) de Carrión, the fourteenth-century poet who composed in both Castilian and Hebrew, flippantly quips in his *Proverbios morales:*[24]

Las mis cañas tenilas;	My gray hair I had dyed,
Non por las aborreçer,	Not to look just like a lad,
Menos por desdeçirlas,	Nor because I would deride
Nin moço pareçer	Or disdain that which I had.
Mas con miedo sobejo,	It was rather from dismay,
Que honbres buscarian	Lest now men would try to sound
En mi seso de viejo,	Out age's wisdom – but would say
Y non lo fallarian.	That there's none here to be found.

No, the prevailing mood was rather more sombre. Abraham ibn Ezra, the twelfth-century Andalusian exegete and poet, writes:

His days of waste at fifty do encroach;
He mourns for mourning does indeed approach;
The splendour of this world's a mere reproach;
He shan't be long alive.

---

[22] In an unpointed Hebrew text the spelling of the two words is the same.

[23] See, e.g., Jonah ben Abraham Gerondi, *Perush rabbenu Yonah mi-Gerondi ʿal massekhet 'avot* (Jerusalem, 1968-1969), p. 95; Simeon ben Zemah Duran, *Magen 'avot*, p. 214; Bahya ben Asher, *Kitvei rabbenu Bahya*, ed. Charles B. Chavel (Jerusalem, 1969-1970), p. 460. The dour fifteenth-century Lisbon scholar Joseph Hayyun is even more negative: "'Ninety for decrepitude' (la-shuah) from shuhah ʿamuqqah ('deep pit,' Prov. 22:14, 23:27), i.e. the grave ... for he is of no use. Or it may be from siah la-'ares ve-torekka ('or speak to the earth and it shall teach you,' Job 12:8), i.e. he is good only for speaking and reminiscing" (*Millei de-'avot* [Venice, 1595], p. 60a).

[24] Shem Tob de Carrión, *Proverbios morales*, ed. Guzmán Alvarez (Salamanca, 1970), p. 44, lines 129-136. See A. Loewenthal, *Musrei ha-pilosofim* (Frankfurt-am-Main, 1896), 1.8, p. 7.

> What is the fate of one who is three-score?
> Are now his deeds to vanish evermore?
> His limbs are all too feeble and too sore
>   To help him in his battle to survive.
> If three-score and ten he does attain,
> To listen to his speech will be a strain;
> The patience of his friends he'll surely drain;
>   A burden he can't bear although he strive.
> At four-score his sons must bear the yoke.
> He has no eyes, no mind he can invoke.
> To all about he is a sorry joke;
>   Of sustenance he's painfully deprived.[25]

Abravanel finds Ibn Ezra just a bit extreme in hastening the aging process,[26] but the fact remains that any advance in years entails decline in physical strength. If one is weak in body then, how can he be strong in mind? The answer is that it is precisely this weakening in bodily strength that is conducive to mental vigour. Thus Rimoch can conclude his enumeration of the decades by pointing out that "'He satisfies your old age with good things' (Ps. 103:5) alludes to the strengthening of the intellect with the weakening of the corporeal powers, ... so that 'your youth (ne^{c}uraikhi, with an additional *yod*) is [renewed] like an eagle' (ibid.). This *yod* alludes [to the period from] sixty to seventy, for during that time one increases in power and strength" (Oxford, Bodl. MS. Hunt. 485, fol. 175r), and it is, of course, of intellectual strength that he speaks. Thus "'The Lord shall bless you [out of Zion]' (Ps. 128:5) by virtue of the intellect which comes from Zion, and 'You shall see the good of Jerusalem' (ibid.), when you shall attain the divine merit called the 'good of Jerusalem' 'all the days of your life' (ibid.), that is, even in old age when your powers weaken, you will see the good of Jerusalem, which is intellectual apprehension" (ibid., fol. 223v).[27] Yes, life may be all too brief and, with the psalmist, Rimoch complains: "You have made my days as handbreadths and my age is as nothing before You" (Ps. 39:5).

---

[25] Abraham ibn Ezra, "Ben 'adamah yizkor be-moladto," in *Shirei ha-qodesh le-rabbi 'Avraham 'Ibn ʿEzra*, ed. Israel Levin, 2 vols. (Jerusalem, 1980), 2: 544, lines 23-38. On the introduction, see Levin's introductory note to the poem, ibid. Cf. also the similar poem of Samuel ha-Nagid (eleventh century), *Ha-shirah ha-ʿivrit*, 1: 132. These two poems are the two medieval Hebrew precursors of Jacques' "All the world's a stage" speech in *As You Like It*, Act 2, scene 7.

[26] Abravanel, *Naḥalat 'avot*, p. 372.

[27] Rimoch is making use of kabbalistic exegesis, which he frequently interprets in Aristotelian terms. See Talmage, "Trauma at Tortosa." The "good of Jerusalem" is the effulgence bestowed by the *sefirah tif'eret* upon Zion, *malkhut*, through *yesod*. See Zohar 3:13a.

Dividing life into four periods, he laments that in the first, early youth (*yaldut*), and in the fourth, advanced old age (*yeshishut*), wisdom cannot be acquired because of hotbloodedness[28] in the former case or weakness in the latter, leaving only early manhood (*baharut*) and old age (*ziqnah*)[29] (ibid., fols. 76v-77r). Yet, on the other hand, he can sing:

> "I will praise the Lord while I live" (Ps. 146:2). This refers to old age when I shall praise Him because He has kept me alive until now and aided me, while "I will sing praises unto God while I have my being" (ibid.) refers to advanced old age (*sevah*), that is, as long as my soul's strength is within me, even though my [physical] strength has waned. I shall utter his praise because my intellect is healthy and strong despite the waning of physical power. (Escorial MS. G-I-7, fol. 8r)

The same concept is expressed in the allegorical commentary on talmudic aggadot or legends of Rimoch's contemporary, Shem Tov ben Isaac Shaprut. In tractate "Bava Batra," there is a series of fanciful parables concerning Leviathan, in one of which it is stated that when Leviathan "is thirsty, he makes furrows in the sea, as it is said 'He makes a path to shine after him; one would think the deep to be hoary' (Job 41:24 [32]). R. Aha bar Jacob said: The deep does not return to its strength until after a period of seventy years, as it is said 'one would think the deep to be hoary' and one is hoary only at the age of seventy" (*T.B. Bava Batra* 75b). Ibn Shaprut comments: "R. Aha explained that one apprehends true principles only when he diminishes his corporeal strength and refrains from physical desires, like one who is old, as Scripture says: 'Wisdom is with aged men' (Job 12:12)."[30]

The "decrepitude," as it were, of old age may then be seen as a token of special grace, but one that must be used to advantage. The riper years must be exploited in a way that will profit the soul in this world and the next. The psalmist had entreated: "So teach us to number our days, that we may get us a heart of wisdom" (Ps. 90:12). Kimhi took this as a petition to know when one's end would come in order that one might prepare for it. But Anatoli's insightful remarks implicitly reject such an interpretation as naive. He interprets the verse:

---

[28] See *Comm.* to Ps. 90:3, Oxford, Bodl. MS. Hunt. 485, fol. 161r-v; Ps. 119:40, ibid., fol. 209r.

[29] In some classifications, *yeshishut* precedes *ziqnah*. See Löw, *Lebensalter*, pp. 30-35 and nn.; Abravanel to 1 Kings 1:1 (Jerusalem, 1954-1955), p. 32, who distinguished between the *yashish* who is advanced in years (*ba ba-yamim*) and the *zaqen* who has the appearance of old age. Other classifications, however, place it at the end of life. See Ben Yehuda, *Millon*, s.v. "yeshishut"; Abravanel, *Perush ʿal ha-torah*, Gen. 23:1, p. 54a; Exod. 12:15, p. 21a: "*ziqnah* with maintenance of strength, *yeshishut* with loss of strength"; Abraham Shalom, *Nevey shalom* 10.8, p. 184b.

[30] Shem Tov ben Isaac Shaprut, *Pardes rimmonim* (Zhitomir, 1866), p. 22.

Teach us in this way to number our days so that we shall be sensitive
enough to know the "power of your anger" (v. 11). "We may get us a
heart of wisdom" (v. 12) alludes to the acquired intellect which exists *in
actu* and is the everlasting form of man. There is no doubt that [the
psalmist] does not seek to know when he will die, for a wise man would
not ask such a thing, but he must act as if tomorrow were his last day so
that he will spend his life in penitence.[31]

Anatoli tells us that there are many interpretations of Psalm 90 and one is
free to choose as one wishes. "But," he petitions the reader, "do not disre-
gard the intent of 'numbering the days of your life,' for I have no doubt
that this is the point of this psalm."

Throughout all these considerations there is little heard of what we call
senility. The *senex* who numbers his days and increases in wisdom will
never become a *senilis*. Any physical frailty that may exist is only a guarantee of renewed spiritual and mental power – surely a not unpleasant
prospect for the intellectual of the Middle Ages, nor, one should think, of
any age.

[31] Anatoli, *Malmad*, p. 186b.

5

Aging and the Desert Fathers
The Process Reversed

John T. Wortley

The University of Manitoba

By the "desert fathers" we mean here those thousands of men – and some women – who withdrew from "the world" into the solitude of the Egyptian and Syrian deserts, in the fourth through seventh centuries of our era, the earliest Christian monks.[1] Their object was to obey literally the dominical call to perfection, to "leave all and follow Me." Their legacy is an extensive literary corpus of "sayings" (*apophthegmata*), of tales they told to and about each other (what the Bollandists call *narrationes animae utiles*), and of other hagiographical material. For the most part, we owe this literary heritage, not to the monks themselves who told the tales and uttered the sayings, but to others who visited them and set their oral lore down in writing for posterity: the author of *Historia monachorum in Ægypto,* Palladius of *Historia Lausiaca,* and John Moschos of *Pratum spirituale,* to name the best known (not to mention the anonymous collectors of *apophthegmata*).[2]

---

[1] For a good introduction to the subject, see Derwas J. Chitty, *The Desert a City* (Oxford, 1966).

[2] *Historia monachorum in Ægypto* [henceforth *HME*], ed. André-J. Festugière, Subsidia hagiographica 34 (Brussels, 1961), and trans. Festugière, *Enquête sur les moines d'Egypte: Les Moines d'Orient* 4.1 (Paris, 1964) with copious notes. The work is "[une] enquête ... menée par un groupe de moines du Jardin des Oliviers à Jérusalem au cours d'un voyage accompli en 394-395 depuis la Thébaïde jusqu'à la côte," Festugière in *Les Moines d'Orient,* Vol. 1 (Paris, 1961), p. 19. There are about 40 tales in this collection; an English translation of *HME* and of some variant passages found elsewhere has recently appeared, with a very useful introductory essay by Sister Benedicta Ward, SLG: *The Lives of the Desert Fathers,* trans. Norman Russel (Oxford, 1980). Palladius' *Historia Lausiaca,* ed. E. C. Butler, Texts and Studies 6.1-2 (Cambridge, 1898, 1904), trans. W. K. Lowther

Aging and the Aged in Medieval Europe, ed. Michael M. Sheehan, CSB. Papers in Mediaeval Studies 11 (Toronto: Pontifical Institute of Mediaeval Studies, 1990), pp. 63-73. © P.I.M.S., 1990.

From these writings there emerges a lively picture of life in the desert,
and something of the relationship between those who embraced it and the
ones who remained "in the world." And if that picture is less complete
and not so detailed as we might wish, we must remember that it is nevertheless unique. For no other body of literature has come down to us that
affords a comparable glimpse of the life of any other social group characteristic of the twilight period of the ancient world. Let us then ask: what
can it tell us about the desert fathers' attitudes to age and aging?

Rather disappointingly, the *prima facie* answer to this question seems
to be: not very much at all. For, and the point is by no means unimportant, it seems as though aging was something the desert fathers neither
talked nor thought about very much. In fact, they seem rather to have
ignored it – so far as themselves were concerned. But when it came to
secular persons, that was a different matter. Thus when David the bandit-
chief tired of his life of sex and violence and sought admission to a monastery, the abba looked him over and saw that he was "an old man
(*gerōn*)." "You can't stay here," he said, "the brethren labour hard and
lead a very ascetic life." The implication is clear: that David is no longer
capable of the required effort. Which in the event David proves not to be
the case, for he gains entry to the monastic community by threatening to
destroy it, and turns out to be a most exemplary monk.[3]

Now the curious thing about this tale is that the abba first refuses entry
to David because he is *gerōn*.[4] It is the very word that is used most commonly by and of monks to denote each other. And it is the despair of
translators. One will render it *senex* or the equivalent thereof, for which

---

Clarke, *The Lausiac History* (London, 1918), is an enquiry concerning monks written for one
Lausus ca. 419; it contains about 40 tales of one kind or another. The systematic collection of *apophthegmata* that was initiated at the beginning of the sixth century, the so-called "Pelagius and John"
collection [henceforth P&J], now contains about 120 tales; in Patrologia Latina [PL] 73: 855-1022,
trans. Jean Dion and Guy-M. Oury, *Les Sentences des pères du désert* (Solesmes, 1966). The alpha-
betical collection dating from the middle of the sixth century has about 50 tales; see Patrologia
Graeca [PG] 65: 75-440, trans. Benedicta Ward, *The Sayings of the Desert Fathers* (London and
Kalamazoo, 1975). Cf. Jean-C. Guy, *Recherches sur la tradition grecque des Apophthegmata
patrum*, Subsidia hagiographica 36 (Brussels, 1962). John Moschus' *Pratum spirituale* (PG 87:
2851-3112) records stories heard by the author in his travels around the monasteries of the east
around the year 600. It contains about 125 tales as the text stands in PG, but we have neither a critical edition nor an English translation as yet; both are in preparation. Many more tales are listed
under *narrationes animae utiles* and *patrum vitae* in the third edition of *Bibliotheca hagiographica
Graeca* [BHG], ed. François Halkin, 3 vols. (Brussels, 1957), and its *Novum auctarium*, ed. Halkin
(Brussels, 1984).

   [3] *Pratum spirituale*, ch. 143, PG 87: 3005A.

   [4] The term is also found, on occasion, used to designate secular persons of great piety, e.g. in
BHG, 1: 180, no. 1322g, *Synaxarium ecclesiae Constantinopolitanae* 232.31-235.54, where a distinguished Byzantine (John) and a poor leather-worker (Zacharias) use it of each other.

there is good precedent, as we have just seen. Another will lay emphasis on an equally valid aspect of its meaning, found already several times in Homer,[5] and render it "senior" or "elder," in the sense of one who has acquired some degree of superiority or excellence. But the truth of the matter is that *gerōn* is used often enough to denote somebody who is advanced neither in years nor in the monastic profession, somebody whose sole claim to the title is that he has received the monastic habit. In other words, often enough *gerōn* means no more and no less than *monk*, and should be translated thus, except that this would raise the further difficulty of how then to represent the word *monachos,* which occurs almost as frequently as *gerōn*.

Exactly how and why the term *gerōn* came to connote a monk may be something that a Coptic scholar could explain, but clearly something nevertheless remained of both its chronic and its qualitative aspects when used in this way. Qualitative in that a person was held to have passed to a higher estate in receiving the tonsure, chronic because admission to that estate was normally limited to those who were already somewhat advanced in years. We can, it is true, cite instances of persons being tonsured whilst still in their teens, even in their early teens, but these must surely have been exceptional.[6] There are far more instances that suggest that those who embraced the monastic life were already fairly mature, persons who had seen enough of the world to sicken of it, to long for more "solid joys and lasting pleasures."

Were monks perhaps called *gerōntes* because they tended to be more longevitous than persons living "in the world"? From *Historia monachorum in Ægypto* in particular, one gains the impression that ninety-plus was the expected life span of the monk,[7] but this must surely be deceptive. We have to remember that the literature speaks only of outstanding monks for the most part, not of the generality. The most outstanding of them all, Abba Anthony, is said to have attained the age of

---

[5] *Il.* 2.53, 4.344; *Od.* 2.14.

[6] Daniel the Stylite is said to have been received into a monastery at the age of twelve, *Vita,* ch. 4, trans. Elizabeth Dawes and Norman H. Baynes, *Three Byzantine Saints* (Oxford, 1948), from *Les Saints stylites,* ed. Hippolyte Delehaye, Subsidia hagiographica 14 (Brussels, 1923), pp. 1-94. On the other hand, the writer feels a need to emphasize the obviously surprising facts that "young Silvanus" (who had been an actor) was only twenty when he became a monk, and that he made good progress *kaitoi paidion ōn*, "even though he was a child." *Paralipomena de SS. Pachomio et Theodoro,* ch. 2, ed. François Halkin in *Le Corpus athénien de Saint Pachôme* (Geneva, 1982), pp. 74 (text) and 124 (trans.).

[7] John of Lycopolis and Abba Or are said to be "about ninety years old" (the former having spent forty years in a grotto); Abba Copres was "nearly ninety," Abba Elias "would be a hundred now," whilst Abba Apollo had founded a new monastery at the age of eighty. It is to be noted that these assertions of longevity are rarely found in later tales and sayings.

one hundred six.[8] The temptation to attribute his longevity, as well as
something of his other virtues, to the great ones who stood in his tradition
must have been very strong indeed. And there is a practical consideration:
is it likely that those fathers, who spent half a lifetime rejecting the things
of this world, would have troubled to retain anything so insignificant to
them as the memory of the year of their physical entry into the world? Or
that, being men of so few words, they would waste words in communi-
cating such trivial information to others? Then again, the very fact that so
many of the fathers are said to be ninety-plus should itself urge caution; it
may be no more than a conventional term for "many years," comparable
to the forty years that so many fathers are credited with in this or that
activity. Indeed, ninety-plus may not even be a chronic statement at all,
but a qualitative one, meaning that in being only a little short of the century the monk in question was approaching, but had not yet attained, perfection.[9]

That some few monks did far outlive their contemporaries there can be
little doubt; it is what we might expect, though not that these should be
the outstandingly virtuous ones, and they probably were not. For the rest,
death appears to have overtaken them at varying points in their earthly
pilgrimage. Again, it is what one would expect, and the great Abba
Anthony confirms it in his second apophthegm: "Lord, how is it that
some die having lived only a short time, whilst others become exceedingly old (hypergērōsi)?"[10] Whether or not, on the whole, monks lived
longer than men "in the world" there is as yet no way of telling – though
the fortuitous discovery of, say, a sixth-century monastic cemetery could
tell us a lot. The likelihood, it seems to me, is that the advantages of the
monastic life were at least offset by its privations, and thus, that they did
not. Which means, if we can trust the only available evidence, that half of
them died before they reached the age of forty-four, and half the remainder before they attained sixty-four.[11]

---

[8] See *Vita Antonii* by Athanasius, PG 26: 837-976. So far as I am aware, only Saint Paul of
Thebes is said to have lived longer than Anthony (one hundred sixteen), and that in a *Vita* (by
Jerome) which seems in part an attempt to assert that there was a yet greater ascetic who preceded
and exceeded Anthony in several ways: see *Studies in the Text-Tradition of Saint Jerome's Vitae
patrum,* ed. William A. Oldfather (Urbana, 1943), pp. 158-172.

[9] I am indebted for this suggestion to Sister Benedicta Ward, SLG of Oxford.

[10] PG 65: 76B.

[11] See Evelyne Patlagean, *Pauvreté économique et pauvreté sociale à Byzance, 4ᵉ-7ᵉ siècles*
(Paris, 1977), ch.3.3, "Durées de vie," pp. 95-101. The figures given are for males only (one has to
subtract about ten years for females), and only for those males who survived into adulthood. The
findings are based on tombstone inscriptions at Moab. Patlagean notes that saints in general are
often said to have lived to much greater ages than the rest of mankind.

With desert fathers, then, we are dealing with an aged and aging segment of the population. What can we learn of them as they advanced
from profession to the grave?[12] Well, to start with the very obvious, old
age brought sickness and failing strength. "Having grown old, he became
ill (*kai gērasas ēsthenēse*)" is a phrase that often recurs.[13] It was expected
and, in a sense, prepared for. Thus Amma Syncletica: "Fast whilst you are
young and healthy, for old age with its sickness (*meta astheneias*) will
come."[14] When it did come, concessions were to be made to it, but we
only hear of those cases in which concessions were refused. Thus did
Peter the Pionite refuse the cup of wine and water that his disciples
offered him "for his stomach's sake" when he, who had never drunk
wine, reached the weakness of old age.[15] Thus did Isidore the priest not
heed his disciples when they urged him to rest a little from his manual
labours, now that extreme old age had befallen him.[16] Thus too did Abba
Sisoes refuse to move a little closer to civilization (*hē oikoumenē*) and its
comforts.[17] From all this we can conclude that concessions of various
kinds were normally expected to be made to the ravages of old age.

Thinking that old age also brought decreasing resistance to temptation,
the demons, the eternal antagonists of the desert fathers, seem not in the
least to have abated their attacks on the very aged. Abba Joseph of Panu-
pho was subject to such an attack at the very point of death, but he rallied
himself, called for his staff, and put the demon to flight.[18] It is no surprise
to anybody who is familiar with the desert literature to read that, most
of all, it was the demons of *porneia* who menaced the aged, as they
menaced monks of all ages; for no temptations seem to have more sorely
tried the endurance of the desert fathers than those of the various sins of

---

[12] Space will not allow for a comprehensive treatment here of all the aspects of monastic "progress," which were many. We should, however, at least note the third apophthegm of Matoes (PG 65:
289D): "When I was younger (*neōteros*) I said to myself, 'perhaps this day I shall do something
good'; but now I have grown old (*hōs egērasa*), I see that I have not one good deed in me."

[13] Sometimes with the addition of *kai lelōbēmenos* (e.g. P&J 6.20, Nau 260), meaning perhaps
"disfigured" rather than "a leper" (see below, p. 70). See Theodore of Pherme 26 (PG 65: 194): "[he]
... became old and sick. So the brethren brought him some things to eat. But what the first brought,
he gave to the second, and so forth ...." The *gerōn* who refuses material comfort in his old age is in
stark contrast to the secular gardener who sought to assure himself of it, P&J 6.21, Nau 261/493.
François Nau published many *narrationes animae utiles* from Paris, BN, MS. Coislin 126 in a series
of articles, entitled "Histoires des solitaires égyptiens," in *Revue de l'Orient chrétien* 12 (1907)
through 18 (1913). For access to Nau 260, etc., see *Les Sentences des pères du désert: Nouveau
recueil*, 2nd ed. (Sablé-sur-Sarthe, 1977).

[14] Syncletica 15, PG 65: 425D.

[15] PG 65: 375BC.

[16] PG 65: 220D-221A.

[17] PG 65: 392D.

[18] PG 65: 232B.

concupiscence. Saint Benedict is reported to have said that after the age of fifty the flesh begins to cool and its attendant problems to go away.[19] Which may have been the case in the northern latitudes of Italy, but it seems not to have been the case in the deserts of Egypt and Syria – where, incidentally, a man of fifty years was considered to be on the threshold of old age, if he had survived that long.[20] Abba Sisoes, already mentioned, gave as his reason for not moving a little closer to civilization (and thus greatly facilitating the business of his obviously proximate funeral) that he would rather go where there were no women, that is, no additional inducements to *porneia*. And Macarius the Great, the Egyptian, lamented in these words: "See how many years I have led an ascetic life, held in honour by everybody, and the spirit of *porneia* troubles me in my old age (*tōi gerōnti*)."[21]

Nor were these temptations always successfully resisted, as we learn from the story of an anonymous monk of Scētē. Old and sick, he regretted being a burden to his brethren, so he took himself off to civilization in search of medical care. There he was nursed back from the gates of death by a religious lady, with whom he fell into sin, so that she conceived and bore him a child. He returned to Scētē with the infant, "the child of disobedience" as he called it, warning the brethren to beware, for he had gotten this "in my old age (*eis to gēras mou*)." He then returned to his cell and started to rebuild his ascetic life – by no means the only indication that the monastic community could be as forgiving of sins of *porneia* as it was prone to them.[22]

We are not told what became of "the child of disobedience." It is most unlikely that he would have been suffered to remain at Scētē, or in any other monastic community, for the literature reveals an almost paranoid antipathy to the young, *ta paidia,* on the part of the *gerōntes*. It is an antipathy that is particularly surprising in the light of the dominical charge "Suffer little children (*ta paidia*) to come unto me and hinder them not, for of such is the kingdom of God."[23] But there is no denying it; there was a yawning generation gap between the *gerōntes* of the desert and *paidia* in general. "Where there is wine and *paidia,* there is no need of Satan," says one sage.[24] "Satan, not God, sends *paidia* into the desert

---

[19] "ab anno quinquagesima, calor corporis frigescat," Gregory, *Dialogues* 2.2.4 (PL 66: 134).

[20] Patlagean, *Pauvreté économique,* notes in the seventh-century *Miracula Sancti Artemii* (ed. Athanasios Papadopoulos-Kerameus in *Varia Graeca sacra* [St. Petersburg, 1909]) a fifty-year-old man described as "grey-haired and entering old age" (Miracle 13) and a sixty-year-old who has become incapable of doing his work (Miracle 16).

[21] Macarios 3, PG 65: 264A.

[22] P&J 5.35, Nau 187.

[23] Mark 10: 14 etc.

[24] Nau 545, Paris, BN, MS. Coislin 126, fol. 290v.

to win monks' lives," says another.[25] And there is the tale in which the devil, coming to a monastery gate, finds a boy (*paidion*) there. "No need of me if you are here," he says, and goes his way.[26] These and similar sentiments are expressed over and over again.

It is not difficult to understand why. Young people could indeed literally raise the very devil in a monastery, as they can in any establishment. We have the story of a *gerōn* who had a *paidion* living with him, whom he reproved for a fault. The youth promptly locked up the pantry and made off with the key, leaving the father without food for three days.[27] The point of this story is that the father withstood this severe test of his patience, but this must have been an exceptionally gifted father. Another problem was that youths are given to speaking unseemly words. "A youth who expresses an opinion before those who are senior to him is like a man who throws fire into his brother's breast," declares one aphorism.[28] This explains why the disciples of Pachomius so bitterly resented it when he appointed Theodore to be their teacher. "He is a mere beginner (*archarios*)," they complain, "you have appointed a *paidion* to be teacher of us who are so many *gerōntes* and ancient brethren."[29] Since Theodore is said already to have been twenty years – another suspiciously round figure – in the monastic profession, this should be a warning not to take the word *paidion* too literally when it is used of the desert fathers.[30]

But monastic antipathy to *paidia* goes deeper than this; here too there is the all-pervasive demon of *porneia* lurking in the background. "Even more so than women, *paidia* amongst monks are the snare of the devil."[31] Thus when Abba Eudaimōn tried to join the community at Scētē whilst still quite young, Abba Paphnutius sent him away, saying: "I do not allow the face of a woman to dwell in Scētē because of the conflict with the enemy."[32] This explains the otherwise incomprehensible tale of Carion, who abandoned wife and family to join the same community. There came a famine in Egypt, and he was obliged to take his son Theodore into the monastery with him. The brethren were very distressed about this, but

---

[25] Nau 458, Paris, BN, MS. Coislin 126, fol. 268v, adding "to win those who would live piously."

[26] Nau 457, Paris, BN, MS. Coislin 126, fol. 268v. Note also Matoes 11: "Take care to have neither friendship with a *paidion*, nor acquaintance with a woman, nor a heretic as a friend." PG 65: 293B.

[27] Nau 341, P&J 16.24/15.

[28] Nau 542, Paris, BN, MS. Coislin 126, fol. 290v.

[29] Halkin, *Paralipomena*, pp. 73-74, 123-124. We learn elsewhere (*Epistola Ammonis* 9, ibid. p. 102) that, everything said here notwithstanding, the great Pachomius took in Theodore when he was only thirteen years old, and raised him as his own son.

[30] *Paidion* originally meant only a child of up to seven years.

[31] Nau 544, Paris, BN, MS. Coislin 126, fol. 290v.

[32] PG 65: 176B.

young Theodore set their hearts at rest in a most curious way. He submerged himself in nitre for many hours, "until his body was changed and he became like a leper" (perhaps "like a diseased old man" would be a better translation of the difficult word *lelōbēmenos*). "Now he has become like an angel," declared Isidore the priest of Scētē. It should be added that he went on to become an outstanding monk; clearly Theodore's was an exceptional case.[33]

For the most part, *paidia* presented severe problems in monastic communities. "A monk who lives with a youth, falls if he is not stable. But even if he is stable and does not fall, he still does not make progress," says one apophthegm recently discovered.[34] John Colobros went even further: "He who talks with a boy has already committed fornication with him in his thoughts."[35] "Four churches at Scētē were deserted because of boys," claimed Isaac of the Cells,[36] so "when you see *paidia*, take your sheepskin and go away," was the advice of Macarius the Great.[37]

So far we have stated little more than the obvious: that young persons constituted a danger to older ones who sought to "progress" by, *inter alia*, suppressing their physical desires. It was not so much that age despised youth; rather, that youth was feared. But the matter goes a little deeper still. Here is one of the apophthegms of "Abba Poimēn":

> A man who lives with a youth (*paidion*) and is incited (*energoumenos*) by him to no matter what passions of the old man (*pathos tou palaiou anthrōpou*) and yet keeps him with him – that man is like someone who has a field eaten up with maggots.[38]

In other words, the youth is the agent of the "old man," which is a nice paradox. The latter reference is, of course, scriptural; the Christian's "old man" is crucified with Christ, the Christian life is a "putting off" of the "old man" and all his works in Pauline thought[39] – which "Poimēn" takes up elsewhere: "God gave this pattern of behaviour to Israel: to abstain from everything that is contrary to nature ... and the rest of the oldness (*tēs palaiotētos*)."[40] "Is there not something of the old man still left in

---

[33] PG 65: 249D-252C. This is a most unusually long tale for the *Alphabetikon*, and there is much more to it than I have suggested here.

[34] Karion 3, in Jean-C. Guy, *Apophthegmata des pères du désert* (Begrolles, 1966).

[35] PG 65: 205AB.

[36] PG 65: 225AB.

[37] PG 65: 264D.

[38] "Poimēn" (i.e. "the shepherd," therefore perhaps equivalent to "anon.") 176, PG 65: 365A.

[39] Rom. 6:6 (cf. 7:6), Col. 3:9, Eph. 4:22. *Palaios anthrōpos* and *gerōn* are, to a certain extent, interchangeable terms, though the latter is innocent of the somewhat pejorative connotation of the former.

[40] Poimēn 68, PG 65: 337C.

you?" he asks Pelousios the priest in another passage.[41] "Putting off the old man" is the monk's profession; it is in this that he progresses, growing away and out of the "old man" as he himself grows physically older. And one of the greatest threats to his progress comes from those who, whilst physically young, are largely under the domain of the "old man."

But how on earth, you may well ask, did the desert fathers reconcile these curious paradoxes and their own paedophobia, nay, "misopaedy," with that saying of the Lord of the Christians, "Unless you change altogether and become as children (*hōs paidia*), you shall no wise enter the kingdom of heaven," and "Of such is the kingdom of God"?[42] It should be fairly clear from many of the foregoing quotations that they simply did not resolve it in any practical sense whatsoever; that, far from suffering (*aphiēmi*) *paidia,* they held them very much at arm's length, and effectively cut themselves off from the younger generation, willingly and deliberately. But then it could scarcely have been otherwise, given some of the qualities for which the monk strove: silence (*hēsuchia*), compunction (*katanuxis*), self-control and self-sufficiency (*autarkeia*), long-suffering, discretion (*diakrisis*), vigilance and perseverence in prayer. Having raised three children myself and taught many hundreds of others, I suggest to you that these are not the qualities one normally finds in *ta paidia;* and that, if "of such is the kingdom of God," it must be by virtue of certain qualities other than those just mentioned. This is not to say that all young people are a noisy, reckless, undisciplined bunch of barbarians; merely, that many of them do tend in that direction. They can and do "get on one's nerves" – if I may so translate the *energoumenos* of "Poimēn's" apophthegm; they can and do drive one to all sorts of "passions of the old man," whether we like it or not, even those of us whose profession is the raising and training of youths rather than the saving of our souls in the desert.

But there is another side to the young, especially to the very young, which is a very different matter indeed. There is a side that is lovable, wholesome, and praiseworthy, a side that seems to be the very antithesis of the "old man" and all his machinations. It is characterised by innocence, generosity, warmth, kindness, trust, purity, honesty, and a number of other equally desirable qualities. Was it not by seeking to emulate these qualities that the desert fathers attempted to "become as *paidia*"? Was it not precisely in "turning around" – we might say turning the clock back – that they attempted to recapture that freshness and those excellent

---

[41] Poimēn 11, PG 65: 325A. Cf. the monk in Nau 660 who agonizes "until [God] make me come out of the *palaios anthrōpos.*"

[42] Mark 10:14 (cf. *a fortiori* 9:37), etc.

qualities of youth, which most of us lose once and for all as we grow "older and wickeder"? Thus, to cite but a few of the more obvious examples, the monk strives to disembarrass himself of worldly possessions (the great monastic virtue of *aktēmonsunē*), and to become wholly dependent on a heavenly father, as the child depends on his earthly parent. He seeks to put aside physical passions and to regain the purity and innocence of the very young. He tries to shed the sophistication and intellectualism that cloud the clear sight of youth, to humble himself and obey, like the ideal good child, and so forth. In a word, it seems that in a certain sense the monk did not so much progress as regress into a second, purer, childhood, as he strove to attain the idealized qualities of the very young. And this may largely explain why he seems to have been so indifferent to the process of physical aging. His belly might slacken and his eyes grow dim, but he was not concerned with that aspect of his being. He did not think of himself as getting older, but rather as becoming ever younger, and that not by a negative regression but by a very positive rejuvenation and renewal, through a second and more excellent childhood, tending at the last (and first) to glorious rebirth, a passing through the mirror into the kingdom, at the moment of death. Or, putting it another way, one might say that his entire *askēsis* was an entering into the womb of his mother, the angelic community, in order that he might truly be born again.

Now this may be going a little further than the documents will support, but it may also have revealed a yet more curious aspect of the fathers' antipathy to youth. There is something analogous to it in the Byzantine antipathy to the Jews. Of all Christian people, the East Romans seem to have taken the Christian vocation to be "the New Israel" the most seriously, even to the extent that it became an integral part of their political ideology.[43] On the one hand, this meant that they most warmly espoused and earnestly tried to emulate the nobler aspects of the Old Israel, cherishing its scriptures and some of its other traditions. But on the other hand, for the surviving remnants of the Old Israel, the Jews, they entertained a lively antipathy that all too often erupted into overt persecution. In part, no doubt, this was because the continued survival of the Old Israel was a condemnation of their own claim to have supplanted it. But was it not also, and even more so, because they saw in it a too blemished and imperfect foreshadowing of the ideal they believed to be their destiny and to which they strove, a fearful reminder that the whole endeavour

---

[43] See John Wortley, "Israel and Byzantium: A Case of Socio-Religious Acculturation," in *Traditions in Contact and Change: Selected Proceedings of the XIVth Congress of the International Association for the History of Religions (1980)* (Waterloo, 1983), pp. 361-375, 719-723.

might yet come crashing down around their ears? Something very much like this (I suggest) lay behind the monk's rejection of youths. They were just too much both the image and the caricature of what he was striving to achieve, too much the tatty old remnants of what were but obsolete prefigurings of the glorious new life he would lead. So he simply did to them what the Byzantines in general would have liked to do to the Jews: he shut them out of his life.

*   *   *

We have been speaking of "the monastic community," which was surprisingly large at certain times, to be sure, but which nevertheless was at no time more than a small proportion of the population. Small though it may have been, its influence spread far and wide beyond the confines of the desert. Monastic lore not only permeated "the world" to a remarkable extent, it even inspired a number of secular imitators who devised and retailed "tales" in the monastic mold. In time, these were to provide Byzantium with the nearest thing she ever possessed to a genuine folk-lore of her own. As one might expect, in common with many other characteristically monastic modes of thought, something of the attitudes we have been discussing – to aging and youth – passed into that lore. The question that one would dearly like to see answered is: to what extent did these attitudes thus communicate themselves to the population at large? It is, alas, difficult if not impossible to say. The only clue I have been able to find, and it is an ambiguous one, lies in a growing tendency for men (and also some women) to take the monastic habit when death was obvi-ously nigh. Could it be that they did so in the hope of thus being able to share something of the rejuvenation and new birth of the *gerōn*? We can only speculate. But we can be fairly sure that many, many people shared the monastic conviction that, in the New Israel, aging was no longer a degenerative but a regenerative process.

6

Beyond the Topos of Senescence
The Political Problems of
Aged Carolingian Rulers

Paul Edward Dutton

Simon Fraser University

Historians have, by and large, been reluctant to deal directly with topoi, since they seem to belong more properly to the realm of poetic fancy. But the topos of senescence is to be found buried in historical narratives. Curtius charged that historians often fail to recognize the theme when they encounter it and instead unwittingly take such statements as "the world is in gray old age" as self-expressions of the Middle Ages.[1] Just as often, one suspects, historians have knowingly employed such topoi as structuring principles on which to build huge historical edifices: Spengler is an obvious example. On a day-to-day basis, historians of the Middle Ages are more likely to dismiss outright such commonplace expressions as irrelevant to the reconstruction of a factual history. Even Curtius, despite his encyclopedic treatment of topoi, seldom stopped to ask what might lie behind the use of a given figure in a given time. The question asked here is what place the theme of senescence had in the ninth century.

Senescence is a very special topos, since it is a subset of the organic metaphor, the metaphor most frequently applied to the state.[2] Whenever we find the state compared to a diseased body, a poisoned body, or a body naturally growing old, we are in the presence of this organic metaphor,

---

[1] Ernst R. Curtius, *European Literature and the Latin Middle Ages,* trans. Willard R. Trask, Bollingen Series 36 (Princeton, 1953; repr. 1973), p. 28.

[2] See Robert Nisbet, *Social Change and History: Aspects of the Western Theory of Development* (Oxford, 1969), p. 3; Victor W. Turner, *Dramas, Fields, and Metaphors: Symbolic Action in Human Society* (Ithaca, 1974), pp. 24-29.

Aging and the Aged in Medieval Europe, ed. Michael M. Sheehan, CSB. Papers in Mediaeval Studies 11 (Toronto: Pontifical Institute of Mediaeval Studies, 1990), pp. 75-94. © P.I.M.S., 1990.

and it is one that imposes a situational model on its user.[3] If the state, for example, is said to be declining into old age, the implication is rather drastic: a body once youthful and full of energy, now thought to be old and decrepit, must eventually die. There can be some prolongation of life, but no reversals. If, however, the state is compared to a diseased body, the underlying intention of the author may be to urge someone to effect a cure. Historians need occasionally to be reminded that the state is not a body, and that they are not "country doctors" capable of diagnosing an amorphous historical corpse.[4]

Carolingian historiography has not been free from the influence of this metaphor.[5] Heinrich Fichtenau, in particular, has argued that "the Carolingian empire, itself a late manifestation of the *regnum francorum*, seemed to enter the period of old age" during Charlemagne's latter years.[6] Doubtless an organic conception of Carolingian history underlies the work of most modern historians. They see, in other words, Pepin the Short as representing the youthful period of the Carolingian historical experience, Charlemagne its maturity, and Louis the Pious and his successors its old age and decline. Fichtenau and Ganshof only tinkered with the model when they observed that the first signs of decline had really appeared during the last period of Charlemagne's reign.[7] The received pattern of ninth-century history, therefore, is one of senescence. I say "received," because this pattern is not the invention of any modern historian but is rather imbedded in the Carolingian sources we read.[8] Senescence is a historiographical theme of the ninth century, one that first burst into prominence at the beginning of the century.

---

[3] See Randolph Starn, "Meaning-Levels in the Theme of Historical Decline," *History and Theory* 14 (1975) 15-16; Paul Edward Dutton, "Awareness of Historical Decline in the Carolingian Empire, 800-887" (Ph.D. diss., University of Toronto, 1981), pp. 5-12.

[4] Randolph Starn, "Historians and 'Crisis'," *Past and Present* 52 (1971) 3-22.

[5] For various uses of the metaphor, see Dutton, "Awareness of Historical Decline," pp. 19-64.

[6] *The Carolingian Empire: The Age of Charlemagne*, trans. Peter Munz, Studies in Medieval History 9 (Oxford, 1957; repr. Toronto, 1979), p. 187. It should be noted that this is not a full translation of Fichtenau's *Das karolingische Imperium: Soziale und geistige Problematik eines Grossreiches* (Zurich, 1949).

[7] Fichtenau ibid.; François L. Ganshof, "La Fin du règne de Charlemagne: Une décomposition," *Zeitschrift für schweizerische Geschichte* 28 (1948) 533-552 [trans. Janet Sondheimer in Ganshof, *The Carolingians and the Frankish Monarchy* (Ithaca, 1971), pp. 240-255], and "L'Echec de Charlemagne," *Académie des inscriptions et belles lettres: Comptes rendus des séances* (1947), pp. 248-254 [trans. Sondheimer in *Carolingians and the Frankish Monarchy*, pp. 256-260].

[8] The anonymous author (sometimes called the Astronomer) of the *Vita Hludowici imperatoris*, ed. Georg H. Pertz in Monumenta Germaniae historica (henceforth MGH), *Scriptorum* 2 (Hanover, 1829) 3, p. 608, said that Charlemagne knew the kingdom was like a body that needed ministering and spoke (61, p. 645) of the body of the empire as diseased in Louis' own time.

The later writings of Alcuin are, in one sense, a mournful song on the subject of his senescence. When he became abbot of Saint-Martin of Tours in 796, Alcuin was already over sixty and in poor health. He wrote to Charlemagne that in the morning of his life and at the height of his powers he had worked in Britain, but now, in the evening of his life, he laboured in Francia.[9] His body, he admitted to the king, was broken, and he urged his royal reader to turn to one of Jerome's letters on the failure of the body and the strengthening of the mind in old age.[10] To a friend he complained that he was beset by the double burden of infirmity and old age.[11] It should be noted that Carolingians generally linked sickness and agedness as though these two conditions belonged together.[12] Indeed, after one has often encountered descriptions of infirm old men and phrases like *debilitata senectus,* "crippled old age," in Carolingian sources,[13] one begins to wonder what awareness of agedness the Carolingians had beyond the merely pathological. Furthermore, like many ninth-century men, Alcuin employed this double burden as an excuse for not attending to the king's demands upon him.[14] But his invocation of the theme of senescence, even by way of excuse, was not without literary sophistication. Alcuin likened himself to old Entellus fending off the assaults of a young Dares, who would persecute his old age.[15] He called upon the king and his friends to defend the old poet.[16] In letters to friends he aped Ovid, complaining that now "tired old age enters my room with

---

[9] Ep. 121 of *Epistolae Alcuini,* ed. Ernst Dümmler in MGH *Epistolae* 4 (Hanover, 1895), p. 178. Alcuin here draws an allusion to Eccl. 11:6.

[10] The reference is to Jerome, Ep. 52, *Ad Nepotianum presbyterum* 2, ed. Jérôme Labourt in St. Jérôme, *Lettres* 2 (Paris, 1951), p. 173.

[11] Ep. 114 addressed to Eanbald, archbishop of York in 796, in MGH *Epistolae* 4: 169, "Ecce ego duplici fatigatus molestia, id est senectute et infirmitate." See also Ep. 229 of 801 to Charles (ibid., pp. 373-374), where weakness and old age are again linked.

[12] To give but a few examples of this persistent theme, see Candidus, *De uita Æigili* 11, ed. Ernst Dümmler in MGH *Poetae* 2 (Berlin, 1883), pp. 102-103, lines 1-5; Einhard, Ep. 10, ed. Karl Hampe in MGH *Epistolae* 5 (Hanover, 1899), p. 114, and Ep. 28, p. 123; the so-called *Narratio clericorum Remensium,* ed. Albert Werminghoff in MGH *Concilia* 2.1.2 (Hanover, 1908), p. 813; *Epistolae uariorum* 31.3, ed. Ernst Dümmler in MGH *Epistolae* 6 (Hanover, 1925), p. 196.

[13] Candidus, *De uita Æigili* 11, line 18, in MGH *Poetae* 2: 103.

[14] See Alcuin, Ep. 241 in MGH *Epistolae* 4: 387; Ep. 240, p. 385; and Ep. 238, p. 383 for some of the excuses for not appearing at court. Einhard, in Ep. 10 to Louis the Pious in 830, MGH *Epistolae* 5: 114, line 16, describes himself as "iam senex et ualde infirmus" and pleads in a series of letters to be allowed to be absent from the court: see Ep. 13, pp. 116-117; Ep. 14, p. 117; Ep. 15, p. 118; and Ep. 25, p. 122.

[15] Drawing on Virgil, *Aen.* 5.437 ff., Alcuin frequently employed this imagery. See Ep. 145 to Charles (ca. 798), p. 231; Ep. 164 to Charles (799), p. 266; and Carm. 42, ed. Ernst Dümmler in MGH *Poetae* 1 (Berlin, 1881), p. 254, lines 19-20.

[16] Carm. 42, in MGH *Poetae* 1: 254, line 18, and Ep. 229 to Charlemagne (801), p. 374. In Carm. 16, p. 239, lines 5-6, Alcuin asks Angilbert to help old Alcuin.

quiet foot."[17] Indeed Theodulf, full of bitter fun, may have grown tired of the excuses of the whining dotard of Tours: let old Flaccus answer for himself, says Theodulf on the matter of Alcuin's non-appearance at court, "he has the time."[18] Time, in other words, before he dies.

Alcuin did not, however, reduce the topos of senescence to a purely personal theme; rather, he tied it to his pessimistic view of contemporary history. His formulaic response to the events he witnessed at the end of his life was that "the times were full of danger."[19] He believed that he saw the good fortune of his times turning everywhere to misfortune. In his long poem on the sack of the monastery of Lindisfarne, he linked the fall of the four ancient kingdoms (Babylon, Persia, Greece, and Rome) and his own world overrun by pagans (in Africa, Asia, Spain, and even Rome) with the example of a single aging man, whose body had begun to fail him: "What more can I say? All youth grows feeble, and all beauty of the body now passes and fails. Slack skin just scarcely adheres to the bones and the old man does not even recognize his own body."[20] In this image, we may perceive an aged Alcuin who pretended not to recognize his changing times. In an awful and impermanent age, comfort could lie only in belief in God. Alcuin seemed to think that if he alerted the brothers of Lindisfarne to the sadness of all times, the worst of which was his own, the blow of their recent sack at the hands of the Norsemen would somehow be bearable.[21]

Alcuin's conviction of the mutability of all things is not without its personal dimension, since he had been part of a world of intimate court camaraderie that was vanishing. There had been a certain youthfulness and joy among the poets gathered around Charlemagne after 780: one thinks, for example, of Angilbert's poems of pomp and play, and of the charming nicknames given to the close circle of men fashioning the Carolingian renaissance. After 796, however, these poets had gone their own separate ways: Paul the Deacon, Peter of Pisa, and Paulinus of Aquileia had returned to Lombardy, Alcuin had exchanged Aachen for

---

[17] From Ovid, *Ars amat.* 2.670. Alcuin, Ep. 310 to Remedius (803-804), p. 479: "tacito pede fessa senectus ingreditur cubile nostrum." See also Ep. 225 to Theodulf, p. 369.

[18] Carm. 27 "Ad Corvinianum," in MGH *Poetae* 1: 491, line 37: "Ille habet aetatem ...."

[19] For variations of the phrase "tempora sunt periculosa" see Alcuin, Ep. 116, in MGH *Epistolae* 4: 171; Ep. 74, p. 117; Ep. 193, p. 320; and Carm. 48, in MGH *Poetae* 1: 261, line 21.

[20] Carm. 9 "De clade Lindisfarnensis monasterii," in MGH *Poetae* 1: 232, lines 111-114:
>   Quid iam plura canam? marcescit tota iuventus,
>   Iam perit atque cadit corporis omne decus,
>   Et pellis tantum vacua vix ossibus haeret,
>   Nec cognoscit homo propria membra senex.

[21] For an analysis of the images of senescence in Alcuin's writings, see Dutton, "Awareness of Historical Decline," pp. 230-234.

Tours, and Angilbert spent most of his time at Saint-Riquier. A sense of separation and loss pervades the post-796 poems of these men, who increasingly styled themselves *senes vates,* "the old poets."[22] They shared an awareness of agedness as a common condition.[23] In his poem "O mea cella," Alcuin laments the silencing of the poets, the absence of Alcuin and Angilbert from court, and the stilling of the singing boys. He again describes his times as changed, as "the youth who once hunted deer in the fields is now a tired old man leaning on his walking stick."[24] Theodulf of Orléans, who had remained behind after the other poets had parted, also coupled the theme of senescence and an awareness of changed times. In one of his later poems, perhaps written after he was sent into exile in 818, he contemplated the evident end and ruin of all things. The old world was failing, and the embittered Theodulf was convinced that now "nothing stands fixed as it stood before."[25] Everywhere he saw the defeat of youthful qualities, which now wearied the old. Dreadful old age, he grumbled, devours all things.[26] Thus the topos of senescence assumed historiographical proportions in the early ninth century, because Charlemagne's poets allowed the issue of their personal aging to symbolize the times in which they lived. These men did not go gently into their old age, they went complaining.

---

[22] Others thought of them in this way as well. Modoin, the young contemporary called Naso at court, wrote a poem in hexameters to Charles in the form of a dialogue between a *puer* and a *senex.* The young interlocutor asks for admission to the closed circle of *senes uates* (Angilbert, Alcuin, and Theodulf). See "Nasonis Ecloga" in MGH *Poetae* 1: 385-387.

For another Carolingian dialogue based on the conflict of generations, see the one attributed to Sedulius Scottus: *Senex et adolescens,* ed. Siegmund Hellmann in his *Sedulius Scottus,* Quellen und Untersuchungen zur lateinischen Philologie des Mittelalters 1.1 (Munich, 1906; repr. Frankfurt, 1966), p. 120.

[23] See, e.g., Paul the Deacon, Carm. 12, verse 12, in MGH *Poetae* 1: 50; Peter of Pisa, Carm. 15 "Versus Petri ad Paulum," ibid., p. 54, line 45.

[24] Carm. 23 in MGH *Poetae* 1: 244, lines 29-30:
        Qua campis cervos agitabat sacra iuventus,
        Incumbit fessus nunc baculo senior.
On the attribution of this poem to Alcuin, see Peter Godman, "Alcuin's Poetic Style and the Authenticity of 'O mea cella'," *Studi medievali* 3rd ser. 20 (1979) 555-583. Godman points out (577) that the "ponderous spondaic movement" of line 30 reflects "the old man's weary step." Cf. also Carm. 9, p. 231, lines 101-102.

[25] Carm. 14 "Quod multis indiciis finis proximus esse monstretur," in MGH *Poetae* 1: 469, line 16: "fixum nil stat ut ante stetit."

[26] Ibid., lines 21-22:
        Non viget, ut viguit dudum, vegetata iuventa,
        Cuncta senectus atrox ore nigrante vorat.
In this poem, Theodulf draws extensively on a letter of Cyprian to Demetrian that described in dramatic fashion the physical exhaustion of the world: see Cyprian, Ep. 10.3, ed. Wilhelm Hartel in Corpus scriptorum ecclesiasticorum Latinorum (henceforth CSEL) 3.1 (Vienna, 1868), pp. 352-353, and printed in MGH *Poetae* 1: 468, n. 2.

In more subtle fashion, the theme of senescence colours some important histories of Charlemagne's reign. We need to remember that these
historians were primarily witnesses of Charlemagne's later years. Einhard
was only in his early twenties when he arrived at the court of Charlemagne, who was already fifty. But his biography of the emperor was not
written until much later, when, as an old man himself, he recalled his
younger days. The *Vita Karoli Magni,* thus, contains the youthful impressions of Einhard at the court of an old king. Evidence for this is not hard
to find: Einhard admitted that nothing was known about the early period
of Charlemagne's life.[27] Indeed, he leaves us with a portrait of an aged
ruler, who loved to soak in hot springs, who wept over the deaths of his
children, and who took up writing too late in life to become proficient.[28]
Of the physical traits mentioned by Einhard, the most striking is a glorious head of grey hair.[29] The later medieval, and doubtless romantic,
image of Charlemagne as an old and holy emperor with a flowing white
beard derives, in part, from Einhard's biography. Louis the Pious's historians (the so-called Astronomer, Thegan, Ermold, and even Nithard) all
remembered a Charlemagne who was, as they said, "full of days in his
fine old age."[30] In fact, in Ermold the Black's poem in praise of Louis,
Charlemagne is made to speak directly to the issue of his old age. He
reminds his gathered nobles in 813 that when his body was young and
vigorous he had employed arms, and every enemy of the Franks had
feared him. But now his blood had grown sluggish and cold, harsh old
age made him listless, and flowing grey hair covered his white neck. His
warlike right hand, once famous throughout the world, now trembled. His
children had died before him, except Louis, whom he now took up as
coemperor.[31] Like so much else about ninth-century kingship, the great
length of Charlemagne's reign became an influential model for his successors. In his mirror of the prince, Sedulius Scottus contrasted the brief
and unhappy days allowed to the reprobate with the many and happy
years given to just and holy rulers.[32] In the major annals, in fact, one can

[27] *Vita Karoli Magni* 4, ed. Oswald Holder-Egger in MGH *Scriptores rerum Germanicarum in
usum scholarum,* 6th ed. (Hanover, 1911; repr. 1947), pp. 6-7.

[28] *Vita Karoli Magni* 22, p. 27; 19, p. 25; and 25, p. 30.

[29] *Vita Karoli Magni* 22, p. 26: "canitie pulchra ...."

[30] See, e.g., Thegan, *Vita Hludowici imperatoris* 7, ed. Georg H. Pertz in MGH *Scriptorum* 2:
592, who describes Charlemagne as "in senectute bona plenus dierum." See also *Nithard His-
toriarum libri IIII* 1.1, ed. Georg H. Pertz and Ernst Müller in MGH *Scriptores rerum Germanicarum
in usum scholarum,* 3rd ed. (Hanover, 1907), p. 1, on Charlemagne "in senectute bona decedens ...."

[31] "In honorem Hludowici" 2, lines 3-30, ed. Ernst Dümmler in MGH *Poetae* 2: 24-25 and ed.
Edmond Faral, *Poème sur Louis le Pieux et épitres au roi Pepin* (Paris, 1932), pp. 52-54, lines 654-
681.

[32] *Liber de rectoribus Christianis* 20, ed. Hellmann in *Sedulius Scottus,* p. 89.

identify this as a central theme: bad kings die disastrous, violent, and premature deaths, while good kings die in peaceful old age.

The topos of senescence, thus, assumes an important place in ninth-century historiography because of the conjunction of Charlemagne's own aging alongside the aging of his highly vocal poets and the expansion of historical writing. The remembered Charlemagne was aged and his latter years were characterized as a period of spreading senescence. The Carolingian interest in the theme did not end with Charlemagne, but rather continued to arise throughout the century in conjunction with the aging of later kings. What I would like to ask is whether we can account for this coincidence of aged rulers and the expression of the theme of senescence. Granted that this topos is clothed in age-old figures[33] and is not directly descriptive of historical events, could it not be that there were real reasons why aged Carolingian rulers were beset by political and familial problems, and that the topos of senescence exists as a parallel structure beside them, one reflecting through the rhetoric of disorder an indirect, yet deeper impression left by the time? Beside the ancient and borrowed guise of the topos of senescence,[34] then, we need to set the actual activities of aged Carolingian rulers. Perhaps we should, in general, turn away from overmuch examination of attitudes towards the aged and move towards a consideration of the activities of aged medieval man in his social and group setting in society. For even when we lack a plentiful set of direct observations on old age, as we do for the ninth century, we still possess examples of the lives of aged men and women.

To begin with, if we can overcome our general reluctance to employ statistical evidence for the upper class (the only group, incidentally, for which we have sufficient information of this kind), I believe that we can calculate with some rough accuracy the average life expectancies of members of the royal family. For the thirty-eight males born between

---

[33] An example of traditional imagery would be that of the "senex puer." On this theme in western literature, see Curtius, *European Literature,* pp. 98-101. For a few examples of its usage in the Carolingian period, see Paul the Deacon, "Versus in laude Sancti Benedicti," in MGH *Poetae* 1: 37, lines 6-7; Alcuin, Ep. 270, in MGH *Epistolae* 4: 429; Einhard, Ep. 3, in MGH *Epistolae* 5: 110; the so-called Astronomer, *Vita Hludowici imperatoris* 19, in MGH *Scriptorum* 2: 617; Aimo, *Liber translationis beati Vincentii* 1.1, in PL 126: 1013B9-10; and Notker, *Gesta Karoli Magni* 2.10, ed. Hans F. Haefele in MGH *Scriptores rerum Germanicarum,* n.s. 12 (Berlin, 1962), p. 65.

[34] Carolingian authors quite consciously drew on models for their understanding of senescence. As we have seen, Alcuin drew on Virgil (n. 15 above), Ovid (n. 17), and Jerome (n. 10), and Theodulf on Cyprian (n. 26). Paschasius Radbertus, in his preface-letter to his commentary on the Gospel of Matthew, employed Cicero's *Cato maior De senectute:* see MGH *Epistolae* 6 (Berlin, 1925), pp. 144-147. In addition, when weighed down by old age and grief at his wife's death in 836, Einhard sought out the opinions of Cyprian, Jerome, Augustine, and perhaps Cicero: see Ep. 3, in MGH *Epistolae* 6: 9-10 and also in *Loup de Ferrières, Correspondance,* 2 vols., Les Classiques de l'histoire de France au moyen âge 10, 16, ed. and trans. Léon Levillain (Paris, 1927, 1935), 1: 12-18.

Charlemagne in 742 and Louis the Child in 893 for whom we possess fairly good birth and death dates (the possible series is forty-nine) we obtain a life expectancy at birth of 33.5 years.[35] If one removes six infant deaths from the calculations, the average normal life expectancy of a male Carolingian rises to 39.6 years. These figures do not seem at all unreasonable when we remember that Charlemagne's brother Carloman died at nineteen and his own two vigorous sons Charles and Carloman (renamed Pepin) at thirty-nine and thirty-three respectively.[36] Moreover, royal males seem generally to have died from natural causes, and almost never from wounds sustained in battle or from assassination.[37] Unfortunately we have firm birth and death dates for only three Carolingian queens, and the average of their lives is thirty-four years. Carolingian queens seem to have married young and died young. Although Hildegard, "the mother of kings" as Paul the Deacon described her,[38] bore Charlemagne nine children, she had married him at twelve and died at twenty-five. Indeed, few first wives outlived their royal husbands, though Emma, the wife of Louis the German, reigned for thirty-nine years and only died a few months before her husband in 876. When a queen did survive her husband, she often assumed an important matriarchal position in the house of her son the king. Bertrada, Charlemagne's mother, pursued a policy of conciliating her two antagonistic sons and even managed to lead Charlemagne into a marriage of political convenience with a Lombard princess.[39] After Carloman died in 771, however, Charlemagne repudiated this wife and relegated his mother to a subordinate position within his household. More common was the situation described by Hrabanus Maurus: Ermengard, the wife of Lothar I, had just passed from her juvenile years to a mature age when she died.[40] During the same period one can obtain sure dates for ten women born in the royal family (from a

---

[35] For the royal family members considered and the means of calculation, see the appendix below, pp. 91-94.

[36] Regino of Prüm, *Chronicon* A.880, ed. Friedrich Kurze in MGH *Scriptores rerum Germanicarum in usum scholarum* (Hanover, 1890), pp. 116-117, claimed that the Carolingian line was dying out because of the premature deaths of the Carolingians and the infertility of their wives.

[37] Two possible exceptions are Charles, son of Charles the Bald, and Carloman, son of Louis the Stammerer, both of whom died young under suspicious circumstances: see *Annales de Saint-Bertin* A.864 and A.866, ed. Felix Grat et al. (Paris, 1964), pp. 105, 130; and Regino, *Chronicon* A.884, p. 121.

[38] "Epitaphium Hildegardis reginae," in MGH *Poetae* 1: 59, line 24: "genitrix regum." On this queen, see Klaus Schreiner, "'Hildegardis regina': Wirklichkeit und Legende einer karolingischen Herrscherin," *Archiv für Kulturgeschichte* 57 (1975) 1-70.

[39] See Einhard, *Vita Karoli Magni* 18, ed. Holder-Egger, pp. 22-23.

[40] "Epitaphium Irmingardis," in MGH *Poetae* 2: 240, lines 15-16:
Haec quoque dum expleret iuvenile hic tempus, et annos
Maturae aetatis inciperet, iam obiit.

possible series of forty-one); these had an average life expectancy at birth of 32.6 years and a normal life expectancy past infancy of 40.5 years.

These figures suggest that the average Carolingian male or female from the royal family could expect to live somewhere in the vicinity of thirty-five to forty years. While the average life expectancy figures at birth are doubtless somewhat high, perhaps not fully incorporating infant deaths, the normal life expectancy figures for individuals who survived the childhood years would seem fairly close to the mark. The length of life of members of the royal family should no doubt be counted the upper limit for a group within society as a whole.[41] Palaeodemographers have suggested, on the basis of early medieval skeletons that reveal approximate ages at death, a much lower figure for the life expectancy of common individuals.[42] I do not think, moreover, that we can assume that a Carolingian who lived the average life of thirty-five years necessarily felt that he had attained old age. Maximum life span could, after all, reach eighty or slightly more in a few cases.[43] Probably we hear less talk about agedness in the ninth century, because fewer people lived out lives that reached into old age. Instead they often died, as Hrabanus said of Ermengard, in their mature years. But here we enter the realm of subjective age classifications. How old was *old* for the Carolingians? We should guard against equating the Carolingian use of *senex* with modern notions about the elderly. For the one was an informal type of social stratification based

[41] Creighton G. Gilbert, "When Did a Man in the Renaissance Grow Old?" *Studies in the Renaissance* 14 (1967) 31, makes this point for Renaissance princes and popes.

[42] István Kiszely, *The Anthropology of the Lombards,* trans. Catherine Simán, B.A.R. International Series 61.1 (Oxford, 1979), pp. 163-164, on the basis of 870 skeletons, placed the average age of mortality for early medieval Lombard men at 34 years 9 months and for women at 34 years 2 months; but since virtually no skeletons of infants were found, the figures were lowered to 24 years 8 months and 24 years 3 months respectively. See also the parallel results provided in György T. Acsádi and Janós Nemeskéri, *History of Human Life Span and Mortality,* trans. K. Balás (Budapest, 1970), pp. 215-234; Winfried Henke and Karl-Heinz Nedder, "Zur Anthropologie der fränkischen Bevölkerung von Rubenach," *Bonner Jahrbuch* 181 (1981) 395-419; Peter Laslett, *The World We Have Lost,* 2nd ed. (London, 1971), p. 97; and Laslett, "Societal Development and Aging," in *Handbook of Aging and the Social Sciences,* ed. Robert H. Binstock and Ethel Shanas (New York, 1976), pp. 97-98.

[43] Adalhard, the cousin of Charlemagne, was reputed to have lived to eighty: see "The Eclogue of the Two Nuns" appended to Paschasius Radbertus' *Vita Sancti Adalhardi* in PL 120: 1555A5. Elipandus, the bishop of Toledo, claimed in a letter of 25 July 799 to be eighty-two: see Alcuin, Ep. 183.2 in MGH *Epistolae* 4: 308. Finally, and more scientifically datable, is the case of Egino of Verona, a relative of Queen Hildegard. A study of his skeleton has confirmed that he was indeed an octogenarian, who was born before 720 and died 26-27 February 802: see Alfred Czarnetzki, "Die Skelettreste aus dem sogenannten Egino Grab," in *Die Abtei Reichenau: Neue Beiträge zur Geschichte und Kultur des Inselklosters,* ed. Helmut Mauer (Sigmaringen, 1974), pp. 563-572, and with W. Erdmann, pp. 575-576.

on an estimation of outward appearance, health, and social position in which one was labelled old by individuals who had few objective standards by which to call one old, while the other is a formal means of classification instituted through the state and its legislative programmes according to a determination of one's exact age. In the ninth century, a thirty-five-year-old poor woman with grey hair, poor health, and a walking stick would immediately have been called an old woman (*anus*); today the same woman would simply be thirty years away from collecting an old-age pension. Following Isidore, Hrabanus said that the period of *gravitas* began at fifty and lasted until seventy, and then was followed by *senectus,* which lasted until death.[44] But nothing suggests that Isidore's sixfold classification of ages gained currency during the ninth century.[45] Working Carolingian authors from annalists to hagiographers tended, instead, to reduce the ages of man to three: *puer, iuvenis,* and *senex.*[46] Since we rarely meet *iuvenes* over forty in the sources,[47] *senectus* might apply to some members of society over forty, but perhaps not all.

In the case of kings and princes, the line that marked the passage into old age was never clearly defined. In part, this was because ninth-century writers seldom spoke of a king as old while he still lived and was healthy. They had no need, moreover, to identify a king by age, since he was obviously well known. Princes were, on the other hand, frequently characterized as young; age labels served the function of identifying the countless

---

[44] Isidore, *Etymologiae* 11.2.1-8, ed. Wallace M. Lindsay, Vol. 2 (Oxford, 1911); Hrabanus Maurus, *De universo* 7.1, in PL 111: 179D.

[45] E.g. Alcuin in his *Disputatio de rhetorica et de virtutibus sapientissimi regis Karoli et Albini magistri* employed a four-part division (based on Cicero's *De inventione* 1.24.35): "in aetate puer an adulescens, natu grandior an senex" (ed. Wilbur S. Howell, *The Rhetoric of Alcuin and Charlemagne* [Princeton, 1941], p. 104, lines 609-610).

[46] E.g. Alcuin, Carm. 1 "Versus de sanctis Euboricensis ecclesiae," in MGH *Poetae* 1: 181, line 528: "... pueros iuvenesque senesque"; Anon., "Planctus de obitu Karoli," ibid., p. 435, verse 4: "Infantes, senes, gloriosi praesules"; Paulinus of Aquileia, "Versus de destructione Aquilegiae numquam restaurandae," ibid., p. 143, verse 10: "iuvenes, senes, mulieres, parvulos ..."; Aurelianus of Orléans, the postscript to his *De disciplina musicae,* ed. Ernst Dümmler in MGH *Epistolae* 6: 131: "Audiet me semper de te loquentem sexus uterque, senex, iuvenis, puer, advena, cives"; and Ermoldus Nigellus, "In laudem Pippini regis" 1, in MGH *Poetae* 2: 80, lines 23-24, says that at the palace of Pepin in Aquitaine there were found clerics, old men (*patres*), youths (*iuvencli*), and a procession of boys (*puerile agmen*). This Carolingian tendency follows a pattern of age classification into children, adults, and aged to be found in many societies: see Bernice L. Neugarten and Gunhild O. Hagestad, "Age and the Life Course," in *Handbook of Aging and the Social Sciences,* p. 36.

[47] E.g. in 830, when Lothar I was already thirty-five years old, Einhard, Ep. 18, in MGH *Epistolae* 5: 119, line 24, referred to him as "Hlotharius iuvenis augustus." Thegan, *Vita Hludowici imperatoris,* in MGH *Scriptorum* 2: 590, refers to the twenty-nine-year-old Charlemagne in 771 as "in iuventute."

Charleses, Carlomans, Louises, and Pepins of the Carolingian line. As well, what marked off the royal boy from the royal man was an initiation rite in which boys coming of age at puberty were invested with sword, shield, and horse by their father.[48] The act of accepting the boy into the rank of manhood also had the effect of impressing upon him his subordination in terms of age and authority to his father. But no formal act surrounded the aging of a king. Perhaps he only became aware of his agedness with the onset of illness and the consequent diminishment of his ability to execute his orders in person. The deaths of old and trusted friends also reminded Carolingian kings of their own advancing age. By 805 Charlemagne must have noted the passing of his generation; his son Louis suffered the same fate in 836-837 as contemporaries began to die.[49]

The most famous Carolingian rulers lived relatively long lives: Charlemagne died at seventy-one, Louis the German at seventy, Louis the Pious at sixty-two, Lothar I at sixty, and Charles the Bald at fifty-four. They are the most famous precisely because they lived long enough to accumulate extensive power, for there were political advantages for the long-reigning king. Power and territorial control tended to accrue to the one who outlived his relatives. Thus Charlemagne gained undisputed control of Francia upon the timely death of his brother Carloman late in 771. The historian Thegan, exploiting a biblical theme, begins his biography of Louis the Pious with the argument that the youngest son is often the best of sons,[50] but in fact Louis was only the best of Charlemagne's sons in one regard: he outlived his more dynamic brothers and so inherited the entire empire on his father's death in 814. Charles the Bald quickly seized the opportunities presented by the deaths of his nephew Lothar II in 869 and his brother Louis the German in 876 to invade their territories. Even the imperial title fell to him after the death of his nephew Louis II in 875. But, as I hope to show briefly, Carolingian rulers faced a special set of problems if they lived long lives, problems that arose out of the very fact of their agedness and that they could not very well have anticipated when young.

In the first place, since Carolingian kingship was largely personal, anything that affected the ruler personally affected his governance of the

---

[48] On the Germanic customs of male initiation, see Tacitus, *Germania* 13; the so-called Astronomer, *Vita Hludowici imperatoris* 6, in MGH *Scriptorum* 2: 610: "Ibique ense, iam appellens adolescentiae tempora, accinctus est ...."

[49] It was as though, said the Astronomer, *Vita Hludowici imperatoris* 56, in MGH *Scriptorum* 2: 642, the very nerves of the land had been severed.

[50] Thegan, *Vita Hludowici imperatoris* 3, in MGH *Scriptorum* 2: 591.

kingdom, and agedness was one of these things. Efficient government depended more on the king's willingness and ability to respond to outbreaks of trouble than it did on any administrative agencies within the kingdom. Old age impaired the peripatetic function of Carolingian kings. Charlemagne, for example, made Aachen his principal palace during the last twenty years of his life and only infrequently left there after 808. The *Royal Frankish Annals* reflect this new-found sedentary life, as in the period after 800 Charlemagne is seemingly always at Aachen, receiving foreign ambassadors and legations, convoking councils, and making laws. The last of these does seem to have been an increasing activity of the latter years of Charlemagne's reign. We seem to see, if we may judge by the volume and tenor of his capitularies, the transformation of Charlemagne from warrior into lawmaker and settler of disputes. In part, Charlemagne's later juridical activities represented an attempt to overcome the weakness of central royal power when an aged king decided to settle down. But the palace administration, which was not sophisticated enough to handle the large numbers of petitioners attracted by Charlemagne's fixed residence, often suffered from confusing congestion. Moreover, even if Charlemagne was increasingly concerned with obedience to his laws, he could not be sure that they were being instituted unless he himself was constantly on the move and could judge for himself local situations. The *missi dominici,* who were supposed to oversee the implementation of law in the provinces and to correct local abuses, were themselves often the instigators of local trouble, especially if they remained in office in one place for too long. We should recall that Louis the Pious began his reign with the stated intention of reforming the abuses of justice that had gone unchecked during Charlemagne's last decade. One of his first acts was to send out handpicked *missi* to investigate; they reported back that they had found many people who had been deprived of their hereditary lands or their freedom under Charlemagne.[51]

Even more importantly, old Carolingian rulers were reluctant to initiate wars of conquest that might, in the long run, have checked future invasions and suppressed rebellious peoples. Charlemagne's last campaign was in 810, against the Danish king Godefred, but it was only in response to a threatened invasion. When Carolingian kings began in the ninth century merely to respond to incursions instead of anticipating them, as Charlemagne had done with the Lombards, Saxons, and Avars,

---

[51] See *Annales regni Francorum* A.814, ed. Friedrich Kurze in MGH *Scriptores rerum Germanicarum in usum scholarum* (Hanover, 1895), p. 141; Thegan, *Vita Hludowici imperatoris* 13, in MGH *Scriptorum* 2: 593.

they played a dangerous game they could not win; they were always two steps behind their many enemies. It is no coincidence that aged Carolingian rulers experienced military difficulties: one thinks of the threats posed by the Danish in the north and the Saracens in the south during Charlemagne's last years, Louis the Pious' problems with Viking raids, Charles the Bald and the Saracen assault on Italy in 877, and Charles the Fat's utter inability to respond effectively against the Vikings in the 880s. It was not so much that these were special attacks as it was that aged rulers were unable to mount vigorous and far-sighted campaigns: the potential for invasion of the huge Carolingian empire was always there threatening, but, as Ermold had expressed it, the warlike right hand of the old Carolingian king trembled. In all fairness, it must not have been a happy prospect for an old king to set out personally for war. During his last military operation, when already sixty-eight years old, Charlemagne fell from his horse, much to the shock of his assembled troops.[52]

One way around this problem was for the aged ruler to employ his sons to carry out his military campaigns. Both Charlemagne and Louis the Pious pursued this policy. Perhaps the most famous of these wars was the one that Pepin waged against the Avars in 796. In a poem celebrating Pepin's victory, an anonymous poet asked not only for long life for Pepin but also for his father Charlemagne to continue to reign, to grow old, and to beget sons who would maintain his palaces during his life and after his death.[53] In truth, it was very difficult for a ruler to grow old peacefully if he had sons, and even odder that a living son of Charlemagne should have welcomed newborn brothers. Germanic tradition, of course, extended a privileged place in law to fathers: a son ought not to oust his father while he was still strong and able to perform his duties, Bavarian law said.[54] But Lupus of Ferrières prudently advised Charles the Bald not to give power to his sons during his lifetime; better that they should beg favours from him than the reverse.[55] Nevertheless, Carolingian sons frequently rebelled against their old fathers. Charlemagne was fifty when his son Pepin the Hunchback led a revolt against him in 792, Louis the Pious

---

[52] Einhard, *Vita Karoli Magni* 32, pp. 36-37. It should be noted that an epizootic attacking both cattle and other animals raged while Charlemagne was on campaign in 810, and that his horse may have been weakened by the disease; on this incident see Dutton, "Awareness of Historical Decline," pp. 91-92.

[53] "Carmen de Pippini regis victoria Avarica," in MGH *Poetae* 1: 117, verse 14. On this poem in general, see Alfred Ebenbauer, *Carmen historicum: Untersuchungen zur historischen Dichtung im karolingischen Europa*, Vol. 1, Philologica Germanica 4 (Vienna, 1978), pp. 30-33.

[54] See *Lex Baiwariorum* 2.9, ed. Ernst M. von Schwind in MGH *Leges nationum Germanicarum* 5.2 (Hanover, 1926), pp. 302-303.

[55] See Lupus, Ep. 31 to Charles the Bald, ed. Levillain, *Loup de Ferrières*, 1: 142.

was fifty-two when his elder sons first rebelled in 830, Louis the German suffered the first of a series of rebellious machinations by his sons in 860 when he was fifty-four, and Charles the Bald's son Carloman revolted in 871 when his father was forty-eight. The reasons for these revolts are complex. In part they were bred by the royal policy of setting up young sons in specific regions of the kingdom. This had the double effect of distancing the young princes from their fathers and at the same time allowing them to establish regional power bases from which they could resist their fathers. Although Charlemagne followed this practice, he was saved from open revolt by the deaths of two of his contending sons and by his clever policy of keeping his sons engaged in wars of expansion. Louis the Pious and Louis the German were not, however, as fortunate. Indeed, throughout his last years, Louis the Pious constantly attempted to assert his paternal and royal authority over his son Louis the German, never with very much success. In 840 he chased his rebellious son from Thuringia into Bavaria, where he belonged, but ill health forced the beleaguered father to give up the campaign. He died a short distance from his favourite palace of Ingelheim on an island in the Rhine. On his deathbed Louis forgave his recalcitrant son, but wanted him to know that it was he who had led his grey-haired father to his death.[56] Ironically enough, late in life Louis the German himself was to suffer many revolts by his own sons. The fact of the matter is that a Carolingian ruler who lived a long life and had many middle-aged sons simply could not satisfy their natural desire to exercise power independently of their father.

There is another issue, a moral one, about Charlemagne's life after 800, that needs to be framed in terms of the policies of an aged ruler. I will let the good Anglican Edward Gibbon present the charge in his best dudgeon:

> Without injustice to his fame, I may discern some blemishes in the sanctity and greatness of the restorer of the Western empire. Of his moral virtues, chastity is not the most conspicuous: but the public happiness could not be materially injured by his nine wives or concubines, the various indulgence of meaner or more transient amours, the multitude of his bastards whom he bestowed on the church, and the long celibacy and licentious manners of his daughters, whom the father was suspected of loving with too fond a passion.[57]

Indeed, ten years after the emperor's death Wettin, a monk of Reichenau, was supposed to have had a vision in which he saw an animal gnawing at

---

[56] The Astronomer, *Vita Hludowici imperatoris* 63, in MGH *Scriptorum* 2: 647: "qui canos paternos deducit cum dolore ad mortem ...."

[57] *The History of the Decline and Fall of the Roman Empire*, ed. John B. Bury, Vol. 5 (London, 1911), p. 303.

the genitals of Charlemagne. When the shocked visionary asked his angelic guide how such a man, who had been almost alone in the modern age in defence of the church, could suffer so, the angel answered that, although he had done many remarkable things that had pleased God, he had given himself up to the delight of debauchery and had wished to end the great length of his life in the sin of lust.[58] What the critics of Charlemagne's personal life did not fully recognize was that they were witnessing the deliberate policy of an aged ruler. Charlemagne was reluctant to marry off his daughters because he feared that the offspring of such legitimate marriages would threaten his dynastic line: his bitter enemy Tassilo had been the product of such a marriage by one of Charles Martel's daughters.[59] In his own case, I suspect that Charlemagne did not marry again after Queen Luitgard's death in 800 in order not to sire any more legitimate sons. At that time he still had three living legitimate heirs, and that must have seemed enough. The *Divisio regnorum* of 806 by which the emperor divided his kingdom into three parts, in the manner in which it had been divided earlier between Charlemagne and Carloman, is a meticulous document.[60] It anticipated every eventuality but one: what should happen if a new legitimate heir should be born to Charlemagne. Of course, he could have made a new division of territories, but it seems more likely that Charlemagne intended to remain unwed, despite ecclesiastical criticism, in order not to confuse the question of his succession. The three sons he sired after 800, one in 807 when he was sixty-five, were all illegitimate.

Unfortunately Louis the Pious did not pay close attention to the example of his father.[61] Louis already had three legitimate heirs by 817 when, frightened by a near-fatal accident, he divided his territories into three in the *Ordinatio imperii*.[62] Ignoring the older Frankish form of

---

[58] See Heito, *Visio Wettini* 11, in MGH *Poetae* 2: 271, and the poetic rendering of Walafrid Strabo, ibid., pp. 318-319, lines 446-465, also ed. David A. Traill in *Walahfrid Strabo's Visio Wettini*, Lateinische Sprache und Literatur des Mittelalters 2 (Bern, 1974), p. 197. On Charlemagne's role in Carolingian dream literature, see Dutton, "Awareness of Historical Decline," pp. 260-279.

[59] According to the Astronomer, the Carolingians, including Louis the Pious, were aware of this threat: see *Vita Hludowici imperatoris* 21, in MGH *Scriptorum* 2: 618.

[60] In MGH *Capitularia* 1, ed. Alfred Boretius (Hanover, 1883), pp. 126-130. On it, see Walter Schlesinger, "Kaisertum und Reichsteilung zur *Diuisio regnorum* von 806," (1958) in *Zum Kaisertum Karls des Grossen*, ed. Gunther Wolf, Wege der Forschung 38 (Darmstadt, 1972), pp. 116-173.

[61] His son Lothar I, however, knew of the practice, since after the death of his wife Ermengard in 851 he took two concubines, but never remarried: see *Annales de Saint-Bertin* A.853, p. 67.

[62] See Peter R. McKeon, "817: Une Année désastreuse et presque fatale pour les Carolingiens," *Le Moyen Age* 84 (1978) 5-12. For the *Ordinatio imperii*, see MGH *Capitularia*, 1: 270-273, and François L. Ganshof, "Some Observations on the *Ordinatio imperii* of 817," (1955) in *Carolingians and the Frankish Monarchy*, pp. 273-288.

patrimonial division, Louis decided that the empire (though not the kingdom) should pass united to his son Lothar. Again there was no provision
made for the birth of another legitimate heir, but that is just what happened. When Queen Ermengard died in 818, Louis at first seems to have
thought of not marrying again, which would have preserved his succession as outlined in 817. Under pressure from his nobles, however, Louis
eventually married Judith, who bore him Charles the Bald in 823.[63] On
the urging of his queen, he attempted to overthrow the previous agreement with his sons, in order to make room in the kingdom for his new
son. When his sons revolted in 830, they justified their action on the
grounds that they only wanted to restore their father to his proper position
in his house, for Louis was widely reputed to be a cuckold: Judith was
said to have committed adultery with Bernard of Septimania.[64] Agobard
of Lyons wrote works in which he demonstrated, by way of biblical
examples, the dangers of a young wife for an old king.[65] On his side
Louis and his supporters attempted to invoke the positive commandment
that children ought to honour and obey their parents.[66] A good deal of
this debate centred specifically around the respect due to an aged parent,
an issue that became highly politicized during the last decade of Louis'
life.[67]

Finally, as Carolingian kings succumbed to old age, they were subjected to the pressure of suitors attempting to jockey for position around
them. Einhard and the imperial party at court, for example, pressured
Charlemagne into accepting Louis as coemperor in 813. Judith and her
advisors, in their turn, badgered Louis late in life to guarantee protection
for Charles the Bald after his death. Old age was, in a sense, a natural
transition period in the passage of Carolingian power. For the aged ruler
it was a time fraught with difficulties. If he was not fending off ambitious
sons, he was often faced with the opposite: a dearth of heirs.[68] No wonder
that many of them thought of retiring in their last days to a monastery in
imitation of Pepin the Short's brother Carloman. Even Charlemagne suggested in the testamentary statement recorded by Einhard that he might

---

[63]   See the Astronomer, *Vita Hludowici imperatoris* 32, in MGH *Scriptorum* 2: 624.

[64]   See Thegan, *Vita Hludowici imperatoris* 36, in MGH *Scriptorum* 2: 597; the Astronomer,
Vita Hludowici imperatoris 44, ibid., p. 633.

[65]   *Libri duo pro filiis et contra Iudith uxorem Ludovici pii,* sometimes called the *Liber apolo-
geticus,* ed. Georg Waitz in MGH *Scriptorum* 15.1 (Hanover, 1887), pp. 275-279.

[66]   Hrabanus Maurus wrote a short treatise for Louis, *De honore parentibus a filiis exhibendo,*
ed. Ernst Dümmler in MGH *Epistolae* 5: 404-415.

[67]   On the emergence of these arguments about the obligations of fathers and sons towards each
other, see Dutton, "Awareness of Historical Decline," pp. 178-186.

[68]   This was the fate, in particular, of Charles the Fat.

withdraw from worldly affairs.[69] Louis the Pious constantly raised the possibility of his retreat, and Lothar I did end his days as a monk at the monastery of Prüm. One cannot blame these troubled rulers for wishing to find relief from the particular condition of their political positions as aged Carolingian rulers.

In conclusion, I wonder if it is not now possible to account for the importance of the topos of senescence in the ninth century. On the one hand, at the level of events, it is possible to see that aged Carolingian rulers faced a special set of political and familial problems that made their latter years a turbulent time for the kingdom as a whole. On the other, at the level of ideas, we encounter the topos of senescence wrapped in the ancient imagery of decline and not directly descriptive of current history. Somehow the poets of the ninth century felt at a deep-seated and personal level the mood that embraced the kingdom when it was in the "quavering grip" of an old king. Conscious of their art, if not of the underlying reasons for their anxiety, they transformed a historical given into its poetical correlative.

Appendix

The dates for the Carolingian royal family are taken from Siegfried Rösch, *Caroli Magni progenies* 1, Genealogie und Landesgeschichte 30 (Neustadt an der Aisch, 1977). The dates used here are based on the direct male line including illegitimate children, though not the children of illegitimate royal males or legitimate princesses. This may at first seem arbitrary, but when the series of all Carolingian offspring is studied as a whole it becomes apparent that the greater the distance from the direct male line, the vaguer and more unreliable the dates for the putative offspring become.

The following are the royal males, listed in reverse order of longevity, who were considered in the calculation. The ages of individuals have been estimated in cases where precise dates for either birth or death are lacking. The greatest variation can never be greater than three years, and this in only a few cases. Eleven individuals for whom dates were unreliable were omitted.

The total of estimated years lived by these individuals is 1272.6, thus producing an average life expectancy at birth of 33.5 years. Disregarding the first six individuals who died in infancy, a total of 1266 years was lived by thirty-two individuals, thus producing an average life expectancy past infancy of 39.6 years.

---

[69]   *Vita Karoli Magni* 33, p. 39.

Name	Birthdate	Deathdate	Life Span
Infant son of Charles the Bald	875 Mar 23	875 Apr	0.1 yr
Charles, son of Charles the Bald	876 Oct 10	877 Apr 7	0.5 yr
Pepin, son of Charles the Bald	872-873	873-874	1 yr
Drogo, son of Charles the Bald	872-873	873-874	1 yr
Louis, son of Louis III of Bavaria	877	879 Nov	2 yrs
Lothar, son of Charlemagne	778 Apr 16	779-780	2 yrs
Carloman, son of Louis the Stammerer	866	884 Dec 12	17 yrs
Louis IV, the Child	893	911 Nov 24	18 yrs
Charles jr, son of Charles the Bald	847-848	866 Sept 29	18 yrs
Louis III, son of Louis the Stammerer	863-865	882 Aug 5	18 yrs
Charles, son of Lothar I	845	863 Jan 24	18 yrs
Carloman, brother of Charlemagne	751	771 Dec 4	19 yrs
Bernard, son of Carloman (aka Pepin)	797	818 Apr 17	21 yrs
Hugo, son of Louis III of Bavaria	855-860	880 Feb	22 yrs
Zwentibold, son of Arnulf of Carinthia	870-871	900 Aug 13	29 yrs
Louis the Stammerer, son of Charles the Bald	846 Nov 1	879 Apr 10	32 yrs
Carloman (renamed Pepin), son of Charlemagne	777	810 July 8	33 yrs
Lothar II, son of Lothar I	835	869 Aug 8	34 yrs
Charles, son of Pepin I of Aquitaine	825-830	863 June 4	36 yrs
Hugo, son of Lothar II of Lotharingia	855-860	895	38 yrs
Charles jr, son of Charlemagne	772-773	811 Dec 4	39 yrs
Hugo, son of Charlemagne	802-806	844 June 16	40 yrs
Pepin I, son of Louis the Pious	797	838 Dec 13	41 yrs
Pepin II, son of Pepin I of Aquitaine	823	864	41 yrs
Pepin the Hunchback, son of Charlemagne	770	811	41 yrs
Louis III of Bavaria, son of Louis the German	835	881 Jan 20	46 yrs
Arnulf, son of Louis the Pious	794	841 Mar	47 yrs
Charles the Fat, son of Louis the German	839	888 Jan 13	48 yrs
Arnulf of Carinthia, son of Carloman of Bavaria	850	899 Dec 8	49 yrs
Charles the Simple, son of Louis the Stammerer	879 Sept 17	929 Oct 7	50 yrs
Carloman, son of Louis the German	830	880 Sept 29	50 yrs
Louis II, son of Lothar I	825	875 Aug 12	50 yrs
Charles the Bald, son of Louis the Pious	823 June 13	877 Oct 6	54 yrs
Drogo, son of Charlemagne	801 June 17	855 Dec 8	54 yrs
Lothar I, son of Louis the Pious	795	855 Sept 29	60 yrs
Louis the Pious, son of Charlemagne	778 Apr 16	840 June 20	62 yrs
Louis the German, son of Louis the Pious	806	876 Aug 28	70 yrs
Charlemagne	742 Apr 2	814 Jan 28	71 yrs

The following graph indicates the percentage of mortality of the series of thirty-eight royal males distributed according to decades.

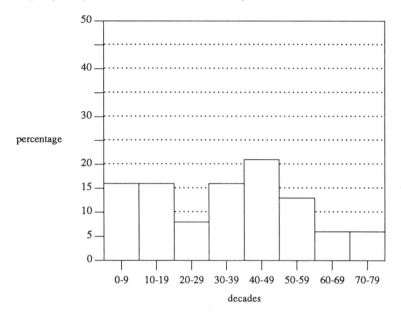

Notice that the distribution of mortality in decennial groups is remarkably even until the seventh decade. Even if infant mortality is too low because of under-reporting, the distribution as a whole is quite different from a graph of modern mortality rates, which would reveal a steady rise in the sixth and seventh decades and much lower percentages during the earlier decades. The graph supports what we know from the sources: illness at any age could be and often was fatal. Old age itself contributed less to overall mortality than it would in twentieth-century society.

Reliable dates for both the births and deaths of Carolingian queens are rare. Although their deaths and the lengths of their reigns are often recorded, their birthdates are mostly unrecorded. In fact, only three queens can be safely dated:

Name	Birthdate	Deathdate	Life Span
Hildegard, wife of Charlemagne	758	783 Apr 30	25 yrs
Judith, wife of Louis the Pious	805	843 Apr 19	38 yrs
Irmintrude, wife of Charles the Bald	830 Sept 27	869 Oct 6	39 yrs

It is virtually impossible to draw a conclusion from these three examples, though the average life of these three was 34 years.

For the female offspring of the Carolingian line, our information is also of a particular kind. Whereas for the queens few birthdates were available, for the female offspring birthdates are often available but deathdates scarcer. Again this specific reporting reflects proximity to the royal house: queens were born outside of it and, therefore, their births occasioned little interest. They died, however, in contact with the royal court, and, thus, their deaths and the ends of their reigns were of great interest to the annalists. The princesses, however, were born in royal circumstances, and their births were frequently noted as important events; but when they left the royal house, either to marry or to take up religious life, track of them was lost by the historians connected with the court.

Reliable dates are obtained for ten princesses:

Name	Birthdate	Deathdate	Life Span
Hildegard, daughter of Charlemagne	782 June 8	783 July 8	1 yr
Adalhaid, daughter of Charlemagne	773-774	774 July-Aug	1 yr
Gisela, daughter of Louis III	852-855	868 Apr 28	14 yrs
Hildegard, daughter of Louis the German	828	856 Dec 23	28 yrs
Rotrud, daughter of Charlemagne	775	810 June 6	35 yrs
Hiltrud, daughter of Lothar I	826	865-866	40 yrs
Ermengard, daughter of Louis III	852-855	896	43 yrs
Gisela, daughter of Lothar II	860-865	907	45 yrs
Rothilde, daughter of Charles the Bald	871	928-929	57 yrs
Bertha, daughter of Lothar II	863	925	62 yrs

The average of 326 years lived by these ten individuals is 32.6. Again, one suspects that infant mortality is greatly underreported. If one subtracts the two infants from the calculations, the life expectancy of the remainder rises to 40.5 years. The possible series of royal females is forty-one individuals, thus making the ten available sets of dates open to serious qualification.

7

Old English Words for *Old*

Ashley Crandell Amos †

Pontifical Institute of Mediaeval Studies

The word *old* is itself very old, apparently deriving from the past parti-
ciple of a common Indo-European verb meaning "to grow up" or "to
nourish" (cf. Go. *alan,* ON *ala,* Lat. *alere*).[1] *Old* must originally have
meant "grown up, fully nourished, mature," and the other members of its
word family only extend its range of meaning. The Old English adjective
eald "old" is related to a number of words: *yldu* "old age," *ylde* "men,"
ealda "an elder, a chief," and *ealdor* "leader, prince, chief," and, in a further sense, "life."[2] These words document the early connection of oldness
or maturity with primacy and leadership on the one hand and with life
itself and the world on the other. The word *world* is in fact part of this
group, for it is composed of *wer* "man" plus *eald* "time, age, life" – the
wer-eald, or *weorold,* as it was more often spelled, is literally "the time

---

[1] Charles T. Onions, with the assistance of George W. S. Friedrichsen and Robert W.
Burchfield, *The Oxford Dictionary of English Etymology* (Oxford, 1966) [henceforth *ODEE*], s.v.
old; Ernest Klein, *A Comprehensive Etymological Dictionary of the English Language,* 2 vols.
(Amsterdam, 1966-1967), s.v. *old;* Ferdinand Holthausen, *Altenglisches etymologisches Wörterbuch*
(Heidelberg, 1934), s.v. *eald.*

The following abbreviations are used for the names of languages: Gmc. for Germanic, Go. for
Gothic, Lat. for Latin, ModE for Modern English, OE for Old English, OFr. for Old Frisian, OHG for
Old High German, ON for Old Norse, OS for Old Saxon.

[2] Unless otherwise noted, meanings cited for OE words are well established and represent the
agreement of the major dictionaries and editions. The major dictionaries are: Joseph Bosworth and
T. Northcote Toller, *An Anglo-Saxon Dictionary* (Oxford, 1898), with *Supplement* by Toller (Oxford,
1921), and *Enlarged Addenda and Corrigenda* by Alistair Campbell (Oxford, 1972); John R. Clark
Hall, *A Concise Anglo-Saxon Dictionary,* 4th ed. with supplement by Herbert D. Meritt (Cambridge,
1960).

Aging and the Aged in Medieval Europe, ed. Michael M. Sheehan, CSB. Papers in Mediaeval Studies
11 (Toronto: Pontifical Institute of Mediaeval Studies, 1990), pp. 95-106. © P.I.M.S., 1990.

of man" (cf. OHG *weralt*); in a complementary way *saeculum* "age, generation, the age of man" developed senses associated with the world (the secular is worldly or mundane).[3] Oldness and age have longstanding semantic associations not only with time and life and with the world, but also with space, for the Latin reflex of Gmc. *old* is *altus* "high, great, tall," perhaps originally "something that has grown or become great."[4] The high parallels the old, and distance in space suggests distance in time. The Latin parallel is intriguing, because the connection between age and distance, between measurement in space and time, is basic: "how far back?" frequently means "how long ago?"[5]

There are four Old English words meaning "old": *eald*, the most basic and by far the most frequent of the words, ancestor to ModE *old; har*, ModE *hoary;* and two adjectives that do not survive into Modern English, *frod* and *gamol*. *Eald* is the standard Old English word for the concept "old"; it occurs almost 3000 times, and is documented in almost every text that survives in Old English – in the poetry, the homilies, the saints' lives, and the laws, the medical and scientific texts, the charters, the translations, and the glosses, biblical and monastic texts, scribbles, and inscriptions.[6] It is one of the fifty most frequent words in the Old English language, after the function words, and to call it "common," as a lexicographer would, indicating that it was in general use without restrictions of dialect, period, or register, is massively an understatement.

Its synonyms are all chiefly poetic. *Har* occurs 27 times in the poetry, and up to another 50 or so in charter boundaries and plant names. It is derived from a Germanic stem referring to the colour white or grey, and is paralleled by the ON *harr* "old, grey, hoar" and the OS, OHG *her,* which, like *altus,* means "high, sublime, raised, elevated, venerated."[7]

---

[3] Stephen A. Barney, with the assistance of Ellen Wertheimer and David Stevens, *Word-Hoard: An Introduction to Old English Vocabulary* (New Haven, 1977), pp. 7, 43.

[4] Alois Walde, *Vergleichendes Wörterbuch der indogermanischen Sprachen,* rev. Julius Pokorny, 3 vols. (Berlin, 1927-1932), s.v. 2.*al-* (1: 86-87); Julius Pokorny, *Indogermanisches etymologisches Wörterbuch,* 2 vols. (Bern, 1948-1969), s.v. 2.*al-* (1: 26-27). Cf. Klein, s.v. *old.*

[5] See A. G. Rigg, "Clocks, Dials, and Other Terms," in *Middle English Studies Presented to Norman Davis in Honour of his Seventieth Birthday,* ed. Douglas Gray and E. G. Stanley (Oxford, 1983), pp. 255, 274.

[6] Richard L. Venezky and Antonette diPaolo Healey, *A Microfiche Concordance to Old English,* Publications of the Dictionary of Old English 1 (Toronto, 1980). All statistics cited below on the frequency of occurrence, range of attestation, and number of compounds of OE words are derived from the data analysed in this concordance and its accompanying lists of spellings and reversed spellings. For the purposes of this paper Old English refers to the surviving OE texts included in the OE corpus of the *Dictionary of Old English* and catalogued in the *Microfiche Concordance.* Variant spellings and lexical variants in multiple MSS of a single text and OE names cited outside an OE context (e.g., in a Latin charter) are excluded from the corpus; such items may have been overlooked in the discussion that follows.

[7] Holthausen, s.v. *har;* ODEE, s.v. *hoar;* Klein, s.v. *hoar.* Cf. James A. H. Murray, Henry

Other Germanic relatives mean "bright," although, in the frustrating fashion of colour words, the apparent cognate in Middle Irish (*ciar*) means "dark." *Frod* is a little more frequent, occurring just under 100 times, chiefly in the poetry, but also in a handful of glosses in the early glossaries. It is derived from a word family that in the Germanic languages denotes "wisdom": OFr. and OS *frod*, OHG *fruot*, ON *froðr*, and Go. *froþs* all mean "wise," and related words refer to sense and understanding.[8] Its Indo-European word family (**pero-*, **pere-*) has the meaning "to be experienced" and is indeed the stem underlying the Latin *peritus* "experienced," *interpres* "interpreter," and *experior* "to try, to experience."[9] The experienced, it seems, can become wise, but by the time they do so, at least in Old English, they are old. The fourth of the words, *gamol*, is the least common and the most perplexing. It occurs about 40 times (except for an occasional use as a proper name), all of them in the poetry and almost half of them in *Beowulf* alone (15 in the part of the poem copied by the second scribe, lines 1939-3182). *Gamall* is the ordinary word for "old" in Old Norse, but there are few other cognates in Germanic or other language groups, and the derivation of the word is uncertain. Some scholars are convinced it derives from **gá-mal* (**gemæl*), the common *ge-* prefix and the word meaning "spotted" or "stained"; its original sense would thus have been "grizzled," referring to grey hair.[10] Just as plausible would be a derivation from *mæl* "time," but the phonological development is hard to explain in either case if the first element of the word is the unstressed prefix, *ge-*, so neither etymology is satisfactory. It may be that the word is in some way related to one of the Old English words for man, *guma*, in a different vowel grade.[11] Marko Minkov calls *gamol* the clearest example of Norse influence on West Germanic poetry, but it is not clear whether the word is a loanword from Old Norse, or what exactly it means – simply "old" or "grey and grizzled, hence old."[12]

Bradley, William A. Craigie, and Charles T. Onions, *A New English Dictionary on Historical Principles* (Oxford, 1884-1928), reissued as *The Oxford English Dictionary* [*OED*], 12 vols. and *Supplement* (Oxford, 1933), with *A Supplement*, ed. Robert W. Burchfield, 4 vols. (Oxford, 1972-1986), s.v. *Hoar*, a. and sb.; and Hans Kurath, Sherman Kuhn, and Robert Lewis, *Middle English Dictionary* (Ann Arbor, 1954-), s.v. *hor*.

[8] Holthausen, s.v. *frod*.

[9] Samuel Kroesch, "The Semasiological Development of Words for *perceive*, etc., in the Older Germanic Dialects," *Modern Philology* 8 (1911) 478.

[10] Holthausen, s.v. *gamol*.

[11] Holthausen, s.v. *guma*.

[12] "Es ist wohl der eindeutigste Fall von nordischem Einfluss in der westgermanischen Poesie," in *Zur angelsächsischen Dichtersprache*, Godishnik na universitet Sv. Kliment Okhridski [Jahrbuch der Universität des heiligen Kliment von Ochrid, historisch-philologische Fakultät] 39.2 (Sofia, 1943), p. 30.

There are over 3000 instances of words meaning "old" in the Old English corpus. The word comes up about once in every thousand words on the average. In comparison, "young" occurs less than 500 times, about one-sixth as often. This is partly because *geong* "young" is by and large limited to animate referents, while almost anything, animate or inanimate, can be "old," and partly because certain fixed expressions use *old* but not *young* – in Old English as in Modern English people are *ten years old,* not *ten years young.* But even when these factors have been taken into account "old" words crop up much more frequently than "young" words – the concept "old" is more frequently attested in the Old English corpus than "young" is.

Almost all of these instances involve *eald. Eald* modifies an enormous range of referents: things, animals, people, words, abstractions, time, and place-names. After a year's wear a cloak or cowl is old and may be changed for new; the ointment, soap, butter, and spices used in making medicines must sometimes be old ones; there is an old moon as well as a new moon, and wine and treasure hoards may be old, and are the better for it.[13] Buildings and settlements are old – *hus* "house" and *ham* "villages," *burg, ceaster,* and *tun* "town," *cyrice* "church," *mylne* "mill," and *geweorc* "fortification." Some, perhaps most, of these references are neutral, few are clearly negative. An old weapon, for example, has been proved, as has often been pointed out: it is precious, perhaps an heirloom, and less likely to fail at battle than an untested blade.[14] People are old, too: man and woman, father and mother, scholar and prophet, priest and pauper, Saxon, Roman, Israelite and heathen, servant and monk, *ceorl* "freeman" and king, pupil and writer, fisherman and smith, and specifically Plautus, Saturn, Hannibal, Enoch, and the good Samaritan, among others. The devil is also old: the old fiend, the old accuser, the old opponent, the old demon, the old devil, old Satan. In the Lindisfarne Gospels the Pharisees are "old men or elders, old wise men" (*alda, aldwuta*), but old need not have any negative connotation in the gloss, for elsewhere the word is rendered *sundorhalga* "especially holy man" or *ælareow* "scholar of the law," presumably without negative overtones.[15] Proverbs, books, tales, sayings, and parables are all old, and the more

---

[13] Citations for *eald* may be found in the *Microfiche Concordance* under the following basic spellings with various inflectional endings: eald-, ald-, æld-, eæld-, eld-, ield-, ild-, and yld- (the latter spellings chiefly in comparative and superlative forms).

[14] Hertha Marquardt, *Die altenglischen Kenningar: Ein Beitrag zur Stilkunde altgermanischer Dichtung* (Halle, 1938), p. 131.

[15] See the editions by Walter W. Skeat, *The Gospel According to St. Mark in Anglo Saxon and Northumbrian Versions* (Cambridge, 1871), ... *St. Luke* ... (1874), ... *St. John* ... (1878), ... *St. Matthew* ... (1887); cf. William J. P. Boyd, "Aldrediana VII: Hebraica," *English Philological Studies* 10 (1967) 23-26.

authoritative because of their age. The old law, *eald riht* or *eald æ* is a frequent phrase, especially in Ælfric, referring to the law before the coming of Christ, Old Testament law or, sometimes, pre-Mosaic natural law. *Eald heafoðece* is a persistent or chronic pain in the head; some medical recipes use *eald* in the technical sense of "chronic." Many of the abstractions described as *old* are of dubious merit: error, ignorance, sin, and vice; evil, deceit, bad habits, and guilt; theft, heresy, enmity, unrighteousness, and death are all old; and there are many fewer positive abstractions to set against them – only old mercy, freedom, peace, glory, knowledge, sanctification, and a few others. The earth itself is old, as are day and night, age and life; these too are good things, though the old night is sometimes associated with Satan. There are scores of place-names based on *eald-*: the old dike, street, furrow, town, ford, fire, church, prison, quarry, hill, stile, lake, river, island, tree, field, thorn, wood, path, gate, orchard, hedge, cross, meadow, heath, stone, brook, creek, boundary, and so on.[16] These place-names refer to ancient and sometimes to disused forts, homesteads, streets, or paths, to the former course of rivers or brooks, and to plots of land or topographical features long known or long used, in some cases formerly used and now idle. There are also scores of personal names with the first element *Eald-* or, in its Anglian form, *Ald-*: Aldhelm, Aldfrith, and Aldred are well known, but there are 263 other individuals listed in the standard Old English onomasticon with *eald-* names, on *-beald* and *-beorht* and *-gifu* and *-mund* and *-ric* and *-wine* and *-wulf* and twenty other suffixes.[17] Names based on *Old-* are less common today, but any municipal telephone directory will provide a long list.[18]

Eald, like most Old English words, forms compounds readily: there are forty-three compounds with *eald-* as a first element and six with it as a final element.[19] In only eight of these is *eald* clearly used in a negative

---

[16] Albert H. Smith, *English Place-Name Elements* Pt. 1, English Place-Name Society 25 (Cambridge, 1970), s.v. *ald;* Eilert Ekwall, *The Concise Oxford Dictionary of English Place-Names,* 4th ed. (Oxford, 1960), names beginning *Ald-* and *Old-;* and compounds attested in the *Microfiche Concordance.*

[17] William George Searle, *Onomasticon Anglo-Saxonicum: A List of Anglo-Saxon Proper Names from the Time of Beda to that of King John* (Cambridge, 1897).

[18] Compare the listings in modern onomasticons: Percy H. Reaney, *A Dictionary of British Surnames,* 2nd ed. by Richard M. Wilson (London, 1976), pp. 3-5, 255; Basil Cottle, *The Penguin Dictionary of Surnames,* 2nd ed. (London, 1978), pp. 34-35, 276.

[19] *ealdbacen* "stale," *ealdcot* "old cottage," *ealdgecynd* "original nature," *ealdcypþ* "old home," *ealddagas* "former times," *ealddom* "age," *ealdgefa* "ancient foe," *ealdfæder* "forefather," *ealdefæder* "grandfather, forefather," *ealdfeond* "old enemy, devil," *ealdgefera* "old comrade," *ealdgeddung* "old saying," *ealdhad* "old age," *ealdhettende* "old foes," *ealdhlaford* "hereditary lord," *ealdhlafordcynn* "old royal family," *ealdhriþer* "old ox," *ealdhriþerflæsc* "aged meat," *ealdland* "ancestral land, land long untilled," *ealdlandræden* "law of landed property," *ealdlic* "old," *ealdgemære* "ancient boundary," *ealdemodor* "grandmother," *ealdgeneat* "old comrade," *ealdnes* "old age," *ealdgeniþla* "old foe, devil," *ealdriht* "ancient right," *ealdgeriht* "ancient right," *ealdgesegen*

sense: *ealdbacen* "stale," *ealdgewinn* "ancient conflict between man and the devil," and six compounds for the devil, the "old enemy or old foe," "accursed from old." A number are neutral in connotation, like *healfeald* "half-grown," *efeneald* "contemporary," *ofer-, or-,* or *fram-eald* "very old," *ealdnes, ealdung* "old age," or *ealddagas* "former times." In a majority of the compounds, however, *eald* has positive connotations: *ealdhlaford* "hereditary lord," *ealdcyþþ* "old home," *ealdgestreon* "ancient treasure," *ealdgesegen* "ancient tradition," *ealdgeþungen* "old and distinguished," *ealdwita* "venerable man, sage, prophet," and so forth. In many of these cases *eald-* functions almost as an intensive prefix. A recent study of words with first elements in *eald-* "old," *ær-* "former," *fyrn-* "long ago," *lang-* "long ago," and *geo-* "formerly, of yore," concludes that although the denotation always reflects age, in connotation the first elements act as intensifiers.[20] *Ealdgestreon*, like *ærgestreon* and *langgestreon*, is "ancient or long-accumulated, and hence precious, treasure." *Ærdagas, ealddagas,* and *fyrndagas* are "the good old days." An *ealdsweord* is "an ancient, and therefore good, sword," *ær-* or *fyrngeweorc* is "an old, and therefore great, construction," and so forth. Similarly the *eald enta geweorc* "the old (and marvellous, though now ruined) structures of the giants, those who came before" are the more valuable because they are old. For a number of words *eald* has a strong nexus of positive association, for people – the *ealdwine* ("old and good friend"), *ealdhlaford,* or *ealdgesiþ* ("old and loyal comrade") – as well as for objects. Great age often implies special value.

The words an adjective collocates with can be especially informative. By far the most common collocation for *eald* is old and young. "He was young in years," Wærferth writes, translating Gregory's *Dialogues,* "but old and sober in his habits."[21] Or, according to the *Rule of Chrodegang,* "the young should always honour the old, and the old love the young."[22]

"ancient tradition, *ealdgesiþ* "old comrade," *ealdspel* "old saying," *ealdspræc* "old proverb, byword," *ealdgestreon* "ancient treasure," *ealdgeþungen* "old and distinguished," *ealdung* "process of growing old," *ealdgeweorc* "old work or creation," *ealdwerig* "accursed from old," *ealdwif* "old woman," *ealdgewinn* "old conflict," *ealdgewinna* "old enemy," *ealdwita* "venerable man, sage," *ealdwritere* "old writer, scribe," *ealdgewyrht* "former deeds," *efeneald* "contemporary, coeval," *frameald* "very old," *healfeald* "half-grown," *nihteald* "that happened yesterday," *ofereald* "very old," *oreald* "very old."

[20] Sheila Most Ingersoll, *Intensive and Restrictive Modification in Old English,* Anglistische Forschungen 124 (Heidelberg, 1978), pp. 128-134.

[21] "Se wæs wintrum geong ⁊ on his þeawum eald ⁊ gedefe," in Bk. 3, ch. 18 of *Bischof Wærferths von Worcester Übersetzung der Dialoge Gregors des Grossen,* ed. Hans Hecht, Bibliothek der angelsächsischen Prosa 5 (Leipzig, 1900; repr. Darmstadt, 1965), p. 219, line 3.

[22] "⁊ æfre þa geongan wurðian þa ealdan ⁊ þa ealdan lufien þa gingran," in Ch. 2 of *The Old*

"Don't try to judge the old and the young, the sick and the healthy, the rich and the poor, or the learned and the lewd by the same rules," a confessional text warns, echoing the *Cura pastoralis*.[23] Oddly, the old and the new rarely collocate. "No man drinks old wine and then asks for new," the West Saxon Gospels translate Luke 5:39, "for the old is better."[24] Apart from collocating with its opposites, young and new, old collocates with some of the various qualities of the old; "old and grey" and "old and wise" are both extremely frequent; and "old and full of days" is an idiom used in Bede's *Ecclesiastical History,* echoing Job 42:16, and thoughtfully explained by the translator: "old and full of days, that is, of good deeds."[25] *Eald* also collocates with negative qualities, but more rarely: "old and foolish" (once) or "old and envious" (once).[26] Some collocations prefigure modern idioms to an almost eerie extent: in the entry for 1003 the Abingdon Chronicle refers to someone who is up to "his old tricks," *his ealdan wrencas.*[27]

The synonyms for *eald* complement it. *Har* is originally a colour word, "white- or grey-haired," and only by extension "old." It has been suggested that *har* has positive connotations even when used as a colour.[28] In the poetry it is applied to stone, cliffs, armour, swords, the ocean and heaths, as well as wolves, warriors, and hoarfrost. It is frequently used in references to boundary markers and place-names, though it is often hard to distinguish in any individual place-name from *hara* "hare, rabbit." It is most commonly used of stones and stone objects, and

English Version, with the Latin Original, of the Enlarged Rule of Chrodegang, ed. Arthur S. Napier, Early English Text Society (henceforth EETS), o.s. 150 (London, 1916), p. 9, lines 23-25.

[23] "And geþengc ðu þæt þu ne scealt næfre gelice deman þam rican and þam heanan, þam freon and þam þeowan, þam ealdan and þam geongan, þam halan and þam unhalan, þam eadmodan and þam ofermodan, þam strangan and þam unmagan, þam gehadodum and þam læwedum," in Ch. 3 of "A Late Old English Handbook for the Use of a Confessor," ed. Roger Fowler, *Anglia* 83 (1965) 1-34 at p. 19, lines 91-96. Cf. Ch. 25 of *King Alfred's West-Saxon Version of Gregory's Pastoral Care,* ed. Henry Sweet, EETS o.s. 45 (London, 1871), p. 179, lines 19-22, p. 180, lines 1-2.

[24] "And ne drincð nan man eald win ⁊ wylle sona þæt niwe, he cwyþ, þæt ealde is betere." *The Gospel According to St. Luke ...,* ed. Skeat, p. 60.

[25] "eald ⁊ dagana full, þæt is godra dæda," in Bk. 2, ch. 16 of *The Old English Version of Bede's Ecclesiastical History of the English People,* ed. Thomas Miller, 4 vols., EETS o.s. 95, 96, 110, 111 (London, 1890-1898), 1: 152, lines 1-2. Cf. "senex ac plenus dierum," in Bk. 2, ch. 20 of *Bede's Ecclesiastical History of the English People,* ed. Bertram Colgrave and Roger A. B. Mynors (Oxford, 1969), p. 206.

[26] "eald ond infrod," *Beowulf* 2449, ed. Friedrich Klaeber, *Beowulf and the Fight at Finnsburg,* 3rd ed. (Boston, 1950), p. 92. "eald and ... æfestig," in *The Old English Apollonius of Tyre,* ed. Peter Goolden (Oxford, 1958), p. 22, line 16.

[27] *The C-Text of the Old English Chronicles,* ed. Harry A. Rositzke, Beiträge zur englischen Philologie 34 (Bochum-Langendreer, 1940), p. 56.

[28] Ernst Leisi, "Aufschlussreiche altenglische Wortinhalte," in *Sprache – Schlüssel zur Welt: Festschrift für Leo Weisgerber,* ed. Helmut T. Gipper (Düsseldorf, 1959), p. 310.

place-name specialists suggest that it may mean "grey through being overgrown with lichen."[29] Less plausible is the suggestion that *har* refers always to hair or the beard, and that its use in charters referring to boundary markers may represent some kind of totemistic or animistic rite.[30] No personal names built on *har* survive; names like *Harold* derive from the first element *here-* "army." The seven compounds on *har* include the famous crux in *Beowulf* line 357, *unhar*, perhaps for *anhar*, apparently with the sense "old, hoar," but with the form "not hoary." The other six compounds are straightforward: *healfhar* "somewhat hoary," *fulhar* "entirely grey," *feaxhar, harwenge*, and *harwella* "grey-haired," and *ræghar* "grey with lichen." After *harastan* "grey stone," the most common collocations are *har hilderinc, har heaþorinc, har hildfruma*, and the like, expressions for the "old warrior." In the heroic world of Old English poetry grey or white hair was no stigma.

The sense "wise through age and experience" underlies OE *frod*, although its primary sense is simply "old." Like *har* it has positive overtones; it is used almost entirely of animate creatures, especially people. It refers to kings and heroes, Beowulf, Hrothgar, Methuselah and Abraham, Enoch, Sem, Sarah, and Nebuchadnezzar, and also to the dragon in *Beowulf*. It does not occur in place-names and is not common in personal names, where it can be confused with the first element *forþ*, but there are a score or so of people listed in the onomasticon, *Frodbeorhts* and *-friths*, *Frodgars* and *-munds* and *-wines* and *-wulfs*.[31] *Frod* glosses *grandaevus* "old, very old" and *praefectus* "chief, leader, prefect."[32] Just as the compounds on *har* reflect its original meaning as a colour of the hair, so the compounds and collocations on *frod* reflect its connection with wisdom. There are only two compounds, both with the sense "old and wise": Abraham is *hygefrod* and Sarah *geomorfrod*. Collocations strengthen the association with wisdom: *frod in ferþe, on mode frod* "old and wise in spirit," *frode geþeahte, frodum worde* "with wise thoughts or words," *frod wita* "wise old man," *frod and god* "old and wise," *gearum* or *wintrum* or *missarum* or *dægum* or *dægrime frod* "old and wise in years." In Old Norse, *froðr* is used as an appellation for the chroniclers and

---

[29] Smith, *English Place-Name Elements*, s.v. *har²*; cf. Ekwall, *Dictionary of English Place-Names*, s.v. *har*.

[30] Nigel F. Barley, "Old English Colour Classification: Where Do Matters Stand?" *Anglo-Saxon England* 3 (1974) 20 and n. 3.

[31] Searle, *Onomasticon*, p. 250.

[32] Cleopatra Glossary 2852; William Garlington Stryker, "The Latin-Old English Glossary in MS. Cotton Cleopatra A.III" (Stanford diss., 1951), p. 219. Epinal Glossary 758, Erfurt Glossary 758; Joseph D. Pheifer, *Old English Glosses in the Epinal-Erfurt Glossary* (Oxford, 1974), p. 40.

historians: *Ari Froði, Sæmundr Froði,* and even, in what the dictionary suggests is a rare compliment to a foreigner, *Bede Froði.*[33]

Like *frod, gamol* refers chiefly to people, like *har* it may refer to grey or grizzled hair, and it compounds with *-feax* to produce the adjective "grey-haired." *Gamolferhþ* "old, old in spirit" is the only other compound *gamol* forms. *Gamol* does not survive into Middle English, and is attested in only a few personal names and no place-names. It is used several times of swords, especially in the collocation *gomele lafe* "old relic," and it often collocates with *frod.* Its connotations are normally neutral or positive; *Maxims II* affirms that *gomol* [*is*] *snoterost* "the old man is wisest," *fyrngearum frod* "old and wise in former years," *se þe ær feala gebideð* "he who has endured much before."[34]

It is tempting to generalize, since we are bound in any case to impose our own patterns and our own linguistic preconceptions on the words we study. "Words," Virginia Woolf cautions, "do not live in dictionaries; they live in the mind."[35] When Moritz Scheinert wrote his detailed 1905 study of the adjectives in *Beowulf,* he went so far as to treat the adjectives for "old" in the group of adjectives for nobility and power and esteem, including *æþele* "noble," *eacen* "strong," *rice* "powerful, great," *mild* "merciful," *liþ* "gentle," *hold* "kind," *leof* "dear," and *dyre* "kind, dear"; he was convinced that the words for "old" had strong positive connotations in the poem.[36] Does the evidence support that interpretation? Many scholars have assumed that Byrhtwold, the *ealdgeneat* of *Maldon* line 310, literally an "old comrade or follower," was "trusty," "faithful," or "true" rather than "aged."[37] "Of what use," Alfred J. Wyatt asks in 1919, "is an old man in battle?"[38] Is that interpretation reasonable? Or is the line in *Maldon* evidence that old men were valued as warriors on the battlefield? Such questions are hard to answer. It is always dangerous to extrapolate from words to things and to take linguistic usage as evidence of social reality. Too many factors are involved, and their relationship is

---

[33] Richard Cleasby and Gudbrand Vigfusson, *An Icelandic-English Dictionary,* 2nd ed. with a supplement by William A. Craigie (Oxford, 1957), s.v. *froðr.*

[34] *Maxims II,* lines 11-12, in *The Anglo-Saxon Minor Poems,* ed. Elliott Van Kirk Dobbie, Anglo-Saxon Poetic Records 6 (New York, 1942), p. 56.

[35] Virginia Woolf, "Craftsmanship," first read in the BBC series *Words Fail Me,* broadcast 20 April 1937, and published in *The Death of the Moth and Other Essays* (London, 1942), p. 204.

[36] Moritz Scheinert, "Die Adjectiva im Beowulfepos als Darstellungsmittel," *Beiträge zur Geschichte der deutschen Sprache und Literatur* 30 (1905) 355-356.

[37] Fred C. Robinson reviews the scholarship in "Some Aspects of the *Maldon* Poet's Artistry," *Journal of English and Germanic Philology* 75 (1976) 38-40.

[38] Alfred J. Wyatt, ed., *An Anglo-Saxon Reader* (Cambridge, 1919), p. 282; cited in Robinson, "Some Aspects," p. 39.

too complicated for simple equations to have much validity. But comparisons with modern usage can be illuminating if made within careful limits. Statistics must be handled with particular care, since they compare the Old English corpus, with its marked and distinctive composition, with modern corpora of quite different origin and balance. But when the differences in practice are clear and strongly marked, comparison can highlight and throw into relief the early evidence.

Most of the Old English compounds on *old* were neutral or positive in connotation. Although there are a few positive Modern English compounds like *old world,* the majority are neutral or negative: *old-fashioned, old fogey, old-maidish, old timer.* In most collocations and idioms *eald* and the other *old* words were also primarily neutral or positive in Old English, while they are overwhelmingly negative in Modern English. Even the neutral collocations and phrases are not particularly flattering: "faithful as old dog Tray," "easy or comfortable as an old shoe," "shaggy as an old dog," "old line," "old saw," "Old Joe," "Old Ned," "Old Nick," while the negative ones are hair-raising: "let the old cat die," "cross as an old bear," "old filthy," "old hairy," "old loopy," "old mildewed hog-slosh," "so old he ought to be laid away," "your old man's a monkey," "that old bat," "I may be rusty and old, but I'm not a tin can," "old squaw," "old stick-in-the-mud," "old and feeble," "old town turkey," "old witch," "old scratch," "old rounder," "old step and fetch it," "old maid," "old granny hobble gobble," "old greasy," "old rattle-trap," "don't laugh, big boy, you may be old some day, too."[39] Some of these can be used affectionately, and there are, of course, collocations with positive overtones: "grand old man," "an old head on young shoulders," "the old ball game," "the old guard," "the old school tie," "the old masters," but these are few compared to the rest. Particularly striking is the contrast with phrases and idioms using *young.* There are only one-tenth as many, and they are neutral or positive: "young bloods," "young hopeful," "young shaver," "young pup," "wild as a young colt," "ever young and ever fair," "catch 'em while they're young," "go it while you're young," "young baggage," "young man."[40] Reading modern idioms using *old* is a lowering experience, and a drastic contrast to the Old English patterns.

In Shakespeare and early Modern English the differences are less striking, but still significant. *Old* is very common in Shakespeare – the 161st

[39] Words, idioms, and phrases including *old* are listed in C. Edward Wall and Edward Przebienda, *Words and Phrases Index,* 4 vols. (Ann Arbor, 1969-1970), 1: 240, 2: 187, 3: 199, 4: 133-134; and in Laurence Urdang and Frank R. Abate, *Idioms and Phrases Index,* 3 vols. (Detroit, 1983), pp. 977-980.

[40] Wall and Przebienda, 1: 389, 2: 302, 3: 326, 4: 218; Urdang and Abate, pp. 1685-1686.

most frequent word – and it occurs about once every 1300 words, compared to once every 1000 words in the Old English corpus.[41] *Young* is about two-thirds as common as *old,* relatively much more common than it is in Old English.[42] The referents for *old* in Shakespeare are similar to those for *eald* in Old English: things like coat, cloak, ginger, sack, bones, iron, oak, plants, and cheese; people like shepherds and masters, men and maids, jacks and jades, lords and dukes, friends and acquaintances, playfellows and murderers; signs and texts and tunes and tales and sayings; folly and vice and hearts and age and death. But the use of idioms and commonplaces is markedly different. Although Shakespeare uses phrases like "old and plain," "old and rich," or "old and wise," which can be paralleled in Old English, more common are "old and wicked" and "old and miserable."[43] There is scarcely anything in Old English to parallel the Pantaleone figure of comic old age in the comedies – "old, wrinkled, faded, withered" (*Taming of the Shrew* 4.5.43), "deformed, crooked, old, and sere" (*Comedy of Errors* 4.2.19), "old, cold, wither'd, and of intolerable entrails" (*Merry Wives* 5.5.153); or the harsh tragic vision of old age – "hard-favor'd, foul, or wrinkled old" (*Venus and Adonis* 133), "a very foolish fond old man, fourscore and upward" (*King Lear* 4.3.59-60), "a poor, infirm, weak and despis'd old man" (*Lear* 3.2.20).[44] The closest Old English comes to this is mild in comparison: Byrhtferth's likening of an old man to winter because he is cold and *snoflig* "sniffly," or the reflection of a frazzled homilist that in heaven there will be quiet and eternal blessedness, where the old man does not groan nor the child scream.[45] More typical are reflections like Ælfric's that an old man without piety is like a tree bearing leaves and blossoms but never any fruit, or the proverb that the old man who has learned many old saws and maxims should teach them to the young, or Byrhtferth's division of the four times of man's life into *cildhad* "childhood," *cnihtiugoð* "youth," *geðungen yld* "age of maturity," and *swyðe eald yld* "really old age."[46] A particularly

---

[41] Marvin Spevack, *A Complete and Systematic Concordance to the Words of Shakespeare,* 9 vols. (Hildesheim, 1968-1980). *Old* occurs 665 times in the corpus: see 5: 2494, cf. 6: 4178.

[42] *Young* occurs 460 times in the corpus; Spevack, 6: 4134, cf. 6: 4178.

[43] Spevack, 5: 2494-2497.

[44] Citations are from *The Riverside Shakespeare,* ed. G. Blakemore Evans et al. (Boston, 1974).

[45] "Swa byð se ealda man ceald ⁊ snoflig," in *Byrhtferth's Manual,* ed. Samuel J. Crawford, EETS o.s. 177 (London, 1929), p. 12, lines 17-18. "þæt heofenlice rice ... þær eald ne graneð, ne child ne scræmeð," in *Twelfth-Century Homilies in MS. Bodley 343,* Pt. 1, ed. Algernon O. Belfour, EETS o.s. 137 (London, 1909), p. 128, lines 21-23.

[46] "Se ealda mann þe bið butan eawfæstnysse bið þam treowe gelic þe leaf byrð ⁊ blostman ⁊ nænne wæstm ne byrð ⁊ bið unwurð his hlaforde," in *Old English Homilies and Homiletic Treatises,* First Series, ed. Richard Morris, EETS o.s. 29 (London, 1867), p. 299. "Ðonne þu eald sie ⁊ manegra

moving statement about aging comes from Wulfstan in the *Institutes of Polity* when he reminds his readers that, while it is never appropriate for distinguished age to behave in too juvenile a fashion, it is nevertheless no shame if an old man acts like a child in foolish behaviour – in short, becomes senile – when he cannot help himself.[47]

The contrast should not be exaggerated: the old is often suspect or deficient in Old English, too, and old (pagan) customs, old sins, old errors, old heresies, and even, sometimes, the old law are seen as wanting. But, reading through the hundreds upon hundreds of citations about old people in the Old English corpus, one finds that they do much the same things that anyone else does: they talk and they sin, they pray and cry, they rejoice and go places and do things, they eat and drink, teach and learn, groan and sing and make merry.[48] Returning to Byrhtwold, the *ealdgeneat* "old retainer" of *The Battle of Maldon*, there is no reason to doubt that he was an old man as the poem says. The exploits of a number of famous old warriors are recounted in the literature, Beowulf, Onela, and the *ealdormann* Byrhtnoth among them.[49] Old soldiers, like others, sometimes exhort their comrades. The exhortation of Byrhtwold, himself an old man, serves as a statement of the proper response to adversities, including the adversities of aging, illness, and approaching death, from an Old English Christian and heroic perspective: "Hige sceal þe heardra, heorte þe cenre, mod sceal þe mare, þe ure mægen lytlað."[50] Our spirit must be tougher, our hearts bolder, our courage greater, as our strength diminishes.

---

ealdra cwydas ⁊ lara geaxod hæbbe, gedo hi ðonne ðam giongan to witanne," Sec. 9 in "The Old English Dicts of Cato," ed. R. S. Cox, *Anglia* 90 (1972) 1-42 at p. 6; *Byrhtferth's Manual*, ed. Crawford, p. 12, lines 2-3.

[47] "La, utan þæt geþencan ... þæt soð is, þæt næfre ne geriseð geþungenre ylde to geonclic wise ealles to swyðe; ne ealdan esne ne bið buton tale þæt he hine sylfne wyrce to wencle on dollican dædan oþþon on gebæran," No. 14 in *Die "Institutes of Polity, Civil and Ecclesiastical," ein Werk Erzbischof Wulfstans von York,* ed. Karl Jost, Schweizer anglistische Arbeiten 47 (Bern, 1959), p. 267. I follow Jost's interpretation of the passage, which may also be read in a contrary sense.

[48] "Swaswa Anna seo halige wuduwa ⁊ Simeon se ealda sungon ⁊ drymdon, ða hy þæt mycele ⁊ þæt formære bearn mid heora earmum beclypton," in "Die altenglischen Beigaben des Lambeth-Psalters," ed. Max Förster, *Archiv* 132 (1914) 328-335 at p. 333, lines 10-12.

[49] Robinson, "Some Aspects," p. 39.

[50] *Maldon* 312-313, ed. Donald G. Scragg, *The Battle of Maldon* (Manchester, 1981), p. 67.

8

Figures of Old Age in
Fourteenth-Century English Literature

Alicia K. Nitecki

Bentley College

Fourteenth-century English poets knew the tradition that idealized old age. Chaucer, for example, shows a familiarity with Cicero's *De senectute,* and various of his characters draw on biblical passages advising reverence for age.[1] Yet neither Chaucer, nor any other English writer of his period, presents idealized, venerable old people in his works; nor does any of the poets provide us with realistic portrayals of the old and their position in society.[2] They draw, instead, on the counter-tradition that sees in old age an image of man's physical and spiritual corruption.

The immediate – and most influential – sources for fourteenth-century portrayals of old age are the *Elegies* of Maximianus, from the sixth century, and Pope Innocent III's *De contemptu mundi,* from the end of the twelfth.[3] Both these writers, in their turn, derive much from forces outside their period – from Roman literature, in particular from Horace, and, in the case of Pope Innocent, from Christian teaching.

---

[1] Some of the material in this paper, particularly the section on Chaucer's *Pardoner's Tale,* appeared in different form in Alicia K. Nitecki, "The Convention of the Old Man's Lament in the *Pardoner's Tale," Chaucer Review* 16 (1981-1982) 76-84.

[2] See "Convention of the Old Man's Lament," p. 83, n. 3.

[3] On the influence of Maximianus see George L. Kittredge, "Chaucer and Maximian," *American Journal of Philology* 9 (1888) 85-86, and George R. Coffman, "Old Age from Horace to Chaucer: Some Literary Affinities and Adventures of an Idea," *Speculum* 9 (1934) 249-277. Rosemary Woolf, *The English Religious Lyric in the Middle Ages* (Oxford, 1968), pp. 102-104, and John M. Steadman, "Old Age and *contemptus mundi* in The Pardoner's Tale," *Medium Ævum* 33 (1964) 121-130, discuss Innocent III's influence on medieval literature.

Aging and the Aged in Medieval Europe, ed. Michael M. Sheehan, CSB. Papers in Mediaeval Studies 11 (Toronto: Pontifical Institute of Mediaeval Studies, 1990), pp. 107-116. © P.I.M.S., 1990.

The *Elegies* of Maximianus are lamentations on the hardships of old age.[4] The first elegy expresses a desire for death, and juxtaposes the glories of Maximianus' youth and the miseries of his old age. The second, lamenting his impotence, is a plea to his aging mistress not to leave him. The third and fourth elegies recount the sexual adventures of his youth. The fifth tells the story of his affair with a young woman. The last, and shortest, elegy posits the inevitability of death and old age. *Elegy 1*, of which there are two Middle English translations, one from the thirteenth and the other from the fourteenth century, was of particular importance in the Middle Ages because it provided the form and the themes for poetry dealing with old age, as well as influencing the stance taken towards the subject.[5]

Both Maximianus and Innocent III describe the same physical ills of age: the heart weakens, vigour wanes, breath stinks, the back is bent, eyes grow dim, the nose runs, hair turns grey or falls out, hands tremble, teeth decay, ears are stopped up. Both writers stress the same mental traits: a quickness to anger, greed, vanity, love of the past, disdain of the present. Innocent explicitly evokes horror and repugnance for old age in order to evoke horror and repugnance for the world and the flesh: "for we are what he was, someday will be what he is."[6] Maximianus, while less explicitly didactic, also underscores the inevitability of old age, and, like Innocent's treatise, his elegies were read as moral warnings.[7] His focus on the *senex*'s frustration with his sexual impotence, vulnerability, and isolation is shared by fourteenth-century poets.

The physical and mental characteristics of age as listed by Maximianus and Innocent III recur in the descriptions of age in fourteenth-century literature. Chaucer's *Romaunt of the Rose,* for example, tells us:

> Elde was paynted after this,
> That shorter was a foot, iwys,
> Than she was wont in her yonghede.
> Unneth herself she mighte fede;
> So feble and eke so old was she
> That faded was al her beaute.
> Ful salowe was waxen her colour;
> Her heed, for hor, was whyt as flour.[8]

---

[4] *The Elegies of Maximianus,* ed. Richard Webster (Princeton, 1900).

[5] Woolf, *English Religious Lyric,* p. 104.

[6] Lotario dei Segni, *De miseria condicionis humane,* ed. Robert E. Lewis (Athens, Georgia, 1978), pp. 108-109.

[7] Woolf, p. 104.

[8] *Romaunt,* lines 349-356; ed. Fred N. Robinson, *The Works of Geoffrey Chaucer,* 2nd ed. (Boston, 1957), p. 568. (All quotations from Chaucer are from this edition.)

When Venus shows Gower his face in the mirror, in *Confessio amantis,* he notices:

> my colour fade,
> Myn yhen dymme and al unglade,
> Mi chiekes thinne, and al my face
> With Elde I myhte se deface,
> Se riveled and so wo besein,
> That ther was nothing full ne plein,
> I syh also myn heres hore.[9]

The mental characteristics of the aged in the fourteenth century are also those defined by Maximianus and Innocent. The description of the man in black in *The Parlement of the Thre Ages,* for example, identifies him as "Envyous and angrye, and Elde was his name."[10] *The Castle of Persever-ance* notes that in old age man is covetous by nature;[11] Chaucer's Reeve claims, "Foure gleedes han we, which I shal devyse,/ Avauntyng, liyng, anger, coveitise."[12] Where the psychological traits are not overtly listed, they are used to motivate character. The Gawain poet provides Morgan's jealousy of Guinevere as the cause for Gawain's adventure, while his boastfulness about his prowess causes old Lamech to accidentally kill Cain in the N-Town Cycle.[13]

The emphasis on the incommodities and vices of age serves in the poetry as it does in Maximianus' *Elegies* and in *De contemptu mundi* to show the levelling effect of age on man. For example, in *The Romaunt of the Rose* we are told that "The tyme that eldith our auncessours,/ And eldith kynges and emperours,/ ... us alle schal overcomen," and that we, too, will become a "doted thing."[14] The lyric, *Think on Yesterday,* reminds us "þat þer nis non so stif ne stronge,/ Ne no ladi stout ne gay" who can avoid the onslaught of physical decline.[15] Frequently, the poet draws specific attention to the moral thrust of the poem by having the *senex,* or an observer within the poem, make a comment or raise a question about the significance of human aging. In *Think on Yesterday,* for example, the narrator questions why "God let mony mon croke and elde" and then responds:

---

[9] John Gower, *Confessio amantis,* Bk. 8, lines 2826-2831; ed. Russel A. Peck (New York, 1968), p. 483.

[10] *Parlement of the Thre Ages,* line 163; ed. M. Y. Offord, EETS 246 (London, 1959), p. 5.

[11] See Joseph Quincy Adams, *Chief Pre-Shakespearean Dramas* (Boston, 1962), pp. 265-287.

[12] *Reeve's Prologue,* lines 3883-3884; ed. Robinson, *Works of Chaucer,* p. 55.

[13] See Alicia K. Nitecki, "The N-Town Lamech and the Convention of Maximianus' First Elegy," *American Notes and Queries* (1979) 122-124.

[14] *Romaunt,* lines 391-399; ed. Robinson, p. 569.

[15] *Think on Yesterday,* lines 117-120; ed. Carleton Brown, *Religious Lyrics of the XIVth Century,* 2nd ed. rev. G. V. Smithers (Oxford, 1957), p. 144.

> Crist, þat Made boþe flour & felde,
>   Let suche men lyue, forsoþe to say,
> Whon a ȝong mon on hem bi-helde,
>   scholde seo þe schap of ȝesterday.[16]

The ancient in the lyric, *An Old Man's Prayer,* similarly sees his physical decay as unnatural and questions it:

> Euel ant elde ant oþer wo
>   foloweþ me so faste
> Me þunkeþ myn herte brekeþe a-tuo!
>   suete god, whi shal hit swo?[17]

The juxtaposition of this stanza with the following one, which details the man's youthful sins, suggests – as does much of the poetry dealing with age – that the period of miserable old age is either punitive or atoning.

The old people's sense of "otherness" in medieval literature is intensified by the vulnerability and isolation that they feel. Maximianus writes "uncertain and tremulous, the old man believes always in new evils and foolishly fears evils that he creates himself";[18] at the same time he grounds at least some of those fears in reality, since he comments that the old are ridiculed for wearing elegant clothes, and his first elegy closes with the aged narrator being ridiculed by the young. In *An Old Man's Prayer,* the narrator complains bitterly that those who had previously enjoyed his hospitality now not only shun him because he is old, but also begrudge him food. The Pardoner's Old Man fears he will come to harm at the hands of the youths. The aged Reeve is shunned by the other pilgrims, and his complaint is ridiculed.

The old either await death eagerly as a release from the miseries of age or dread its arrival. Maximianus, for example, would like to die but knows that death is fickle: "Death does not obey the wishes of man. Death would be sweet to the unfortunate, but she denies them their prayers; but where she is an object of sorrow, there she runs precipitously."[19] In the English version of the elegy, *Le Regret de Maximian,* the old man wishes he were dead and buried, but his lament is engaged with the misery of his present life rather than with his desire for death.[20] The York Cycle's Simeon bemoans his physical ills and says, "Owte of this

---

[16] *Think on Yesterday,* lines 105-108; ed. Brown/Smithers, *Religious Lyrics,* p. 146.

[17] *Old Man's Prayer,* lines 47-50; ed. Brown/Smithers, p. 5.

[18] *Elegy 1,* lines 195-196; ed. Webster, *Elegies,* p. 32. My translation into English is used throughout this paper.

[19] *Elegy 1,* lines 114-116; ed. Webster, p. 29.

[20] *Regret,* lines 202-213; ed. Carleton Brown, *English Lyrics of the XIIIth Century* (Oxford, 1932), pp. 98-99.

worlde I wolde I were!"[21] Perhaps the most psychologically astute of all
is Langland's treatment of the horror and entrapment that Will feels as a
result of being old. He cowers in a corner and sees Death's approach:

> And as I seet in this sorwe I say how Kynde passed,
> And Deth drowgh niegh me for drede gan I quake,
> And cried to Kynde oute of care me brynge.
> "Loo! Elde the hoore hath me biseye,
> Awreke me, if ʒowre wille be for I wolde ben hennes."[22]

The same physical and mental characteristics govern the portrayal of
the old in fourteenth-century literature regardless of whether the figure is
male or female. The principal difference the poetry makes between aged
men and women is in the attitude adopted towards their sexuality. Maximianus' second elegy pinpoints that difference precisely. In that elegy, he
is grieved because the woman with whom he has lived intimately for
many years is repelled by him, although she is old now herself: "She calls
me a weak, decrepit man, is nauseated by me, vomits at the sight of
me."[23] Unlike him, the woman has retained her former beauty. "Time,"
he exclaims, "you spare a woman's beauty, you do not totally destroy
what previously charmed in her. As for men, the past leaves nothing
behind to remember them by."[24] Although the old women in fourteenth-
century English literature do not retain their beauty, they do retain their
power and are manipulative and threatening to the male. Morgan Le Fay,
cruelly as her age, ugliness, and attention to dress are portrayed in *Sir
Gawain and the Green Knight,* remains the motivating force behind the
hero's adventure and holds a respected position in her society. The old
hag in *The Wife of Bath's Tale* possesses the knowledge that the knight
needs to save his life, and uses it to manipulate him into marrying her.
Moreover, in the next century, Lydgate cautions young men in his
Dietary thus:

> For helthe of body, keep fro cold thyn hed,
> Ete no rawe mete, take good heed herto,
> Drynk holsom wyn, feede the on lyht bred,
> With an appetite ryse from thi mete also;
> With women aged flesshly have na a do.[25]

---

[21] Play 41, lines 91-99; ed. Lucy Toulmin Smith, *York Plays: The Plays Performed by the
Crafts, or Mysteries of York* (New York, 1963), p. 436.

[22] William Langland, *Piers the Plowman,* B. Passus XX, lines 198-202, ed. Walter Skeat, Vol. 1
(Oxford, 1886), p. 590.

[23] *Elegy 2,* lines 6, 15; ed. Webster, p. 36.

[24] *Elegy 2,* lines 31-32; ed. Webster, p. 37.

[25] *Dietary,* lines 25-29; ed. Henry N. MacCracken, *The Minor Poems of John Lydgate,* Pt. 2,
EETS 192 (London, 1934, repr. 1961), p. 703.

It is either her sexuality or her knowledge of sexual secrets that makes the old woman threatening and powerful. By contrast, the old man's impotence causes him to be socially shunned and vulnerable.

Indeed, of all the ills of old age, impotence is the most explored in the poetry of the period. In *Piers Plowman,* Will's wife shuns him once he has become impotent; Gower reluctantly learns the brutal lesson from Venus that "loves lust and lockes hore/ In chambre acorden neveremore";[26] and in *Confessio amantis,* as in many other works, impotence becomes a metaphor for the death of the active life and the beginning of the meditative one. Old men who refuse to let go of their sexuality (like Chaucer's Januarie, for example) become figures of scorn if not of vice.

The old man, impotent, isolated, and vulnerable, is not typically an object of pity. The ancient's moral nature is generally ambiguous; he is frequently ludicrous and contemptible in his own right, regardless of his didactic role as spiritual guide or harbinger of mortality. The ambiguity of his moral nature often derives from the depiction of his physical condition, or from the narrator's reaction to it. In the description of Elde in *The Parlement of the Thre Ages,* the author conveys not only the ills of age but also his own ambivalence towards aging:

> The thirde was a laythe lede lenyde on his syde,
> A beryne bownn alle in blake, with bedis in his hande;
> Croked and courbede, encrampeschett for elde;
> Alle disfygured was his face, and fadit his hewe,
> His berde and browes were blanchede full whitte,
> And the hare one his hede hewede of the same.
> He was ballede and blynde, and alle babirlippide,
> Totheles and tenefull, I telle ȝowe for sothe;
> And euer he momelide and ment and mercy he askede,
> And cried kenely one Criste and his crede sayde,
> With sawtries full sere tymes, to sayntes in heuen;
> Envyous and angrye, and Elde was his name.[27]

Elde in *Piers Plowman* is good insofar as he warns Will against worldly pleasure and fortune and insofar as he fights on the side of Conscience. Yet he is threatening and repulsive to the individual. "Elde manaced me," Will says, and later, outraged by Elde's cruel treatment of him, scolds, "Sire euel-ytauȝte Elde ... vnhende go with the."[28] His final reaction is the vengeance we have seen him seek.

[26] *Confessio amantis,* Bk. 8, lines 2403-2404; ed. Peck, p. 471.
[27] *Parlement,* lines 152-163; ed. Offord, p. 5.
[28] *Piers Plowman,* B. Passus XX, line 185; ed. Skeat, p. 588.

The exposition of the sins to which the old are thought to be prone, and the descriptions of aging flesh, are supposed to be corrective in that they provoke revulsion from the flesh and fear of our own corruption. While in most of the old man's laments, or descriptions of age, the contemptibility of the flesh (and the world) is used didactically, in some the didactic thrust gives way to dramatic effectiveness. Such effective uses leave a sense of the ludicrousness, contemptibility, or idiosyncrasy of the particular portrayal. An example of this tendency may be found in the lyric *Elde,* where the old man rather dwells on the more sordid aspects of impotence and the uglier signs of senility than conveys the moral implications of human aging. At the end of *Le Regret de Maximian,* in a passage that violates the didactic decorum of the poem, the *senex,* enraged by the indignities he suffers as a result of his years, imagines himself taking vengeance on the young by getting them in a dark place and hanging them!

The aged in fourteenth-century poetry, then, are persistently treated rhetorically as figures of man's spiritual corruption. And that view of age persists in the works of Chaucer, where it receives its richest treatment in *The Reeve's Prologue* and *The Pardoner's Tale.*

In *The Reeve's Prologue,* Chaucer exploits the full potential of the tension I have noted between the rhetorical and the dramatic possibilities of the figure of the *senex.* In doing so, Chaucer turns the convention against itself. The aged Reeve delivers his didactic speech on the ills of age as a response to the Miller's tale, which he, alone of all the pilgrims, considers morally reprehensible. The pilgrims immediately recognise the lament as a piece of "sermonyng," its subject as "hooly writ," and the Reeve's manner as "preaching." The lament, far from working effectively as a didactic piece, proves to be a revelation of his own unregenerate desire for sexual pleasure. Although he employs figures and images traditional to lyric poetry on age, the language in which the Reeve casts those figures is often sexually charged and as a result betrays his lustfulness. Sometimes the Reeve explicitly states that the old want to be sexually able, "For in oure wyl ther stiketh evere a nayl,/ To have a hoor heed and a grene tayl,/ As hath a leek."[29] Other times, his sexual obsession is revealed through an evocative use of language: "Deeth drough the tappe of lyf and leet it gon;/ And ever sithe hath so the tappe yronne/ Til that almoost empty is the tonne./ The streem of lyf now droppeth on the chymbe."[30] Particularly suggestive is his use of the following figure:

[29] *Reeve's Prologue,* lines 3877-3879; ed. Robinson, p. 55.
[30] Ibid., lines 3892-3895; ed. Robinson, p. 55.

> But if I fare as dooth an open-ers,
> That ilke fruyt is ever lenger the wers,
> Til it be roten in mullok or in stree.
> We olde men, I drede, so fare we:
> Til we be roten, kan we nat be rype.[31]

He is bemoaning, conventionally enough, the evils of old age, a period he sees as being worse than death. But in addition to the inherent repulsiveness of the analogy he makes between the fruit rotting in refuse and the aging flesh, the choice of the visually descriptive name "open-ers" over the less specific "medlar" is particularly psychologically apt, if contextually insensitive, because it evokes Nicholas' unfortunate position at the end of the preceding story, and thus draws attention to the drift of the Reeve's thoughts.

The Reeve's sexual frustration, then, motivates his didactic lament and undermines his authority. Chaucer's Reeve, for all his pretensions to morality, remains himself uninstructed; his lament, rather than taking the audience out of themselves and asking them to contemplate higher truths, leaves them satisfied with the world they have. As a result of the disparity between the Reeve's intention and effect, the reader projects onto him rather than identifying with him. As in Roman comedy, the old man remains an inferior; the audience learns nothing from him.

In *The Pardoner's Tale,* Chaucer opens the conventional portrayal of the *senex* up to new psychological and rhetorical significance. For this figure, he draws on specific images from Maximianus' first elegy, and on the paradox implicit in youth-age debate poetry like *The Parlement of the Thre Ages* and explicit in *The Romaunt of the Rose* that, although old age is morally preferable to youth, no one "wolde bicomen old."[32] Chaucer derives the formal structure of the scene with the old man from lyric poetry: the youths question the *senex*'s age, he replies with a complaint, he expresses fear of the young men.

Like other authors, Chaucer draws attention to the ambiguity in the ancient's moral nature. Here, that ambiguity derives from the man's relationship to death. In response to their question, "Why lyvestow so longe in so gret age?" he replies that he cannot find a man

> That wolde chaunge his youthe for myn age;
> And therfore moot I han myn age stille,
> As longe tyme as it is Goddes wille.
> Ne Deeth, allas! ne wol nat han my lyf.[33]

---

[31] *Reeve's Prologue,* lines 3871-3875; ed. Robinson, p. 55.
[32] *Romaunt,* line 4965; ed. Robinson, p. 611.
[33] *Pardoner's Tale,* lines 724-727; ed. Robinson, p. 152.

The exclamation, "Ne Deeth, allas! ne wol nat han my lyf," sounds like the conventional impatience for death, but there also hovers the suggestion that death has actively rejected him – a suggestion that is reinforced by Earth's parallel rejection of his plea later in the speech. The impression is of Death and Earth closing ranks against the ancient and leaving him desolate. The image of maternal Earth rejecting her son, which Chaucer derives from Maximianus, stresses the extremity of his exile and isolation.

Chaucer draws attention to the apparent irregularity in the old man's relationship to death by shifting the normal relationship of old age to death in his speech. Where ordinarily the desire to die is the consequence of man's misery in old age, here it appears that his being rejected by death causes his old age. Nor is this mere quibble, since the switch in what is cause and what is effect reinforces the idea that the man's misery lies rather in his being denied death than in his being old. For example, he attributes the fact that his face is "ful pale and welked" to Earth's refusal to hear his plea, and thus the description of his appearance, conventional enough in itself, conveys the extent rather of his sorrow than of his years. The suggestion that the old man is excluded from death, together with the peculiarity of the relationship between age and death in the speech, creates an uncertainty about him and implies that he is being punished. The opening lines of his speech, which point to a failed quest, attribute his continued life to a world that clings to youth and refuses age. In this sense, he may be seen as a victim of a corrupt world.

The idea that the old man's inability to die is connected with worldly corruption is reinforced by the second failure of exchange in the speech:

> Mooder, with yow wolde I chaunge my cheste
> That in my chambre longe tyme hath be,
> Ye, for an heyre clowt to wrappe in me![34]

As man *will not* change youth for age, so the old man *cannot* change his worldly possessions for a shroud. His ability to relinquish the world depends on his ability to find men willing to grow old.

Chaucer's stressing of the old man's longing for death and the implication that death rejects him is thematically and psychologically important. The world without death that the old man inhabits evokes horror, yet it is just such a world that the young men seek in the tale. The deathless world in *The Pardoner's Tale* is not simply a literary conception, but a trope for human longing and need for transcendence. The old man is not so much the opposite of the youths as he is the embodiment of the implications of their quest to kill death. Far from rejecting the old man, as is conventional, the audience identifies with him on a latent level and, instead, rejects the young men's desire to prolong physical life forever. The old man is now a figure of the horror of never-ending existence and of the denial of transcendence. The result of a failed quest to find a man "that wolde chaunge his youthe for myn age," the old man is the creation of a world like the one the youths desire. He is the human spirit trapped by and in the world.

Throughout fourteenth-century English poetry, then, the view of old age is inspired by one dominant convention. It is a view that exposes man's fear and repugnance in the face of aging, that treats the aged as grotesques, as vehicles of metaphor rather than as characters. It is this same view that the period's greatest poet, Chaucer, explores and enlarges but does not radically alter or obliterate. Not until the next century does the idealized view of age familiar from the *Aeneid, De senectute,* and *Beowulf* re-emerge in poems such as *Mum and the Soothsayer* or Henryson's *Prais of Aig,* poems that see the old as wise and experienced, as reconciled to their years.

Part Two

The Elderly

Numbers, Activity, Support

9

How Many of the Population were Aged?

Josiah C. Russell

Professor Emeritus, University of New Mexico

A few years ago my mother died a day after she was ninety-seven years of age. If she had been a Mohammedan, she would have been one hundred years of age. A century, whether Christian or Islamic, is about the upper limit of human life; the time when our human constitution is geared to finish its work.[1] And, unless there is a very radical discovery, no great change in our span of life seems probable in the future. A serious question is, what percentage of alleged centenarians actually passed the hundred years? The tendency to exaggerate is great for the United States Census and was apparently just as strong in the Middle Ages.

However, this tendency need not affect the total number assigned to all of the elderly, whatever the age selected as the lower limit. What should that age be? Bishop Isidore of Seville in the seventh century suggested that seventy should be the age of entrance among the aged: his opinion was spread in a thousand manuscripts.[2] We shall suggest later why he may have chosen such an advanced age. For the most part sixty years has been preferred. In 1914 Rudolf Martin in his *Lehrbuch des Anthropologie in systematischer Darstellung* set sixty years as the beginning of old age,

---

[1] Only fifteen Harvard and Radcliffe graduates are a hundred years of age or older: 104 – one man; 103 – one man; 101 – three men, one woman; 100 – six men, three women. *Harvard Magazine* 85 (1983) 77.

[2] *Isidori Hispalensis episcopi Etymologiarum sive originum libri XX*, ed. Wallace M. Lindsay (Oxford, 1911), 11: ii.

Aging and the Aged in Medieval Europe, ed. Michael M. Sheehan, CSB. Papers in Mediaeval Studies 11 (Toronto: Pontifical Institute of Mediaeval Studies, 1990), pp. 119-127. © P.I.M.S., 1990.

and generally the anthropologists have followed his lead.[3] That age was often accepted as the limit for requiring official services from medieval citizens. There does not seem to be much tendency to exaggerate for sixty-year-olds, so that the total for sixty and above seems reasonably accurate. And anthropologists find that age convenient, even though our skeletons do not change sharply at that time.

Normally one might compare the number of elderly in terms of percentage of the total population. However, the numbers of the very young are so uncertain that it is better to eliminate them as a factor. It is also hard to get secure figures for the slightly older children. There is nearly always a shortage of female infants. It thus seems better to use the percentage of elderly with respect to the adult population, those above the age of twenty.

Since the adult population is usually about one-half of the total population, it is easy to convert to percentage of the adult population by dividing by two. Even those who fear statistics should not worry about this.

The sources of information about age in the medieval period are more extensive than one might have anticipated. The amount depends also upon the limits that we assign to the Middle Ages, particularly to its beginnings. My own choice for the commencement of that period is A.D. 312, the end of the persecution of the Christians. As a Radcliffe student of mine once explained in a freshman ten-minute quiz, "The Edict of Milan made Christianity tolerable." Multitudes now joined the Church who formerly were deterred by the prospect of persecution. By selecting A.D. 312 we include later Roman grave inscriptions, and there are 30,000 of them. Then, there are the inquisitions post mortem and proofs of age from later medieval England, some 3,000 cases. The magnificent Catasto of Tuscany from A.D. 1427 offers the names of some 300,000 inhabitants with their ages. Lastly, the anthropological research of the last forty years has produced skeletal data about age from some 30,000 cases in five hundred cemeteries.

We are interested primarily in the number of the elderly in living populations, rather than in their percentage in the cemeteries. The Tuscan evidence gives this directly. From the skeletal and inscription evidence, it can be worked out by the use of a life table.

The Roman grave inscription was often a sort of "Who's Who" of the deceased, frequently giving ages at death as well as achievements and offices. There was naturally a bias towards the wealthy and towards city dwellers. The number, as mentioned earlier, is over 30,000. They have

---

[3] Jena, 1914. 3rd ed. by Martin and Karl Saller (Munich, 1959-1964).

been compiled a number of times: the latest and best by the Hungarian scholar, Szilágyi, in the *Acta* of the Hungarian Academy of Sciences.[4] Mercifully, they are in English. Szilágyi set the data up in convenient tables by sex and by time periods. The data were originally collected, mostly by German scholars, in the nineteenth century, in the many stout volumes of the *Corpus inscriptionum Latinarum*. Later scholars have added other data in learned periodicals. Since inscribed stones fell an easy prey to the building needs of the increasing population of the last century, the work of those scholars was especially timely.

We shall be using the percentages of the elderly in the adult population, as mentioned earlier. We should keep the range of percentages in mind: from 0 in Greenland's icy mountains to about 25 percent in Italy's marble land.

A third of the Roman data came from Roman North Africa (not including Egypt).[5] From the first to the fifth century that area enjoyed far and away the best health. At age sixty the expectation of life was about eighteen years, contrasted with ten years for the Middle Ages in general. The percentage of the North African aged was 23.4 for men and 22.1 for women. Their great age can be attributed partly to the dry climate, which discouraged malaria and hindered the spread of tuberculosis, which was apparently creeping over Eurasia then.[6] Such favourable conditions with respect to the great white plague (tuberculosis) were not attained again until the middle of the last century. It was amid these healthy conditions that St. Augustine grew up.

The figures for the elderly among the adults are not so high for other parts of the Roman Empire. The mountainous regions, such as central Italy with about 20 percent and the Alpine regions, were good because those regions were freer from tuberculosis and malaria. Other Roman regions had from 9 to 13 percent of the elderly (see Table 1A). It was about what one would expect of regions where length of life was good but not excellent, as in the territory of the Gauls and northern Italy. Figures were lower in the city of Rome and even in Latium, where unhealthy

---

[4] János Szilágyi, *Acta archeologica Academiae scientificarum Hungarica* 13 (1961) 125-155 for western Europe, 14 (1962) 277-396 for Illyrian and North Italian provinces, 15 (1963) 129-224 for the cities of middle and South Italy with Spain, 17 (1965) 309-321 and 18 (1966) 235-262 for North Africa. For the list of editions see my *Late Ancient and Medieval Population Control*, American Philosophical Society, *Memoirs* series 150 (Philadelphia, 1985), pp. 46-52 and p. 260, s.v. Szilágyi.

[5] Szilágyi 1965-1966. The figures used, however, come from my *Late Ancient and Medieval Population*, Transactions of the American Philosophical Society 48.3 (Philadelphia, 1958), pp. 25-29.

[6] See *Late Ancient and Medieval Population Control*, pp. 93-110.

conditions prevailed. In these areas the numbers of the elderly seem too large and may have been augmented by migration from the countryside. We must remember that we are dealing with urban or quasi-urban conditions where the population was not subjected to hard agricultural labour.

A second large body of information, that from skeletal data, has been provided by archaeologists and anthropologists, in the last forty years.[7] Data exist for more than five hundred cemeteries from all over Europe, but largely from the eastern and northern sectors. It is the more valuable because it often comes from areas not well illustrated by documentary or other evidence. Much comes from lands beyond the Iron Curtain. The subject matter is not controversial, because it touches so little on Marxist issues.

These data are not hard to use. They are frequently presented in standardized tables of the vital data. The Slavic and Hungarian accounts are nearly always accompanied by summaries in western European languages. My incursion into these languages involved only the necessary technical terms for use in collecting the skeletal data. This material has been presented with analysis in my *Late Ancient and Medieval Population Control,* published by the American Philosophical Society.[8]

The cemeteries reveal the status of the elderly in the villages of the Middle Ages, mostly outside of the Mediterranean area. The percentage of the elderly there was low at all times, but very low in the plague periods. The first plague (A.D. 542-750) saw only about 2 percent and the second plague period (1348-1500) scarcely more than 3 percent. These very low percentages come in part from the terrible losses of the first epidemics of each plague period (see Table 1B).

The nonplague periods were somewhat kinder to the elderly. The pre-plague period (before A.D. 542) had about 4 and 5 percent of elderly men and women in the adult population. After the first plague both men and women had about 5 percent of the adult population. Then the percentage declined after A.D. 1000 to 4 percent, slightly more for women than for men. During this period (A.D. 1000-1348) the population increase reduced the size of family land holdings and required more hard labour to extract a living from the soil. A partial shift from animal husbandry to field labour also took its toll.[9]

---

[7] Listed ibid., pp. 241-264.

[8] Pp. 26-40. For a good introduction to this material see György T. Acsádi and Janós Nemeskéri, *History of Human Life Span and Mortality,* trans. K. Balás (Budapest, 1970).

[9] Perhaps overemphasized in my data since central European evidence is larger than that of western and southern Europe.

Table 1: Percentage of Elderly in the Adult Population			
A. ROMAN INSCRIPTION DATA			
Area	**Male**	**Female**	**Both**
Africa	23.4	22.1	
Rome	12.0	7.2	
Iberia	15.0	9.9	
Aemilia			12.3
Asia			10.9
Brutii, Campania, Sicily			9.3
Calabria, Apulia, Samnium			20.4
Egypt			11.0
Gaul-Cisalpine			12.5
Gaul-Narbonne			12.3
Latium			13.8
B. SKELETAL DATA			
Nonplague Periods	**Male**	**Female**	**All***
A.D. 1-542	4.6	6.2	5.2
A.D. 750-1000	5.1	5.2	4.3
A.D. 1000-1348	4.2	4.3	4.3
Plague Periods			
A.D. 520-750	1.8	2.2	3.0
A.D. 1348-1500	3.3	3.2	3.7
Mikulcice			
Moravia, 9c.	2.3	1.8	2.1
Canary Islands, 11c.			
– North	11.6		
– South	5.2	2.0	
* "All" includes male and female skeletons and those of unidentified sex.			
C. DATA FROM INQUISITIONS POST MORTEM			
Generation	**Male**		
Born before 1276	8.42		
1276-1300	7.3		
1301-1325	6.9		
1326-6.1348	8.9		
7.1348-1375	10.3		
1376-1400	9.0		
1401-1425	10.6		
1426-1450	12.4		
D. CENSUS-LIST DATA			
Area	**Male**	**Female**	**Both**
France-Reims 1422	6.3	5.2	5.8
Pozzuoli 1489	8.5	12.1	10.3
Tuscany 1427			
Florence (city)	18.9	23.9	
Tuscany (country)	23.2	26.0	
Pistoia	25.1	23.9	
Total			24.7

The third source, the data from the inquisitions post mortem and proofs of age in the English Public Record Office are the most accurate medieval figures about age.[10] At the death of a landholder, the courts held inquisitions with respect to his holdings. These gave, besides information about real estate, the names of the heirs and their ages. In addition, the holders when coming of age (men at twenty-one and women at fourteen) were often required to prove their ages by the testimonies of twelve witnesses.[11] These witnesses not only gave the date of the heirs' births, but also the circumstances by which they remembered the dates. These reminiscences are among the most interesting items about life in the Middle Ages. For us the chief interest is that they show how accurate the information in the inquisitions was. They were quite accurate except for rounding. For adults the proofs show that ages rounded to thirty years averaged thirty-four; those to forty, averaged forty-five; to fifty, fifty-four; and to sixty, sixty-two (see Table 1C).

By 1938 about half of the inquisitions post mortem and proofs of age were in print.[12] The rest I examined in that hectic year 1938-1939. Few American scholars were in the London archives or libraries that year, and relatively few others. At my request the Public Record Office allowed the attendants to bring in large numbers of the documents, so that I could check in short order the few data I needed from each document. In no other year in this century would I have been allowed to examine so many thousand documents in so few months. Eventually I found data about the age at inheritance and at death of 3,400 lives upon which to base the study of their length of life.

Since I had the actual years of birth and death I could set up the data to show change by generations. The first generation was of those before A.D. 1276; the succeeding generations were of twenty-five years apiece to the last born A.D. 1426-1450. The first generation saw the elderly with 8.5 percent of the adult population. The generation born 1301-1325 had the smallest with about 7 percent. The generations during the plague period always had 9 percent or a little more, but in the last one the number of elderly rose to 12.5 percent. This increase in the percentage of the elderly was in part the result of the very heavy death rates for those aged seven to twenty-five years. The plague apparently killed many who would normally have died between twenty-five and sixty, leaving a

[10] Josiah C. Russell, *British Medieval Population* (Albuquerque, 1948), esp. pp. 92-117, 147-154.

[11] Ibid., pp. 92-177.

[12] *Calendars of Inquisitions post Mortem and Other Analogous Documents,* 12 vols. (London, 1906-1937). Vols. 13-16 were published 1955-1974. For other, fifteenth-century inquisitions, see the *Calendar of Inquisitions post Mortem,* Second Series, *1-24 Henry VII,* 3 vols. (London, 1898-1956).

higher proportion of the elderly. This high percentage of the elderly in time of plague may explain why Isidore placed the portal of old age so late.[13]

Apparently the first outbreak of the plague killed off large numbers of the members of small families, such as the clergy and the elderly who lived alone, presumably because rats had fewer people to bite in the smaller households. One question is why, if the death rate of those who took the plague was so high (perhaps 60 to 80 percent), only 25 to 40 percent of the population died in the first attack. The answer possibly is that fleas did not care to bite perhaps half of the people.[14]

The disadvantage of the elderly because of living in small households was overcome partly in the late fourteenth and fifteenth centuries by their inclusion in the larger households that became more common then. Against this advantage must be set the loss of dignity that the elderly suffered by being forced to live as subordinates in larger homes: the increasing stress was one of the factors in the development of the witchcraft mania then.

The fourth and most extensive data are several lists of people by age from fifteenth-century Italy and one from France. The French list of citizens comes from Reims in 1422 and shows a modest number of the elderly among the adults of that city: 6.3 percent of the men and 5.2 percent of the women.[15] This is about half the percentage in the general medieval population, which was largely rural, of course. The city of Pozzuoli in 1489 had a somewhat larger percentage of elderly in the adult population: 8.5 percent of men and 12.1 of women.[16] This was more like the proportions of the Roman provinces of the Mediterranean area. The best record comes from the great Catasto of Tuscany of 1427. The data about Pistoia were presented by Professor Herlihy in his volume of 1967 on that city (see Table 1D).[17] The other evidence about Tuscany that he discovered in the Florentine archives, he presented in collaboration with Dr. Klapisch-Zuber in 1978.[18] Pistoia had 25.1 percent of elderly men and 23.9 percent of women of the adult population. In its countryside the figures were 24.2 for men and 26.0 for women. These were higher than in

---

[13] Data from British Medieval Population, pp. 180-186.

[14] That fleas prefer certain persons is a well-known fact of flea country. Our family learned it in June 1938 when we returned from our year in England to a house in which several cats and dogs had been living.

[15] Pierre Desportes, "La Population de Reims au XVe siècle d'apres le dénombrement de 1422," Le Moyen Age 72 (1966) 497.

[16] K. Julius Beloch, Bevolkerungsgeschichte Italiens, 3 vols. (Berlin, 1937), 1: 29-32.

[17] David Herlihy, Medieval and Renaissance Pistoia (New Haven, 1967), esp. Appendix II.

[18] David Herlihy and Christiane Klapisch-Zuber, Les Toscans et leurs familles (Paris, 1978). The main population data are on pp. 656-663.

Tuscany, which had 23.3 for men and 26.0 for women. In the city of Florence the figures were 18.9 for men and 23.9 for women. Herlihy and Klapisch-Zuber explain these very high figures as the result of recent plague epidemics, which had decimated the younger groups of adults more than the older. It does seem to corroborate the evidence from the English landholder generation born in 1426-1450 that the plague left more of the elderly alive than was normal in nonplague periods.

It will be remembered that Bishop Isidore set seventy as the beginning of old age. He lived in approximately the same later phase of the plague in the seventh century as that in which we find larger percentages of the elderly in the fifteenth century. This period marks the great upturn in the number of religious writings in Europe.[19] The very loss of life concentrated wealth in the hands of fewer people and greatly improved the economic status of the survivors. Upon this century fell the benefits of the eyeglasses, which were invented in the later thirteenth century and came into use rapidly, enabling the elderly and others to enjoy reading more. The new printing press accelerated the availability of written materials. Although the period had its share of death, economic disaster, and social distress, we are not surprised that a Renaissance occurred. The larger percentage of the elderly was a natural part of it.

And now for the two final questions. The first: did women live longer than men? It depends upon their age group. At birth, no. Too many girl babies disappeared at or near birth. Even at Florence in 1427 and in Tuscany the sex ratio in the first year of life was 120 instead of the normal ratio at birth of about 104. At age twenty the expectation of life of men was higher than that of women. The combination of child-bearing, hard work, and greater loss from tuberculosis produced a heavier mortality for women than for men between the ages of twenty and forty. If, however, life began at forty, the case is different. After that age women had a lesser mortality and lived a little longer. In Florence in 1427 men and women were equal in their numbers at age forty-six, but the Tuscan women had to live to eighty-five before they had an equal chance. For the peasant of Europe the conditions of women even declined after the year 1000.

The second question involves the aging of the clergy. One might expect that its simplicity of food and action would lead to longer lives and a larger percentage of the elderly in the adult population. Not much evidence is available, but that little would affirm it. The length of lives of

---

[19] Josiah C. Russell, "Cycles of Late Ancient and Medieval Religious Writers," *Journal of Cycle Research* 10 (1961) 89-93.

monks in monasteries in Canterbury and Florence was greater than that of the laity.[20] The small size of the priests' households, however, probably led to high mortality during plague periods.[21]

Perhaps the most remarkable cases of clerical longevity come from the careers of the pillar saints or Stylites of the late ancient and early medieval period in Syria and Asia Minor. Their position on pillars high above the crowd separated them from contagion, so that they were an experiment in sanitary living. Appropriate clothing, shelters above, and railings about protected them from hazards of weather and falls. At least one was struck by lightning, one of their few occupational hazards. Their morale was strengthened by attention of the crowds who looked to and listened to them. One saint lived a century and many lived to great age. Some even had disciples who also lived on pillars, but not so high, of course. In those auspicious circumstances it is not surprising that the longevity of the saints, like their conversation, was on a high level.

---

[20] Herlihy and Klapisch-Zuber, *Les Toscans*, pp. 203-204.
[21] Russell, *British Medieval Population*, pp. 220-226.

10

Age-Related Data from the Templar Trials

Anne Gilmour-Bryson

University of Melbourne

The Military Order of the Temple was founded in 1118 or 1119 in Jerusalem by Hugues de Payens, a French knight thought to have his origins in Champagne, and six other French noblemen.[1] At some point during the first ten years of the Order's existence, it began to accept, as well as aristocrats, serving brothers who were not members of the nobility. During the early years popes granted many favours to the Order, including the right to possess its own member priests, who formed a third class within the group.[2] The original purpose of this order was to perform a protective function by safeguarding pilgrims on the dangerous roads of the Holy Land.[3] The actual military or fighting role that the Templars carried out for almost two hundred years alongside the knights and serving brothers of the Order of St. John of Jerusalem (the Hospitallers), troops from other military orders, and crusaders, did not begin until somewhat later.

After the Rule of the Templars was approved by the pope in 1128, the importance, wealth, and possessions of the Order grew with remarkable

---

[1] On the origins of the Order, see Malcolm Barber, "The Origins of the Order of the Temple," *Studia monastica* 12 (1970) 219-240.

[2] Papal bulls concerning the Order of the Temple prior to 1255 may be consulted in Rudolph Hiestand, *Papsturkunden für Templer und Johanniter: Archivberichte und Texte* (Göttingen, 1972).

[3] The chronicles of William of Tyre, *Historia rerum in partibus transmarinis gestarum*, and Jacques de Vitry, *Historia Hierosolimitana*, provide some of the rare information available on the Order's early years.

Aging and the Aged in Medieval Europe, ed. Michael M. Sheehan, CSB. Papers in Mediaeval Studies 11 (Toronto: Pontifical Institute of Mediaeval Studies, 1990), pp. 129-142. © P.I.M.S., 1990.

rapidity.[4] It acquired property in virtually every corner of Christendom, although France was always the area where its members were most numerous and Paris was the location of its headquarters outside the Holy Land itself. During the thirteenth century, the Order took on the role of banker or keeper of the treasury for the French kings, and occasionally for other monarchs and pontiffs also. In 1291, when the Holy Land was lost at the battle of St. Jean d'Acre, those Templars who survived fled to Cyprus. From that time until 1307 the Templars continued to exist on their many properties scattered throughout Latin Christendom. At no time in the Order's history did more than a small proportion of its members reside outside Europe. The fighting men, of course, travelled to the Holy Land, from which the Order was governed until 1291. A much larger number managed revenue-earning properties, farms, mills, and other businesses from which the Order earned much of the capital it needed to build fortresses and maintain its very expensive forces in the Middle East.

On 13 October 1307, at dawn, all Templars in France were arrested by order of Philip IV, king of France, at the direction of Pope Clement V. Templars elsewhere were captured at various times throughout the following four years. What percentage of the members escaped altogether will never be known. The Office of the Inquisition, under direct orders of the pope, through local bishops and archbishops, held a series of trials in all countries in which the Order existed. All captured Templars were interrogated on one or more occasions between 1307 and 1311.[5] Although the evidence given in the interrogations varied widely from one country to another, virtually all those questioned in Cyprus, Spain, and Portugal declared their innocence, as did all but three of the members in England, Ireland, and Scotland. In most of France and Italy (with some notable exceptions) more than 95 percent of those questioned confessed guilt concerning at least one of the allegations of heretical practices put to them. Data on the age (where available) and status of almost 900 Templars living between 1307 and 1311 furnished the data used here.

The computer-aided statistics on ages of members of the Order, and years in which numbers of members were recruited, are only as accurate

---

[4] The two best books on the Templars' financial affairs are Léopold Delisle, *Mémoire sur les opérations financières des Templiers* (Paris, 1889; repr. Geneva, 1975), and Léon L. Borelli de Serres, "Le Trésor royal de Philippe IV à Philippe VI," in *Recherches sur divers services publics du XIIIᵉ au XVIIᵉ siècle,* Vol. 3 (Paris, 1909; repr. Geneva, 1974), pp. 5-89.

[5] On the Templar trials, consult Malcolm Barber, *The Trial of the Templars* (Cambridge, 1978). Actual editions of all the various trials have been published: see the bibliography and the footnotes to the Introduction in Anne Gilmour-Bryson, *The Trial of the Templars in the Papal State and the Abruzzi,* Studi e testi 303 (Vatican City, 1982), pp. 11-25.

as the documents themselves. Total reliance on these figures should await a third verification of all the information against the original sources where possible, the editions where necessary. Moreover, age is sometimes given only approximately, in round figures. A man recorded as being 40 might well be anywhere from 35 or so to 45. Some witnesses may not have known their exact ages nor the precise number of years of service they had completed. Nevertheless, I have used all data relating to age for those Templars where it exists in the depositions remaining to us in manuscript or in published editions. My ongoing research project, the computer-aided analysis of the full testimony in all the available depositions, has been fully coded and entered, using the facilities of the Institute for Behavioural Research at York University.[6] Programs have been written to permit counting and correlating this data in all its myriad diversity: by country, by witness, by trial, in order to know precisely how the evidence differed in each trial. Part of this study involved the coding of some thirty elements of data for each witness. Although I have not yet added the testimony of non-Templar witnesses, I intend to add their testimony eventually. The 828 persons whose depositions remain gave in aggregate at least 895 depositions, since 67 of them seem to have testified on more than one occasion. For each of these persons, age (where given), status (knight, sergeant, serving brother, priest), trial at which he testified, rank in the Order (grand master, preceptor, marshall, etc.), age at reception,[7] year of reception, and many other details have been coded along with the answers to the questions themselves. It became evident to me while coding the data that more information was available than had been realised on the age of the members of the Order either at reception or at the time of giving testimony.

It became necessary to remove from the data base (for the purpose of certain of these calculations) those persons who appear to have testified on more than one occasion, since otherwise, had one or more unusually young or unusually old witnesses testified on several occasions, the overall results would have been falsified by the fact that this person and his age would have been counted more than once. The solution was to use two data bases: first, a larger one in which every witness and his testimony appears, and second, a smaller data base eliminating duplicate persons as far as it is possible to do so. The rule adopted in deciding whether a certain witness was reappearing or not was to eliminate those persons

---

[6] This research was funded by a two-year post-doctoral grant awarded by the Social Sciences and Humanities Research Council of Canada, and facilities accorded to me by Glendon College and the Institute for Behavioural Research.

[7] Calculated where age at time of testimony is given, since year of the testimony is available, by subtracting the stated number of years the witness served in the Order from his present age.

with the same, or highly similar, names only when they possessed other identical features. For example, in each deposition such an individual must have stated that he joined the Order in the same geographic location, in approximately the same year,[8] and with the same dignitary named as responsible for the reception ceremony itself. In the hypothetical case of one Iohannes de Viterbio who alleged that he was received in Assisi in 1301 by Stephanus de Tuscanella, and another Iohannes de Viterbio who stated that he was received in Bologna in 1295 by a different person, my decision would have been to consider these men as two different individuals and to retain them both.

The unique data base containing 828 persons, counting each witness only once, contains 112 knights or *milites*, 72 priests or *presbyteres*, 21 sergeants or *sergentes* (a title for serving brothers used primarily in Cyprus), 348 designated only as *fratres* or brothers, 270 qualified by the more usual title of serving brother or *serviens*, as well as 5 for whom no title or status is given. Although one can easily extrapolate statistics from the above figures indicating that 13 percent are knights, 77 percent are either serving brothers or sergeants (assuming also that those simply designated as *frater* are undoubtedly members of this category), and only 8.6 percent hold priestly rank, it is invalid to assume that these percentages necessarily reflect the actual percentage of each group in the Order prior to 13 October 1307. We do not have all the depositions, but only a certain unknown percentage of them. It is possible that members of the noble class had the resources and means by which to escape in greater numbers than did their less fortunate, more lowly brethren. It is also almost certain that large numbers of Templars in some countries were never captured and interrogated. The only sure pronouncement to be made here is to give the figures as they depict the group that was captured and interrogated, and for which the depositions happen to remain.

If we turn to the actual age of witnesses on the date of their testimony, ignoring status and using only those 372 men for whom an age is given in the trial record, the breakdown of age appears as in Table 1. The total number of witnesses under age 50 is 228, of whom 160 fall into the group between 30 and 44. Only 144 Templars are demonstrably over 49; of these, 37 are between 60 and 64, many more than one sees for any other five-year age range examined in those over 54. Two important facts must be taken into consideration here: first, arriving at an age of even 50 must have been no mean achievement during this period in history. However,

---

[8] One cannot expect the same level of accuracy when referring to events in the past from a witness in the early fourteenth century as one would today.

life expectancy figures of the sort usually seen are not properly applicable to this group, since the death rate in the fourteenth century was particularly high in infancy, childhood, and for women during the childbearing years. Templars were not normally admitted to the order until they were about 16 or 18 years old, hence had already survived the dangerous years of infancy and childhood. None of them was female.

Table 1			
Witnesses under 50	Number	Witnesses 50 and over	Number
Under 20 yrs when testifying	2	50-54	73
20-24	15	55-59	17
25-29	26	60-64	37
30-34	54	65-69	1
35-39	30	70-74	11
40-44	76	75-79	0
45-49	25	80-84	4
		85-99	0
		100 yrs (a witness in Navarre)	1

One way to attempt to solve the problem for the more than 456 depositions in which age itself is not given is to calculate a minimum age for each person based on his length of service in the Order and the average age at which members of that rank were received, using those persons whose testimony provided both actual age and length of service. Witnesses did almost always state how many years earlier they had been received as Templars, whether or not they gave their age at the time of testimony. In almost all these cases an actual year of reception was not stated. As mentioned above, however, the date of the testimony is known. In consequence, if a witness testifying in 1310 stated that he had joined the Order twenty-five years before, it is reasonable to assume that he had been received on or about the year 1285. It is, therefore, essential to find out at what age knights, serving brothers, and priests joined the Order, according to the records at our disposal.

Looking at this calculation first on an overall basis, without regard to status and using those persons whose age and year of reception is known, provides the results shown in Table 2. Only seven members were received below the age of 14 (the *Rule*[9] specified that children were not to be received). Since even a boy of 14 or 15 may have been considered close enough to adulthood to join, the practice of admitting younger boys seems to have been exceedingly rare.

---

[9] C. 14 [62], *La Règle du Temple*, ed. Henri de Curzon (Paris, 1886), pp. 25-26.

Table 2	
Age of reception	Number
Less than 14	7
14-15	14
16-20	81
21-25	79
26-30	82
31-35	46
36-40	27
41-45	12
46-50	13
51-55	5
56-60	1
61-65	0
66-70	1
71-75	1
over 75	0

On an overall basis then, without regard to rank, the majority of members were between 16 and 30 at the time of reception. The number of members received between 31 and 35 is only 56 percent of those received in the previous five years. The number of those received between 36 and 45 years of age drops to only 16 percent of those received between 16 and 30. It is essential, nevertheless, and perhaps more useful in any event, to look at age of reception in combination with status on an overall basis; for this data, see Table 3.

Considering first the unique data base concerning knights only, and using those *milites* for whom an age was given, it is clear from Table 3 that almost twice as many knights were received at less than 21 years of age as during all other periods combined.[10] Looking at serving brothers (*servientes, sergentes, fratres*), the age of reception changes noticeably. These three categories together account for 72 brothers received prior to age 21, 210 prior to age 31, and only 86 after the age of 30. It is obvious that these members were received equally often from age 26 to 30 as they were at less than 21, unlike their superiors the knights. Turning to the priests (*presbyteres* or *cappellani*), the known age at reception is seen to be often higher, perhaps because of the studies they undertook for the priesthood prior to joining the Order. The age group 26-30 contributed the largest number of priests received in any one five-year period among those for whom we have data. Reception at a very young age, under 21, constituted only 16.6 percent of the sample, whereas with knights that age group contributed 64.8 percent of those received.

---

[10] Twenty-four in the first instance versus thirteen in the second.

Table 3			
Age of reception	Number of members		
	knights	serving brothers	priests
20 or less	24	72	6
21-25	6	66	7
26-30	0	72	10
31-35	3	39	4
36-40	2	21	4
41-45	0	12	0
46-50	2	10	1
51-55	0	4	1
56-60	0	0	1
61-65	0	0	0
66-70	0	0	1
71-75	0	0	1

The way in which one may calculate age figures for those many Templars for whom no age, either at reception or at moment of testifying, is given, is to look at those for whom we possess a statement as to number of years of service in the Order, to which one can add the usual age of reception for that particular rank. It must be stressed that such a calculated age is only an estimate, within a wide range, based on the previous data as outlined above. It can serve only as an approximation of the exact age of individual members. It does, nevertheless, allow the computing of a probable average age for any member whose length of service in the Order is known.[11] When applied to reasonably large groups of Templars, it should provide a rough guide to the difficult question of the age of those who testified in these trials. But it would be unwise to infer that these figures are accurate for any other period of Templar history or for any other religious order.

The years of service for witnesses who indicated length of service but omitted any data regarding age are classified as shown in Table 4. In the lowest class (serving brothers, *sergentes,* and those qualified as *fratres*), of a total of 231 such witnesses, only 24 had served for more than thirty years. In the knightly class, in which 69 members fall into the category without age data, 39 had served a relatively short time, from one to ten years, while only 11 had been members of the Order for more than thirty years. And among 28 priests in the same category, only 6 had belonged to the Order for more than twenty years, none for more than thirty.

---

[11] E.g., a witness with thirty years of service could not reasonably be assumed to be less than 48 or 50 years of age. He could, of course, be 100, one cannot know.

Table 4			
Length of service	Number of members (age unknown)		
	serving brothers	knights	priests
1-5 years	33	12	6
6-10 yrs	59	27	4
11-15 yrs	34	8	6
16-20 yrs	32	5	6
21-25 yrs	24	0	1
26-30 yrs	25	6	5
31-35 yrs	6	5	0
36-40 yrs	13	2	0
41-45 yrs	2	3	0
46-50 yrs	2	1	0
51-55 yrs	1	0	0
over 55 yrs	0	0	0

Expanding the sample to include all those serving brothers, knights, and priests who indicated year of reception whether or not they stated their age yields the results shown in Table 5.

Table 5			
Length of service	Number of members (age known or unknown)		
	serving brothers	knights	priests
1-10 years	208	55	29
11-20 yrs	157	19	24
21-30 yrs	113	15	10
over 30 yrs	49	23	1

It is not sufficient to look at age only in those depositions in which that matter is documented: an age figure exists for only 372 of the 828 witnesses. But possessing a year of reception, and armed with the average figures of age at reception calculated from those 372, one can estimate probable ages, as mentioned above. All but 126 of the witnesses indicated either a year of reception, or age, or both. It is thus possible to list a definite or presumed age for all but those 126 persons. Since we shall now examine the results trial by trial, we shall be using the entire data base, not the one from which duplicate testimony has been removed. In the few cases in which an individual testified twice at the same trial, only one of his appearances will be counted, nevertheless.

*   *   *

Let us now look at the overall 895-person data base. Looking at "older" witnesses only, and here we shall consider those at or over age 50 to be in the "older" category, the results appear as follows, with each trial considered separately. Naturally, for these separate trials, each witness who testified will be considered only once for each trial at which he appeared.

The trial in the Patrimony of Saint Peter and parts of the Abruzzi included only seven witnesses: one priest and six serving brothers. Only one of these men has an estimated age of over 50, 55 in fact.[12]

In the nearby trial that took place in Florence and Lucca, three of the six witnesses, all serving brothers, fall into this category: two estimated at 56 and one at 76 years of age.[13]

The interrogations at Brindisi leave only two depositions from serving brothers seemingly below the age of 50.[14]

Turning to France, seventy witnesses testified before the pope and/or several cardinals in Poitiers in 1308. The manuscripts edited by Schottmüller and Finke, the only remaining sources, give the testimony of only forty-two of these men, thirty-nine of whom gave age and/or length of service.[15] Three knights and one serving brother appear to be over 50, if one estimates according to years of service. I do not consider percentages valuable in the smaller trials of ten persons or less, but in this case 10 percent of the men may have been 50 or more.

The first great trial in Paris, held in the autumn of 1307, heard from 138 Templar witnesses.[16] Almost every witness has his age stated in the deposition. Of this number, only four knights seem to be 50 or more, none of them over 60. Forty-six serving brothers are in this older age bracket, five of them 70 years of age or more. Three priests are between 50 and 60; one is 70. The percentage of older witnesses in this trial comes to 39.7, ignoring the two persons for whom data is missing.

The even larger hearing known as the Pontifical Commission was held in Paris with testimony given during 1310 and 1311, hearing a total of 227 witnesses, by far the greatest number heard anywhere. Virtually all the men's ages are recorded. Nine knights are 50 or more, as are eight priests and seventy-two serving brothers. Although the oldest knight is only 60, three priests are 70 or more, one of them 80; six serving brothers

---

[12] See Gilmour-Bryson, *Trial of the Templars*.

[13] Published by T. Bini as "Dei Tempieri e del loro processo in Toscana," in *Atti della Reale Accademia lucchese* 13 (1845) 395-506.

[14] Edited by Konrad Schottmüller, *Der Untergang des Templer-Ordens mit urkundlichen und kritischen Beiträgen*, 2 vols. (Berlin, 1887; repr. New York, 1970), 2: 105-140.

[15] Schottmüller, *Untergang*, 2: 103-140; Heinrich Finke, *Papsttum und Untergang des Templerordens*, 2 vols. (Münster, 1907), 2: 329-342.

[16] Trials in Paris in 1307, the Pontifical Commission interrogations in 1310 and 1311, and the trial in the Elne, were edited by Jules Michelet, *Le Procès des Templiers*, 2 vols. (Paris, 1841-1851).

are 70 or more, another two recorded at 80 years of age. The overall percentage of witnesses at or above 50 is 39 percent, a result virtually identical to the earlier Paris trial.

The trial in Cyprus, in which all witnesses strongly pleaded their innocence, was notable for the youth of those testifying.[17] Unfortunately, no exact ages are given, so those seen here have been estimated as already described. Only one of the thirty-seven knights for whom we have data seems to be over 50, estimated at 52. Of the thirty serving brothers indicating their year of reception, only two may be over 49, at 50 and 51 respectively. Two of the three priests, however, seem to be about 55 and 58 respectively. Only two of the knights present in Cyprus in 1310 had joined prior to the fall of Acre in 1291. Only five sergeants or serving brothers dated their reception from that earlier era. The percentage of older witnesses in Cyprus seems to be only 6.9, omitting the four persons for whom the needed information is lacking. But it would be logical to assume that younger members of the Order would still be found in Cyprus, older members having returned to their countries of origin.

Age is not given in any of the English, Irish, or Scottish trials.[18] Since year of reception, on the other hand, is usually present in the London trials, the usual formula has been applied to the calculation of age in this case. Discussing only those men over 49, one finds no priests, two knights of 56 and 61, ten serving brothers of over 50, four of whom are between 60 and 70. The second, third, and fourth London trials, which in general reheard the same witnesses, add little useful data to complete the above figures. The total number of witnesses was fifty-seven; the percentage of older witnesses is 25 percent of those providing necessary information, lower than the figures for both large Paris trials.

The Lincoln trials heard twenty-three Templars, twenty of whom indicated year of reception, of whom only two *fratres* and one priest may have been between 50 and 55, none older. Fifteen percent thus fall into the older category.

York heard twenty-three Templars, of whom only one serving brother and one priest were probably between 50 and 55. Here again age had to be estimated, producing an older witness rate of 8.6 percent.

In Ireland, fifteen Templars testified, of whom twelve indicated length of service, in the only trial for which we have documents. Five of these were likely over 50, all serving brothers. Only one was over 60. In this trial, then, the rate of older witnesses is very slightly higher than that seen in Paris, since it is at 41.6 percent versus 39 percent.

---

[17] Schottmüller, *Untergang*, 2: 143-400.

[18] David Wilkins, *Concilia Magnae Britanniae et Hiberniae*, 4 vols. (London, 1737), 2: 329-401.

Neither of the two Scottish witnesses seems to have been over 49, computing from the year of reception.

The trial in the Elne heard twenty-five Templars, all with the necessary data, of whom one knight, one priest, and four *servientes* seem over 49, only one of whom is over 60.[19] At 24 percent of older witnesses, this trial more closely parallels England than it does either of the two Paris trials.

Caen heard only thirteen Templars, none omitting years of service; according to the remaining documents, one serving brother was probably over 49.[20] The percentage of older witnesses in this small group is 7.6.

Cahors heard fifty Templars, but for thirty-two there is no data relating to either age or year of reception.[21] There seem to be eight *servientes* over 49, of whom two are over 70. Looking only at those over 49, as a percentage of the eighteen for whom there is some data, the older witnesses make up 44 percent.

The trial called "Finke 1" in the data base is undated by him, and the place is also missing.[22] It may well have taken place in Provence, considering the place of reception of many of the twenty-five witnesses. The year is probably prior to 1310, since the full series of allegations posed from that time on is not used. Three knights and three serving brothers are over 49; one of these is over 60. Twenty-five percent of the witnesses are likely over 49, omitting the one for whom there are no figures.

Age is given in the trial in Lerida for all but one of the witnesses.[23] Of the thirty-two Templars, six serving brothers and two knights are between 50 and 60; one priest is 64. These older witnesses account for 29 percent of those under consideration.

Age is also given in the trial in Navarre.[24] Only three witnesses appear, of whom two are in their 40s and one is supposedly 100 years of age.

The trials held at Ravenna and Bigorre include no data on age or year of reception.[25]

Bayeux must be estimated from year of reception.[26] Such calculations, possible for all, indicate only one older witness, a serving brother of 68, among the six witnesses.

---

[19]   Michelet, *Procès*, 2: 423-515.
[20]   Hans Prutz, *Entwicklung und Untergang des Tempelherrenordens* (Berlin, 1888; repr. Wiesbaden, 1972), p. 326; Finke, *Papsttum*, 2: 313-316.
[21]   Prutz, *Entwicklung*, p. 326; Finke, *Papsttum*, 2: 316-321.
[22]   Finke, *Papsttum*, 2: 342-364.
[23]   Finke, 2: 364-378.
[24]   Finke, 2: 378-379.
[25]   For Ravenna, see Renzo Caravita, *Rinaldo da Concorrezzo arcivescovo di Ravenna (1303-1321) al tempo di Dante* (Florence, 1964), pp. 265-307. For Bigorre, see Prutz, *Entwicklung*, pp. 324-325.
[26]   The trial is to be found in Prutz, *Entwicklung*, pp. 321-324.

Six witnesses appeared at Carcassonne, according to the available documents.[27] Only one provides any information on age or length of service, and he is apparently 40 years of age.

Five principal dignitaries of the Order were interrogated at Chinon.[28] No testimony remains for the first witness, not even his name. Understandably, they were all knights and all over 45. One of them, Geffroi de Gonneville, lacks data on age both here and in Paris, where he also appeared. Since he has been a member for twenty-eight years, and is a *miles,* the minimum age estimate for him is 46. The Grand Master, Jacques De Molay, indicated only that he had joined the Order forty-two years earlier, making him presumably about 60. The other three are between 56 and 64.

The small trial at Chaumont heard only two persons, one described as an older man. Since no hard data is present, no estimates can be made.[29]

One of the largest French trials took place at Clermont, where sixty-seven witnesses testified.[30] Twenty of these men were over 49, if age is estimated from years of service where necessary. One was a priest, one a knight, the rest serving brothers. Only one of them is over 60. The percentage of older witnesses works out to 37.7, since fourteen provided no appropriate data.

The remaining three trials at Barcelona, Troyes, and Renneville lack sufficient data to make any remarks on age.[31]

Is it possible to come to any conclusions from this pot pourri of figures? Does age mean anything as far as the members of the Order of the Temple were concerned between 1307 and 1311? There is enough firm evidence to permit some inferences to be made from the available figures. The figures are accurate to within less than 1 percent, but one must not ignore the fact that there is no means of cross-checking the figures the notaries placed in the documents. There would seem to be no reason for them to have falsified the figures in any event.

These trials offer a unique opportunity to examine age-related data concerning a group of men from all classes of society and all parts of Latin Christendom. Historians have stated frequently that this was a group of old men unable to resist the French king and the pope. Looking at the overall ages in the unique 828-person data base, 372 men or 44.9 percent are assigned a precise age. Of these 372, only 144 or 38.7 percent

---

[27] Finke, *Papsttum,* 2: 321-324.

[28] Finke, 2: 324-329.

[29] Prutz, *Entwicklung,* p. 327.

[30] Prutz, pp. 327-334.

[31] For Barcelona see Angelo Mercati, "Interrogatorio di Templari a Barcellona (1311)," in *Gesammelte Aufsatze zur Kulturgeschichte Spanien,* ed. Heinrich Finke, Vol. 6 (Münster, 1937), pp. 240-251; for Troyes and Renneville see Prutz, *Entwicklung,* pp. 334-335.

are definitely over 49. Since age may be estimated for 329 others using their stated length of service, and the average age of reception calculated for the rest, it is safe to presume that 72 men or 21.8 percent of this group were probably 49 or more years old. When those with an actual age and those with an estimated age are added together, they total 701 of the 828, a large data base for us to work with. The number of them who are, or can be presumed to be, 49 or more is 216, a grand total of 30.8 percent for men of all ranks.

Age of reception is lowest for the noble class, intermediate for the serving brothers, sergeants, and *fratres,* highest for priests. Only forty-one persons were admitted to the Order at or after the age of 40. The four oldest men to be received were all priests, who joined the group between 54 and 72 years of age. On the other hand, it was clearly not forbidden to join at an age far higher than the normal.

Some individual trials were large enough that calculating the percentage of older witnesses seems useful. Six trials with a total of 172 men for whom we have age or length of service have a rate of older witnesses (49 or more) of less than 20 percent.[32] These trials took place in France, England, and Cyprus. The men from Cyprus were exceptionally young, as befits those serving *outre-mer.* Another eight trials totalling 547 men, occurring in France, England, Lerida, Navarre, and probably Provence, average an older witness rate from 21 percent to 39 percent.[33] Only a small group of three trials at Chinon, Ireland, and Cahors, show a high rate of older witnesses, that of over 41 percent to 80 percent. Chinon can be explained by the exceptionally high rank of those testifying. Both Cahors and Ireland were somewhat removed from the mainstream of Templar properties. There is evidently no clear pattern pointing to a significant correlation between place of trial and percentage of older members.

If one considers only those Templars with an actual age of 60 or more, there are just thirty-two serving brothers, seven priests, and five knights. Looking next at those whose age was estimated at over 60, one finds twenty serving brothers, four knights, and no priests. Priests, however, do not have a significant correlation between real and estimated age as do serving brothers and knights. It is necessary to remove the four priests who entered the Order at advanced ages to achieve a significant co-efficient of correlation.[34] The percentage of priests who joined the Order at or after the age of 40 was 16.6, as against 11 percent of serving

[32] The trials at Bayeux, Caen, Cyprus, Lincoln, Poitiers, and York.

[33] Trials at Clermont, Elne, Lerida, London, Finke 1 (Provence?), Navarre, Paris, and the Pontifical Commission.

[34] Coefficient of correlation $P < .01$ in the case of all knights, all serving brothers, sergeants, and *fratres,* and the priests after removing the four with very advanced age at reception.

brothers and only 5 percent of knights. Given the highly variable age at which priests joined the Order, there may well have existed more of them whose age exceeded 49.

Looking at status and position within the Order assists us to know whether or not the Order valued older, experienced members. Only one knight known or estimated to be over 59 is not a *preceptor* (head of a house) or higher within the hierarchy. One knight's testimony includes no indication of status whatever. Many older serving brothers also served as heads of houses, nineteen of them in fact.

Why is it that over two-thirds of the Templars were below the age of 49 at the time of the trials, below the age of 45 when many of them were captured? The only discernible reason I have found is connected with the relatively high recruitment rate after 1291, year of the loss of the final bastion in the Holy Land, St. Jean d'Acre. A total of 455 men, serving brothers, knights, and priests, joined in the years from 1291 to 1307, according to the trial records. In the years prior to 1291, only 242 witnesses were received. For a witness to be presumably over 49, he must have been received prior to 1283. In fact, only 123 witnesses were in the Order that long. It is most important not to think that the records under consideration include all those received after 1283, or even most of those who joined before and could be still living. They do not. The additional figures for those men received but not in the Inquisition records because they escaped, died, or left the Order, are not available to us.

These men were substantially younger than others have alleged. Recruitment was surprisingly strong after the loss of the Holy Land. Serving brothers were promoted to the rank of *preceptor* or head of a house in spite of their status. Although they rarely achieved the rank of Templar dignitary at this point, neither of the two men described as treasurer of the king or treasurer of France was a knight. Older men predominated only in the very special interrogation at Chinon. The reason for the high rate of older men in Ireland and in Cahors escapes us. Age was not a necessary obstacle to joining the Templar Order, although only five serving brothers and no knights seem to have done so beyond the age of 50.[35] It is evident, nevertheless, that these documents are surprisingly rich in personal data largely unexploited until now.

---

[35] Means existed for older knights to become associate members of the Order very late in life, or on their death bed. This was a fairly common practice that is not evident in the trial testimony.

11

Age, Property, and Career in Medieval Society

David Herlihy

Brown University

> Give not to your son ... power over yourself while you are alive, and do
> not give your estate to another ... For it is better that your children should
> ask of you, than that you look towards the hands of your children .... At
> the termination of the days of your life, and at the time of your death, dis-
> tribute your inheritance.
>
> Ecclesiasticus 33:20-24

This principle, that the aging father retains control over his property until
his death, is a fundamental rule of behaviour in patriarchal households.
Retention of property assures that the productivity and prosperity of the
family will continuously benefit its elders. In spite of their own declining
powers, the old need not fear impoverishment in their final years. The
promise of patriarchy has always been security for the aged. And were
not most families of medieval Europe patriarchically organized?

But in spite of this counsel, medieval commentators on the stages of
life show a tendency to associate old age not with security and comfort,
but with want and deprivation. To be sure, they do not always forcefully
link poverty and aging. Many, particularly in the early medieval period,
treat the uncertainty of life and the fickleness of fortune as independent
ills, adding to the miseries of the human condition. Gregory the Great,
in his commentary on Job, thus states: "We cannot abide for long in
the company of our possessions; either we loose them in death or they

Aging and the Aged in Medieval Europe, ed. Michael M. Sheehan, CSB. Papers in Mediaeval Studies
11 (Toronto: Pontifical Institute of Mediaeval Studies, 1990), pp. 143-158. © P.I.M.S., 1990.

abandon us while we are still alive."[1] Bad luck can befall us, he implies, as it had befallen Job, at any moment of our earthly existence.

Then, too, medieval commentaries on aging are obscured by a shifting comprehension of what it meant to be poor. As Karl Bosl demonstrates, the term *pauper* in early medieval texts, up really to the eleventh century, implies lack of power and effectiveness more truly than lack of material possessions.[2] The antonym of *pauper* was *potens*, not *dives*.

We must wait, it seems, until the late Middle Ages to find clear and forceful assertions of a linkage between advancing years and deepening poverty. For example, Maurice of Sully, a preacher active in Paris in the twelfth century, identifies as the Lord's poor the widow, the orphan, the sick, the exile, and the destitute, but not the aged.[3] Lotario dei Segni, later Pope Innocent III, in his well-known tract on human miseries, rehearses the ills of old age but does not include poverty among them.[4] He dwells on the instability of material possessions in a separate part of this lachrymose essay. In contrast, some two hundred years later, Bernardine of Siena singles out specifically the old, as those likely to require the support of Christian charity. "Old age," he says flatly, "is filled with numerous infirmities, labours, and complaints."[5] Bernardine's old person is clearly not relaxing in the bosom of a large, supportive family. Underlying many of his allusions to the aged is the assumption that the old run greater risk of destitution than the young and the vigorous. And of course children have the weighty obligation to support their parents. If they fail to do so, they will be subject to a short life, or, even if they live long, they too will experience the same *paupertas magna*, as did their neglected parents. Bernardine, it should be noted, is also addressing his exhortations primarily to an urban audience.

---

[1] *Moralium in Job* 18, ch. 19, cited in a sermon by Bernardino da Feltre, *Sermoni del beato Bernardino Tomitano da Feltre*, ed. P. Carlo Varischi da Milano, OFM Cap. (Milan, 1964), 1: 240: "Dives enim cum rebus nostris durare non possumus, quia, aut nos illas moriendo deserimus, aut ille nos viventes quasi deserunt pereundo ...."

[2] Karl Bosl, *Das Problem der Armut in der hochmittelalterlichen Gesellschaft*, Sitzungs-berichte, Österreichische Akademie der Wissenschaften, philosophisch-historische Klasse 294.5 (Vienna, 1974), with references to his previous studies on the same subject. Bosl argues that this essentially feudal conception of poverty prevailed up to about 1050, then gave way over the years 1050-1300 to one very close to our own. For further studies of poverty in the Middle Ages, see Michel Mollat, ed., *Etudes sur l'histoire de la pauvreté*, 2 vols. (Paris, 1974), and *Les Pauvres au moyen âge: Etude sociale* (Paris, 1978). These works do not note a specific tie between old age and poverty, and tend to treat the poor as marginal to medieval society; this view may not be entirely accurate.

[3] Cited from a MS source by Jean Longère, "Pauvreté et richesse chez quelques predicateurs durant la seconde moitié du XIIᵉ siècle," in *Etudes*, ed. Mollat, 1: 261.

[4] *De contemptu mundi, sive De miseria conditionis humane libri tres*, PL 217: 701-746.

[5] *Opera omnia*, ed. Pp. Collegii S. Bonaventurae, Vol. 6 (Florence, 1959), p. 58: "Senectus enim multis infirmitatibus, laboribus, et gravaminibus plena est."

This quick glance at the medieval moral comments on the stages of life is, of course, highly impressionistic, but perhaps it can still delineate a problem, central to the history of aging. Was there a novel linkage between growing older and growing poorer in the communities of the late Middle Ages? Did impoverishment mount a greater menace against the aged in towns than in rural settings? And if it did, why was it that the aged were failing to follow the sage counsel of Ecclesiasticus?

In this paper, we shall seek to investigate some relationships between aging and destitution within a late-medieval, urban community. The community we shall consider is Florence in the early fifteenth century. With a population of nearly 40,000, Florence was then one of the largest cities in Europe. Florence attracts for two reasons. It was a bastion of early commercial capitalism, and thus offers an opportunity to observe the influence of a commercialized or capitalistic economy on the organization of families and the treatment of the old. The Florentine government seems also to have been one of the first in Europe to register births, or some births, for purely secular purposes. Clearly, if we are to investigate the relationship between aging and impoverishment, we must know how old our subjects were. The life cycle, and its analysis, begins with birth.

Already from the late fourteenth century, the Florentine government was taking an interest in the ages of its citizens and subjects, for several reasons. One was fiscal. The government strove to collect a head tax imposed on able-bodied males between 18 and 60 years of age in the city and 14 and 70 in the countryside. It is clear, however, that in attributing ages to the entire male population, government officials had frequent recourse to rough approximations.[6] The government, from about the same time, was also setting age qualifications for its principal offices. Thus, according to the Statutes of 1415, a citizen had to be over 30 years of age to serve in one of the three great councils of the communal government – the *Tre Maggiori* they were called. These were the eight priors, the twelve "good men," and the sixteen standard-bearers of the city's *gonfaloni* or wards. And only those over 45 years of age were eligible for the commune's highest office, that of standard-bearer of justice.[7] Thirty seems also to have been the required age for all important administrative offices in city and countryside. Only *castellani,* or chiefs of castles, could be as young as 25.

---

[6] The quality of age reporting in the Florentine Catasto of 1427 is examined at length in David Herlihy and Christiane Klapisch-Zuber, *Les Toscans et leurs familles: Une étude du catasto florentin de 1427* (Paris, 1978), pp. 350-392.

[7] *Statuta populi et communis Florentiae ... anno salutis MCCCCXV,* 3 vols. (Fribourg, 1778-1783), 2: 770-772, "De aetate dominorum et collegiorum et deveto." The election of castellans over age 25 was allowed, but other officials in the countryside had to be over 30 (ibid., 2: 793).

To hold these offices was regarded as a high dignity. Indeed, it can be shown that many young men were prone to lie about their ages, to claim to be past 30 when they were still in their 20s.[8] They were evidently eager for public honour and recognition. To counter this abuse, the government in August 1429 required that all who wished to hold office had to present proof of age. Specifically, they had to bring forth their family memoirs, in which were recorded their own births or those of their sons. All urban residents obligated to lend moneys to the government were regarded as eligible for office; they included between a quarter and a third of the urban families. Seemingly, many or most of these approximately 3,000 families were keeping written records of their births, marriages, and deaths. This is dramatic illustration of the extent of literacy within Florentine society. It also enhances the historian's confidence in the accuracy of the data these families were reporting.

After 1429, Florentine heads of households continued to present proof of age to the government, for themselves or their sons. We have registers of these *approbationes etatum* through the fifteenth, into the sixteenth century. They give us an anchor, from which to study the lives of those males who aspired to public office in the last century of the Florentine Republic (1429-1530). The total number of prospective office holders who were registered between 1429 and 1530 is approximately 30,000. They constituted, as we have mentioned, from a quarter to a third of the city's male population. Florence in the fifteenth century was an oligarchy, but not a narrow one.

At what moments in his life was the Florentine citizen likely to experience financial duress? To answer this, we can take advantage of another remarkable set of documents. Florence chose its ruling officers, in both the communal government and the twenty-one guilds, through a kind of lottery.[9] The archival deposit describing the results of the lottery, and the office that recorded them, were called appropriately the *Tratte,* meaning sortitions or drawings. The process of election was complex and was frequently changed, but in crude description it worked largely as follows.[10] Special commissions periodically scrutinized the body of taxpaying citizens, and they entered on slips of paper the names of those deemed likely candidates for office. They excluded a small and shrinking number of magnates, and also political exiles, but otherwise seem to have been quite liberal in including names. For example, in spite of sporadic efforts to

---

[8]   Herlihy and Klapisch-Zuber, *Toscans,* pp. 359-360.

[9]   For a description of the system, see Guidubaldo Guidi, *Il governo della città-repubblica di Firenze del primo Quattrocento,* 3 vols., Biblioteca storica toscana 20 (Florence, 1981), 1: 149 ff.

[10]   Ibid., 2: 3 ff.

prevent it, they entered the names of children and even infants. The fathers of these underaged candidates seem to have thought that their sons' careers would ultimately benefit from this early exposure to the public life.

The slips were then collected into separate purses, corresponding to the various important offices of government and guild. When the time came to fill the offices, a slip containing a name would be drawn from the appropriate purse, in the presence of the outgoing officials and other dignitaries.[11] The name was then read aloud. In the technical language, the candidate was said to be *veduto,* "viewed" or considered for the relevant office. The outgoing officials and the invited dignitaries then judged whether or not the citizen should be awarded the office, *seduto* or "seated" in formal terminology. More often than not, he would be disqualified, for a variety of reasons. He might be too young, or already deceased, or ill, or absent from Florence; he or a close male relative might have held the same office in the recent past, or be already serving the commune in a post of greater dignity. One reason for exclusion has particular interest for us here. The candidate might be disqualified because he owed money to the government, whether from failure to pay his fiscal assessments or for some other reason. The delinquent citizen was said to be *in speculo,* "in the mirror." He was judged ineligible for election to any communal office, and even the slip of paper giving his name was at once ripped up. This public desecration of his name was a kind of symbolic execution, and carried great ritual significance. The government insisted that only those who supported it with their moneys could benefit from its offices and honours. All others endured a type of civic death.

Characteristically, the terms of service for Florentine office holders were very short, often only two months in duration and rarely longer than a year. The citizen as he aged was thus likely to be "viewed" for office scores of times in the course of his life, and the results of the viewing would be dutifully recorded in the registers of the Tratte office. The entries thus inform us when citizens were awarded offices, and when they were considered but excluded, and for what reasons. Exclusion for fiscal delinquency certainly indicates that the citizen had fallen upon hard financial times, and was probably bankrupt. Not only did he lose the honour and remunerations of service in public office, but his name was publicly disgraced. He lost in dignity and reputation, upon which his success as a merchant may well have depended crucially.

11   Ibid., 1: 283 ff.

The computer allows us to do what the officials of the Tratte did not do, and could not have done very easily. We can match names of citizens in our file of birthdates with those found in the mirror of fiscal insolvency, and thus determine at what ages in life the Florentine citizen was likely to encounter financial duress. This should allow us to test whether there was a relationship between age and impoverishment, and what was its strength.

Since 1976, with the aid of a grant from the American National Humanities Foundation, I have been entering these birthdates and the other observations from the Tratte deposit into a machine-readable data base, which will eventually serve to reconstruct many individual careers of Florentine citizens. We are collecting these observations from the time of the earliest surviving registers (most of them date from the late fourteenth century) until the end of the Republic in 1530.[12] The work has progressed with reasonable rapidity, though it remains far from finished. Still, the data base is now sufficiently large to support this preliminary inquiry into the relationships between aging and fiscal and financial insolvency in fifteenth-century Florence.

Of course, the number of citizens found to be in tax arrears is not exclusively a function of their ages and fortunes. It obviously must also reflect the financial demands of the Florentine government, and these varied with states of war and peace, victories and defeats. Then, too, in this attempt as in all attempts at life-cycle analysis, we ought to exclude from the scrutiny persons still living at the termination date of the time series, 1530. Otherwise, an "end effect," as statisticians call it, would bias the observations towards the younger years of life. The best strategy would seem to be to confine our analysis to a single age cohort that together had lived through periods of high and low fiscal demands and that no longer contained living members in 1530. The cohort we choose to study comprises those citizens who were entered into the original registrations of 1429, with additions up to 1435.

In this continuing project, we have not as yet entered into the data base all the electoral records of the Tratte archives. The elections to guild offices are now nearly complete, but a large gap remains after 1435 in the series of drawings to the so-called Tre Maggiori, the three chief councils of communal government. But these gaps in the data base are randomly distributed, and ought not distort the results of this inquiry. There are also problems, which we cannot treat at length here, in linking the names of

---

[12] The episode of Ciompi (1378) represents a watershed in the survival of the Tratte records. Most survive in continuous series only after that date.

those born with those cited as being "in the mirror." False linkages are always possible, but Florentine naming conventions tend to be relatively favourable to the researcher. The records usually give not only the name of the person, but that of his father and often the grandfather's too, as well as a family name if he has one. The record, in sum, carries with it a short genealogy. In testing for linkages across records, we admitted only those for which the Christian name, patronymic, and family name or occupation (which often substituted for a family name) were identical; places of residence cited on the records also had to correspond. By following strict procedures, we doubtlessly rejected many true matches, but at least we are reasonably certain that the accepted linkages are true.

Among the Florentine citizens living in 1429-1435, exactly 1,088 had been or would be excluded from office for failure to pay their fiscal charges. The total number of citizens living in 1429-1435 and cited in the birth registrations is 6,027. Thus, 18 percent of this elite group of Florentines were destined to endure, or at least brush with, bankruptcy at some moment of their lives. And this is a minimal estimate. As mentioned, our file does not yet include all citations for tax delinquency, and we have doubtlessly missed many true matches. The conclusion must be that the menace of financial ruin was not limited to small and marginal groups of urban society. Rather, it cast an extensive shadow even over the elite classes. For example, the richest citizen at Florence enrolled in the great survey of 1427, known as the Catasto, was messer Palla di Nofri Strozzi. His assets after deductions surpassed 100,000 gold florins. But in 1431, when "viewed" for election to the "Six of the Mercanzia," he was declared to be *in speculo,* and was cited again for fiscal delinquency in 1434.[13] In these same years, three of his sons, Lorenzo in 1431, Nofri in 1434, and Palla in 1426, were found to be delinquent, and even two of his grandsons (offspring of the deceased Francesco), Carlo and Giovanni: both were disqualified in 1434. The entire lineage seems to have been in a state of fiscal disarray. More surprising is the appearance in the dread mirror of tax arrears of the head of the Medici faction and architect of its hegemony over Florence, Cosimo di Giovanni di Bicci. The Florentine government after his death would honour him with the title *pater patriae.* But he too was several times caught in the mirror of non-payment of

---

[13] Archivio di Stato di Firenze (henceforth ASF), Mercanzia, reg. 83, fol. 13, 30 August 1431; and ASF, Tratte, reg. 198, fol. 163, 29 August 1434. For his sons, see ASF, Tratte, reg. 198, fol. 91, 28 August 1431 (Lorenzo); reg. 198, fol. 166, 12 September 1434 (Nofri); and reg. 197, fol. 148, 28 April 1426 (Palla). The grandchildren appear in Tratte, reg. 198, fol. 158, 28 June 1434 (Carlo), and reg. 198, fol. 161, 29 August 1434 (Giovanni).

fiscal dues, in 1430, 1439, and 1441.[14] The fortunes of even the most prominent Florentines seem to have been remarkably insecure.

At what ages were these Florentine citizens likely to experience fiscal and financial difficulties? The total number of exclusions for reason of tax arrears, which these 1,088 citizens accumulated, is 2,177. Although the electoral officials destroyed the slip of paper containing the name of the delinquent, that name could easily appear again in the drawings for a different office. We can judge the relationship between age and insolvency by comparing the group of citizens cited for tax delinquency with the entire group of potential office holders living in 1429-1435. In Table 1, the second column shows the distribution by decades of age of those citizens caught "in the mirror." It should be remembered that the same Florentine could be "viewed" and excluded several times, as each office had its separate purse. The third column shows the distribution again by decades of life of the entire group of office holders in the year 1432, the middle year of the range 1429-1435, when the earliest registrations were made. This distribution should roughly approximate the age pyramid of the potential office holders as it might be found at any time in the fifteenth century. The ratio in column four shows the relationship between the two columns, and because of multiple citations of the same person can go well above unity.

Table 1			
Ages of Florentine Citizens in Tax Arrears (Cohort Living in 1429-1435)			
Age	Number of Citations (a)	Distribution in 1432 (b)	Ratio (a/b)
0-9	33	1,850	0.01
10-19	138	1,284	0.10
20-29	262	1,051	0.24
30-39	314	735	0.42
40-49	365	686	0.53
50-59	406	238	1.70
60-69	383	126	3.03
70-79	173	38	4.55
80-89	59	12	4.91
90-99	44	7	6.28

Source: For births, ASF, Tratte, regg. 39 and 1093; for those in tax arrears, ASF, Tratte, regg. 190-198 and Mercanzia, regg. 78-88.

[14] ASF, Mercanzia, reg. 83, fol. 7, 15 September 1430; reg. 84, fol. 202, 16 December 1439; reg. 84, fol. 28, 20 December 1441.

Not surprisingly, the number of very young tax delinquents are few, for evident reasons. Most little children remained under the authority of their fathers, and had no independent fiscal responsibility. Some orphans might have been excluded for reason of age, before it was even discovered that they were also in tax arrears. The few young delinquents represent orphans who received an inheritance containing more debts than assets. Even then, they had the option of refusing the inheritance, as more damaging than profitable to their interests.

The proportions of delinquents increase rapidly in the second and third decades of life, even as the young Florentines were achieving fiscal and financial independence (as we shall see, it was not unusual for fathers to emancipate their children at young ages). The rate of increase falls from about 30 to 50 years of age. The Florentine male would normally marry about age 30, and gain use of the substantial dowry that his bride brought into his household. The children born to him did not place heavy demands on his assets over the first twenty years of his marriage. After age 50, however, the proportion of delinquents soars, and reaches stunning levels in the last decades of life. Many old Florentines must have passed their last years in permanent tax arrears, and in destitution.

This association of old age and impoverishment can be illustrated through the individual careers of many prominent Florentines. Matteo di Niccolo Corsini, a merchant who spent seventeen years abroad, left an encumbered inheritance when he died in 1402, at the age of 79. In 1411 his heirs still had not satisfied the government's claims against it for delinquent taxes.[15] Gregorio di Stagio Dati pursued a long and apparently successful career as a silk merchant, served as standard-bearer of justice, and was seven times consul of his guild. In his memoirs, he describes in mournful numbers his financial situation when he was 71 years old.[16] In 1432 and 1433 the comment "in speculo" flags his name in the electoral lists.[17] Messer Luca di Buonaccorso Pitti, who, with his great palace, gave Florence a hitherto unprecedented display of private magnificence, also ended his life – he died at age 77 – under a financial cloud. In 1480, eight years after his death, one of his heirs declares: "this inheritance of messer Luca my father has many burdens of debts and bequests."[18] He

---

[15] ASF, Tratte reg. 150, 1 June 1411. Niccolo's son is said to be "pro patre in speculo."

[16] Gregorio Dati, *Il libro segreto,* ed. Carlo Gargiolli, Scelta di curiosità letterarie inedite o rare 102 (Bologna, 1869), p. 120.

[17] ASF, Tratte, reg. 155, 1 January 1432 and 1 January 1433.

[18] ASF, Catasto, reg. 997, fol. 322, declaration of Iacopo de messer Luca Pitti: "Questa redita di messer Lucha mio padre a molti incharichei di debiti e di lasci ...." He also affirms: "A me ne tocha la sesta parte della gravezza e non piu." The inheritance, but not the tax claims against it, is described ibid., reg. 998, fol. 415, where each of the six heirs could claim 1,067 florins and 7 *solidi a oro.*

emphasizes that he is heir to only one-sixth of his father's patrimony, clearly implying that Luca's liabilities outweighed his assets. Even the greatest Florentine merchants risked destitution in later life.

Our file of tax delinquents also allows us to ask whether there is a relationship between profession and impoverishment. Table 2 shows the average age of tax delinquents, according to the office for which they were being considered. The offices are the Tre Maggiori, the "Six of the Mercanzia," and the consuls or captains of twenty of the twenty-one recognized guilds. Consuls for the judges and notaries were separately elected, and therefore are not represented in the table.

All Florentine officeholders were required to join a guild, but many of them did not actively pursue the profession. However, we can assume that those who were chosen as captains or consuls really were active in the "art" or craft they represented.

Although we do not know the size of the guild membership, Table 2 at least suggests that tax delinquency and bankruptcy were much more frequent in those professions that operated with large amounts of capital, than in the lesser trades, which required little. Put another way, practitioners of the seven (here, six) major, capital-intensive professions were more likely to experience financial strain than the small shopkeepers and artisans.

They were also likely to experience these financial difficulties later in life than members of the minor guilds. One sharp contrast that emerges out of Table 2 is the high age of candidates excluded from the "Six of the Mercanzia," in relation to all the other communal offices. The Six were a kind of mercantile aristocracy, responsible for promoting the commercial prosperity of the city. The office was comparable in dignity to the priorate, as the priors were the chief governing board in the government. Yet the average age of excluded candidates for the Six was some twenty years higher than that of the rejected candidates for the priorate. This suggests that those actively involved in a mercantile career were likely to face financial duress at advanced ages; members of the urban elite less concerned with commerce faced failure at moments more randomly distributed through their lives.

The same conclusion would seem to follow from an examination of the elections to the major and minor guilds. The guild of Calimala, which included the city's greatest merchants, also shows, with the exception of the innkeepers, the oldest age of insolvency in the entire list, 58.61 years, and the bankers at 56.60 years are not much younger. The wool merchants, who constituted the largest but not the richest of the major guilds, also have the youngest average age among the bankrupt, 49.24 years.

But four of the minor guilds show even younger ages. Again there seems evident an association between the use of large sums of capital in one's profession and fiscal insolvency in later life.

Table 2		
Average Age of Candidates in Tax Arrears, by Office		
A. Communal Offices		
Office	Number	Average Age
Six of the Mercanzia	121	55.97
16 Standard-bearers	188	43.28
12 Good Men	253	42.03
Notary	3	40.00
Standard-bearer of Justice	8	38.75
Prior	171	35.47
B. Captains of Major Guilds		
Office	Number	Average Age
Merchant (Calimala)	132	58.61
Furrier	54	57.81
Banker (Cambio)	104	56.60
Silk Merchant	146	52.57
Spice Merchant	151	51.61
Wool Merchant (Lana)	269	49.24
C. Captains of Minor Guilds		
Office	Number	Average Age
Innkeeper	27	59.51
Locksmith	48	56.68
Old Clothes Merchant	49	55.06
Butcher	34	53.52
Cuirass Maker	36	53.27
Iron Worker	70	53.20
Leather Worker	29	51.82
Shoemaker	22	51.45
Hosier	38	50.63
Master of Stone	19	49.31
Carpenter	21	47.66
Oil and Soap Dealer	64	47.60
Baker	29	46.17
Vintner	88	44.64

Source: Same as Table 1. Observations are limited to males living in 1429-1435 and entered into the birth registrations.

Why should this be? It would seem that patrimonies based largely on real property and those containing chiefly liquid capital imposed quite different constraints on those who would manage them, enlarge them, or at least preserve them over time. And those constraints reverberated back upon the organization of the household and the authority of its chief. The peasant property owner was under little compulsion to divide his holdings and to assign portions to his heirs well before his death. Rather, good management of the land recommended that the holdings be kept integral for as long as possible. As he aged, the peasant owner could look to the energies of his children, growing or already grown, to compensate for his own declining powers. The farm was most efficiently worked by the collective efforts of a family. The association of a large family and an integral patrimony seems especially intimate in a rural setting. If a young peasant should depart from his parents' home, he would usually join, as a hired hand, another big household; or he would quickly marry, and begin recruiting the large menage he needed to manage a farm. Large households under the authority of a single chief, and stable, integral holdings: these were the foundations of productivity and prosperity in the countryside.

To be sure, the peasant owner would likely experience some pressures to convey property to his children before his death. His daughters required dowries, and sons might wish for an independent life on their own parcels. But, at least in Tuscany, the peasant owners were able to accommodate these desires without significantly dismantling their holdings. Dowries were small in the countryside, and departing sons seem not to have taken much property with them.

Similarly, no reason of good management pushed the rentier, or the rich landlord, into dividing his patrimony well before his death. He could support even his grown children from his rents, and manage his properties with the help and counsel of his sons. He gained nothing from the early division of his estate, and the act would probably not enhance the revenues it yielded.

These factors affected the developmental cycle of rural households in regard to wealth – a subject we have examined in previous publications.[19] As can be shown from the Catasto of 1427, household heads in the countryside tend to grow richer as they grow older. The richest chiefs in rural areas are consequently the oldest, with the exception only of minor heirs who have not yet divided their inheritance. But this last type of estate represents as much the last stage in the developmental cycle of the

---

[19] Herlihy and Klapisch-Zuber, *Toscans,* pp. 491-494; David Herlihy, "Mapping Households in Medieval Italy," *Catholic Historical Review* 58 (1972) 1-24.

rural patrimony as it does the first. This correlation of age and wealth establishes that a patriarchal system of property management and household organization prevailed in the countryside. Many heads of rural families could look forward to a materially untroubled senescence. They willingly followed the counsel of Ecclesiasticus, and kept their patrimonies under their own control until their deaths.

Within the commercial economy – and commercial professions – of the city, the family usually did not function as a tight team of workers, and the family head early felt powerful pressures to divide his holdings, well before his final hours. There were several considerations prompting him to convey substantial portions of his patrimony to his children.

First of all, to render his capital productive, the household head had to marry his moneys to the energies of an entrepreneur, usually young, often his own son. This active partner would typically seek to multiply the moneys in distant markets – at Rome or Venice, Bruges or London. He had to be given control over as well as possession of these resources. In the world of long-distance trade, opportunities for profit were often fleeting. The young merchant could not wait for authorization from a distant, uninformed father to buy or sell, lend or borrow, save or speculate. The great Florentine commercial houses were often family based; the enterprise that sustained them was not. Rather, success in long-distance trade demanded individual effort, and favoured the early emancipation of the young.

Then, too, in retaining or dispensing his resources, the urban head of family faced a difficult choice. Doubtlessly he wished to retain his wealth, to support himself in his final years. Doubtlessly too, this desire helped give to the aged a widespread reputation for avarice and stinginess.[20] But he had also to consider the interest of his lineage. By retaining control over his property, he would obstruct the marriages of his daughters and the careers of his sons. Dowries were high within the city, and marriage came early for the urban girl. When he was in his 50s, the father would usually have to decide whether to seek brilliant and expensive marriages for his daughters. He would gain thereby the prospect of grandchildren in the female line, and, perhaps even more important in this male-dominated society, enjoy the support of a *bel parentado*, an influential group of in-laws. It cost less to consign girls into convents, but this choice served only poorly the interests of the lineage.

The urban heads of households, especially those engaged in the mercantile professions, needed early to establish sons in careers as well as

---

[20] On attitudes towards the aged in Tuscany, see Herlihy and Klapisch-Zuber, *Toscans*, pp. 606 ff.

daughters in marriage, and this too required substantial amounts of capital. They looked to their sons to repair and restore the family's fortunes, always threatened by the need to support many heirs. Once successful as merchants, the sons marry, and preserve over time the name and station of the lineage.

Another set of records in the Florentine State Archives captures this early conveyance of property from the older to the younger generations. These are the acts of formal emancipation.[21] According to the Roman law, which Florence respected, the father's power over his children, his *patria potestas,* lasted as long as the father survived. Even when physically mature, unemancipated sons and daughters could not enter into binding legal agreements, or acquire or dispense properties, without their father's agreement. In particular, the unemancipated son could not function as an independent merchant. The Florentine Archives have preserved many acts of emancipation scattered through the notarial chartularies, and two registers in two separate deposits, the Mercanzia and the Repubblica. Our consideration is here limited to the last register, which begins in 1422, and we shall end our scrutiny in 1500.

Florentine fathers, when they freed their sons, almost invariably endowed them with property. This conveyance of property to emancipated sons was called, like the comparable settlement upon daughters, a *dos, dota,* or dowry. The amounts of wealth involved were often substantial. In 1382 Matteo Corsini, when he emancipated his oldest son Piero, gave to the boy – he was only 16 – two farms, which Piero later sold for the considerable sum of 1,600 gold florins.[22] In 1468, when messer Giovannozzo Pitti emancipated his two sons, he gave both of them agricultural lands and, in addition, the sums of 1,200 and 1,300 florins respectively.[23] Emancipation, with an accompanying *dota,* thus conferred upon the son not only judicial capacity, but the material means that he needed to function independently in society and launch a career.

In some few of the acts, both the occupation of the father and the age of the son are stated. Table 3 shows the average age of emancipated sons according to the father's profession. Those fathers who style themselves *civis et mercator florentinus,* "Florentine citizen and merchant," appear with notable frequency. Only notaries are encountered in the registers

---

[21] On emancipations at Florence, see Thomas Kuehn, *Emancipation in Late Medieval Florence* (New Brunswick, New Jersey, 1982).

[22] *Il libro di ricordanze dei Corsini (1362-1457),* ed. Armando Petrucci, Fonti per la storia d'Italia 100 (Rome, 1964), p. 67.

[23] Alfonso describes his *dota* in ASF, Catasto, reg. 906, fol. 49, 1469, and Giovanni ibid., fol. 385. The emancipation of both sons is registered in ASF, Repubblica, Emancipazioni, reg. 8, fol. 200.

more often than the *mercatores,* but notaries also formed the largest
single occupational group within the city of Florence, at least in 1427.[24]
The term, to be sure, is not precise, but seems to have identified members
of all the major guilds.

Table 3		
Ages of Sons at Emancipation, 1422-1500		
Profession	Number	Average Age
Merchant (Mercator)	22	15.50
Retail Merchant (Rigattiere)	8	15.75
Dyer	5	18.00
Spice Dealer	10	19.20
Leather Dealer (Galligarius)	5	19.80
"Worker of the Soil"	9	20.11
Silk Merchant	7	22.57
Notary	11	23.45
Baker	8	27.63
Source: Repubblica, Emancipazioni, regg. 1-13.		

The average age at emancipation, for all groups in society, was 20.09
years, but of all groups in society, the merchants freed their offspring at
the youngest ages. The sons of notaries had usually passed their twenty-
third birthday when they were freed, and sons of bakers their twenty-
seventh. In contrast, most sons of merchants were endowed with the
power and property to make their way in the world before they had
attained age 16. The same impressions follow from a consideration of the
Florentine family memoirs. For example, Matteo di Niccolo Corsini, the
merchant whom we previously encountered, emancipated his sons at the
following ages: Piero in 1382, at age 16; Niccolo in 1383, at age 10;
Lodovico in the same year, at age 9; and Neri, before he had reached his
eighth birthday.[25] Of all groups in society, the merchants were the first to
dismantle the formal authority of the father, and break his exclusive control over the family's resources.

One final consideration prompted the aging merchant to emancipate
his sons and supply them with capital: the threat of debts and taxes. The
moneys the aging chief conveyed to the young generation were effectively sheltered from the claims of his own debtors and of the communal
government. The aged should retain the family's debts and liabilities, but

---

[24] For size of occupations according to the Catasto of 1427, see Herlihy and Klapisch-Zuber,
Toscans, p. 297, Table 35.

[25] *Ricordanze dei Corsini,* pp. 66-75, for the emancipations. The births of the sons are given
ibid., pp. 87-95.

pass on its assets to the entrepreneurial young: this was sensible strategy for a mercantile aristocracy. It held out the best hope that the status and future of the lineage would be maintained. But it also left the old generation exposed to a high risk of deprivation and misery.

These, then, are the conclusions that our study of fiscal delinquency in fifteenth-century Florence would seem to support. In Florence and doubtlessly, too, in other commercial towns of the late Middle Ages, the threat of poverty in old age was not confined to marginal groups in society. Rather, it darkened the final years of many members even of the privileged classes. And poverty in old age was not entirely a social accident, attributable to bad luck. It might better be viewed as structural, in the sense that it was brought about by the very operation of the commercial economy. The economy of the town undermined the solidarity of the family and weakened the authority of its chief. In doing this, it deprived him of the means that might have assured him a comfortable old age. Capital had to be joined to individual enterprise, and enterprise was the monopoly of the young. Resources flowed down the generations much more quickly in the town than in the countryside.[26] Urban conditions thus raised a social issue – widespread poverty among the aged – that seems not to have been a pressing problem under the patriarchal family system found in rural society and in the earlier Middle Ages. Perhaps for this reason the great preachers in the late medieval towns dwelt upon the responsibility of the young to support the old – a duty they did not have to urge upon their hearers in other settings. The urban household may have lost in solidarity, but its members – particularly its older members – still had need of its traditional services. The urban old would doubtlessly have benefited, had they been able to follow the sage counsel of Ecclesiasticus. But this, the character of the urban economy and their own sense of duty towards offspring and lineage did not allow.

---

[26] On the development cycle in relation to wealth, see above, n. 18.

12

Three Medieval Widows and a Second Career

Margaret Wade Labarge

Ottawa

Medieval widows were not all elderly, nor all endowed with the freedom of action that the term "a second career" implies. Nevertheless, among the upper classes widowhood could provide for the first time in a woman's life a freedom of action and choice she had not previously enjoyed, and the personal control of resources that came to her through dower, marriage portion, or her own inheritance. Many widows, especially in their thirties and forties (considered old for women in medieval terms), wanted to avoid remarriage, particularly if they had children whose inheritance might be compromised by the actions of a second husband. They devoted themselves to managing their estates, to safeguarding the heir's inheritance until he reached the age to assume full control, and to properly placing the younger children. Such maintenance of family position was recognized as an overriding obligation, and also provided valuable security for the woman herself. Some took on the widow's mantle, solemnly promising to remain continent and not remarry, but continued to live in ordinary society. Others, after their family tasks had been achieved, used a nunnery as a convenient place of retirement, boarding themselves and some of their retinue in a religious house to which they had ties of family or patronage and where they had been able to arrange a suitable corrody. Such secular boarders often caused considerable uproar among the nuns, and if the terms of the corrody were too generous the nunnery obtained some ready money but carried a heavier burden than it could support. Bishops on visitation usually disapproved because the ladies' fine clothes, little dogs, and very worldly behaviour

Aging and the Aged in Medieval Europe, ed. Michael M. Sheehan, CSB. Papers in Mediaeval Studies 11 (Toronto: Pontifical Institute of Mediaeval Studies, 1990), pp. 159-172. © P.I.M.S., 1990.

gave a bad example to the nuns.[1] However, some widows turned to an active religious life and, in reality, took up a new career.

Because of their superior social position these women had the luxury of a choice among several patterns of religious life, as recluse, or nun, or mystic living a devout life in the world. Three noble widows of the thirteenth and fourteenth centuries provide an example of each type and illustrate such a decision in concrete terms. Loretta, widowed countess of Leicester, became a recluse by 1221 and her sister Annora followed the same route eleven years later. Ela, countess of Salisbury in her own right, founded Lacock Abbey in 1232, entered it as a nun, and served as its abbess for nearly twenty years. St. Birgitta, wife and daughter of high-ranking Swedish nobles, was critic and warning voice to popes and kings of the second half of the fourteenth century through her mystical *Revelations,* written in her widowhood. These widows exercised influence, not only as religious, but also in the life of their time. Although we cannot now be certain of their motives for choosing a religious life, it is reasonable to suggest the possible mix of religious and secular considerations that influenced them. The terms of documents by the countesses Loretta and Ela demonstrate their concern to ensure continued prayers for their own souls and those of their husbands and relations.[2] The expanding influence of the Cistercians, then the Franciscans and Dominicans, encouraged a more personal religion among the laity. Upper-class women were especially affected by these orders because their own relations had joined them and their families were often founders or patrons of their houses. These contacts and the growing popularity of the books of hours for lay use extended the new emotional emphasis on the humanity and sufferings of Christ and on devotion to the Blessed Virgin and increased personal piety.[3] At the same time these widows, despite frequent clerical denigration of marriage, did not look back on married life with distaste. However, they saw the advantages for a widow of the religious state, which not only provided the opportunity for a devout life but also offered legal and moral safeguards against physical harm at a time when violence was prevalent. As well, life in a nunnery was not only stable but socially acceptable, allowing outlets for female talents and the continued exercise of authority. By the mid-fourteenth century female mystics were both popular and influential among the highest ranks.

---

[1] Eileen E. Power, *Medieval English Nunneries c. 1275-1535* (Cambridge, 1922), pp. 306-308, details the excesses of a somewhat later period.

[2] For Loretta see *Calendar of Charter Rolls* (henceforth *CChR*), Vol. 1, *Henry III, 1226-1257* (London, 1903), pp. 52-53; for Ela see William Dugdale, *Monasticon Anglicanum,* ed. John Caley et al., 8 vols. (London, 1817-1830), 6: 502.

[3] Richard W. Southern, *Western Society and the Church in the Middle Ages,* Pelican History of the Church 2 (Harmondsworth, Eng., 1970), pp. 228-230.

These three widows had certain common characteristics. All were part of the medieval establishment, and thus benefited from the privileged physical, educational, and social conditions that the upper classes enjoyed. They were also survivors with great physical stamina. In an era when women frequently died in childbirth, or from its effects – and both Ela and Birgitta bore at least eight children – they lived with apparent vigour into their seventies, often outliving their children. Ela's son and heir was killed on crusade, and her grandson at a tournament, while she still ruled as abbess. Three of Birgitta's sons and a daughter predeceased their mother. Even the childless Loretta lived to hear of the death at Evesham of her great-nephew, Simon de Montfort. These women also shared other advantages from their social position. The tenacious links of marriage and relationship, extended to a degree incomprehensible to us, allowed them an important place in the tightly woven social fabric of their time. They could marshal powerful friends and relations to find the resources and support that they needed to carry out their ideas. All had access to the revenues that allowed them to do what they wished and to support their chosen vocation. In addition, long years of social command had gained them respect in the wider world and enabled them to hold their own against their critics. Sir Richard Southern, in describing the attraction of religious life for women, spoke of the early abbesses as "masterful and formidable ladies ... (who) did not forget that they belonged to a ruling caste,"[4] and the statement was equally true of these three. Relevant information is widely scattered for the affairs of the countesses Loretta and Ela; only for Birgitta are the sources voluminous and personal. The process for her canonization inspired much testimony from eye-witnesses, while her *Revelations,* though edited and occasionally updated by the clerics who put her Swedish into Latin, retain a verbose naiveté and an earthy turn of phrase that suggest the experienced and shrewd woman, rather than her more scholarly secretaries.

The information about Loretta's early days is very sparse.[5] Her birthdate is not known, nor the exact date of her marriage to Robert Beaumont, earl of Leicester, though 1196 seems likely. In 1204 the earl died and Loretta was left a widow. She was childless and probably less than twenty, since she survived till at least 1266. The Leicester inheritance was divided between her husband's two sisters: Margaret, wife of Saer de Quency, earl of Winchester, and Amicia, married to Simon de Montfort,

---

4 Ibid., pp. 309-310.

5 Frederick M. Powicke, "Loretta, Countess of Leicester," in *Historical Essays in Honour of James Tait,* ed. John G. Edwards et al. (Manchester, 1933), pp. 247-272, has gathered most of the available information.

lord of Montfort-l'Amaury in the Ile-de-France and father of the Albigensian crusader. Not surprisingly, the attempted settlement was the subject of continuing litigation. However, Loretta's life interest in the Leicester lands assigned to her as dower, and her control of the lands designated by her father as her maritagium, was arranged expeditiously. Loretta and her sister Annora were among the youngest children of the large family of Maud and William de Briouze, a powerful marcher lord. William had energetically supported King John, and appears to have been closely associated with the king in the murder of Arthur at Rouen in 1203.[6] At the time of the Interdict John turned against William, confiscated his lands, and pursued the family to Ireland. William managed to escape to France, where he died in 1211, but his wife and eldest son were captured and starved to death in Windsor Castle. Loretta's lands were confiscated and Annora was imprisoned in England. Both of the sisters reappear in the records by 1214 – Annora being released from prison at the request of the papal legate, as she was the sister of the bishop of Hereford, and Loretta regaining her dower lands and swearing that she was not married and would not marry without the king's consent.[7]

Loretta was not anxious to marry, for she appears to have already been contemplating religious life. In 1219 she committed her dower lands to the bishop of Winchester and Philip d'Aubigny for three years, after which they would return to the king's hand.[8] Such a commitment suggests that she was arranging for a sufficient sum to provide for her support as a recluse. In addition, in an undated charter probably of about this time that was witnessed by several clerics but also by Philip d'Aubigny, Loretta granted much of her land in the manor of Tawstock (Devon), an important part of her maritagium, in "pure and perpetual gift" to the Hospitaller sisters of Buckland (Somerset) to find and support a chaplain.[9] By 1221 Loretta had been enclosed at Hackington, only a mile or so from Canterbury Cathedral by the old path across the fields. The village is on the rise of the hill from the River Stour, a location described by an early historian of Kent as "tolerably healthy but very damp."[10] Archbishop Langton, who would have had to give permission for Loretta's enclosure, had presided at William de Briouze's funeral while the cleric too was in exile. It has been suggested that Loretta spent part of the time between

---

[6] M. Dominica Legge, "William the Marshal and Arthur of Brittany," *Bulletin of the Institute of Historical Research* 55 (1982) 18-24.

[7] Powicke, "Loretta, Countess of Leicester," pp. 260-261.

[8] *Calendar of Patent Rolls* (henceforth *CPR*), *Henry III*, Vol. 1, *1216-1225* (London, 1901), p. 195.

[9] *CChR 1226-1257*, pp. 52-53.

[10] Edward Hasted, *The History and Topographical Survey of the County of Kent*, 2nd ed., 12 vols. (London, 1797-1801), 9: 42.

1210 and 1214 in France and got to know Stephen Langton then. It appears reasonable that there was some link of friendship between them. As well, six years after Loretta had retired to her cell Simon Langton also came to live at Hackington, as the archbishop had appointed his brother archdeacon of Canterbury and allotted the church of St. Stephen, Hackington as part of the endowment of the archdeaconry. Simon enlarged the church and built himself a house near it and close to the recluse's cell in the churchyard.[11]

Loretta may have adopted the life of a recluse out of devotion, with the desire to pray for her dead, but it is likely that she also regarded it as a stable refuge in a world that had treated her harshly. Even the highly spiritual Ailred of Rievaulx, in his letter of advice to his sister and other recluses on their proper behaviour and life of prayer, suggests several reasons for taking up such a life – not only the desire to cling more closely to Christ, but also the wish to escape the dangers of life or to avoid its troubles.[12] The difficulty and dangers of Loretta's early years of widowhood, and the knowledge that, as a childless widow and member of a family in disfavour she lacked strong natural supporters, would have made her decision seem eminently reasonable to her spiritual advisers. Similar circumstances, reinforced by her sister Loretta's example and the influence of the author of the *Ancrene Riwle*,[13] may have encouraged Annora's decision to become a recluse at Iffley a few years after the death of her husband, Hugh Mortimer. Annora then disappears from public sight, except for royal gifts of firewood annually until 1241 and one warm robe, but Loretta's existence and activity during more than forty years as a recluse at Hackington have left a number of traces. Her friend Alice, countess of Eu and lady of Hastings and Tickhill, sent her annually two quarters of wheat, two of barley, one of oats, and two sides of bacon – rather luxurious fare for a recluse. Henry III continued the grant after Alice's death and also provided her with lambs, cheese, and eggs from the revenues of the archbishopric.[14]

Even in her cell Loretta continued to have a number of contacts with the people around her. Most unusually she had a male servant, who in 1235 was exempted at her request from serving on juries, assizes, or

---

[11] J. Hayes, *The Church of St. Stephen Protomartyr, Hackington, Kent* (1978).

[12] Ælred de Rievaulx, *La Vie de recluse*, ed. Charles Dumont, Sources chrétiennes 76 (Paris, 1961), p. 44.

[13] Eric J. Dobson, *The Origins of the Ancrene Wisse* (Oxford, 1976), pp. 307-309, argues forcefully for Annora and Hugh's patronage of the three sisters for whom the treatise was originally written, and believes that the Anglo-Norman version was arranged specifically for Annora when she was planning her life as a recluse.

[14] *Close Rolls* (henceforth *CR*), *Henry III*, Vol. 5, *1242-1247* (London, 1916), p. 425; *CR 1231-1234*, p. 194.

recognitions during her lifetime.[15] From the records it would appear that she kept him busy, for she frequently interceded with the king or his officials for her neighbours. The prioress and nuns of St. Sepulchre, Canterbury, were quit of suit of court in lands that Hubert de Burgh had given them in Romney Marsh. Also at her request, a man was given a royal pardon for his brother's death, since the inquest Loretta had asked for had proved it was misadventure; a local woman was pardoned of her outlawry; and a poor couple was allowed exemption from tallage.[16] Such traces in the records suggest Loretta's continuing knowledge of and interest in what was happening around her, even in her old age. It is likely, but not provable, that some of the visitors from France to Becket's shrine in Canterbury – perhaps especially her nephew Amaury de Montfort in 1239 – may also have gone the extra mile to visit the distinguished old lady with French family connections who spent more than forty-five years in her recluse's cell.

Two documented occasions show that she was still regarded as a person of influence and importance on the public scene. In 1224 she furthered the cause of the first Franciscans to come to England. Their historian, Thomas of Eccleston, when he listed the early benefactors, mentioned three special patrons: Simon Langton; Sir Henry of Sandwich, a well-respected Kentish knight; and the "noble countess, lady recluse of Hackington." Thomas wrote with enthusiasm that "she cherished them in all things as a mother her sons, sagaciously winning for them the favour of magnates and prelates by whom she was held in the highest regard."[17] It is reasonable to suggest that Simon Langton, then based in France, had known their leader, Agnellus of Pisa, who had been *custos* at Paris, and smoothed the way for them with his brother the archbishop and also with Loretta, still a woman of considerable consequence. One of the magnates whom she influenced may have been Hugh Mortimer, whose nephew later became a friar in the Shrewsbury priory.[18]

More than forty years later, in April 1265, the elderly Loretta received a letter from Henry III, then under the control of Simon de Montfort, asking her to expound to the abbot of St. Augustine's and the prior of Christchurch all she knew about the rights and liberties of the stewardship of England as they pertained to the earldom of Leicester.[19] At this time Earl Simon was searching desperately for a way to legitimize his

---

[15] *CPR 1237-1247*, p. 133.

[16] *CPR 1258-1266*, pp. 10, 351; *CPR 1266-1272*, pp. 51, 32, 727; *CR 1254-1256*, p. 48.

[17] Thomas de Eccleston, *De adventu minorum in Angliam*, in *Monumenta Franciscana*, Vol. 1, ed. John S. Brewer, Rolls Series 4 (London, 1858), p. 16.

[18] Dobson, *Origins*, p. 305.

[19] Leveson W. Vernon-Harcourt, *His Grace the Steward and Trial of Peers* (London, 1907), pp. 125-126.

government, and it is perhaps indicative of his desperation that he should seek such information from an aged recluse whose connection with the earldom of Leicester was sixty years in the past. After so long a time the Countess Loretta had not totally disentangled herself from secular concerns. Ailred might well have thought that she spent far too much time at her parlour window.

Ela, countess of Salisbury, was more independently important than the Countess Loretta, her contemporary. The only child and heiress of Earl William of Salisbury, she became countess in her own right on her father's death in 1196, when she was still young.[20] In 1198 King Richard gave her in marriage to his illegitimate half-brother William Longespee, a respected knight, who was thus rewarded with a title suitable to his status. Ela grew up into an active, energetic woman and bore eight surviving children. There are two glimpses of her during her married life suggesting the religious and secular sides of her character. Edmund Rich – scholar, preacher, archbishop of Canterbury, and later saint – was named treasurer of Salisbury in 1219. Countess Ela appears to have been much influenced by him. Although the earl and countess as the local magnates had followed the bishop in laying the foundation stones for the new cathedral at Salisbury in 1220, Ela worried at her husband's neglect of the sacraments and persuaded him to listen to Edmund's warnings. According to the saint's monastic biographer, the earl was deeply impressed by Edmund's holiness and, moved by his reproaches and prayers, soon returned to his religious duties. The grateful countess was convinced that her husband's soul would otherwise have been doomed to eternal torment.[21] Ela's secular side is displayed in the vivid narrative of the St. Albans chroniclers. In 1225 Earl William had been fighting in Gascony in the expedition officially headed by Henry III's sixteen-year-old brother, Richard of Cornwall. Returning from this expedition across the Bay of Biscay the earl's ship was so buffeted by high winds and turbulent seas that he had to take refuge for a time on the Ile-de-Ré. A rumour came to the English court that Earl William had died, and Hubert de Burgh, the ambitious chancellor, saw the supposed widow as a glittering prize to be captured for one of his relations. With the king's consent he at once commissioned his nephew to go off "in noble knightly array" and try to incline the countess' heart to love. Ela haughtily informed the brash young man that she had now received news of her husband's safety, but that in any case

---

[20] George E. Cokayne, *The Complete Peerage*, 12 vols., ed. Vicary Gibbs et al. (London, 1910-1959), 11: 377-384, gives her birthdate as ca. 1191; the Lacock record, Dugdale, *Monasticon*, 6: 501, says 1188.

[21] Edmond Martène and Ursin Durand, *Thesaurus novus anecdotorum*, 5 vols. (Paris, 1717), 3: 1790-1791.

she would never have married him, since the nobility of her birth prohibited such a union. The embarrassed suitor slunk away, pursued by a final taunt on the foolishness of his errand.[22] Earl William died in 1226, some three months after his return, following a stormy scene at court with the presumptuous Hubert de Burgh and wild – and unfounded – rumours of poison.

From the time of her husband's death until her entrance as a nun at Lacock Ela dealt simultaneously with the requirements of upholding her secular position for the benefit of her eldest son, William Longespee II, who was still a minor, and with her growing interest in establishing a nunnery. One of her secular struggles is particularly interesting, as Countess Ela was one of the few medieval women to hold the position of sheriff, which she normally exercised by deputy. In 1231 she paid a fine of 200 marks to have custody of the county of Wiltshire and Salisbury Castle for life, though she was required to agree that neither she nor her son could claim hereditary rights to either.[23] On at least one occasion she exercised her rights in person. At Marlborough in 1234 the king heard a case between Countess Ela as sheriff of Wiltshire and the abbess of Romsey over their claims to hold the pleas of the hundred court at Whorwelsdon. The royal decision was to divide the pleas: the sheriff of Wiltshire was to have the view of frankpledge and the major pleas, while the abbess retained Romsey's rights over less important matters where felony did not apply and there was no king's writ.[24]

Some years before this suit the widowed countess had decided to found a nunnery on her own manor of Lacock and ultimately to enter it herself. Such a monastic foundation, though less usually made by women, who did not normally command the resources necessary, was an accepted charity by which magnates ensured prayers for the deceased members of their families and gained both the social and religious benefits that flowed to the kin of patrons and founders. The less frequent creation of nunneries (since women might pray but could not offer masses) was usually undertaken by fathers looking for a suitable place to bestow superfluous daughters,[25] or by a widow combining family feeling for her dead with suitable recognition of her own religious concerns and social position. With the advice and encouragement of Edmund Rich,

[22] Matthew Paris, *Chronica majora*, ed. Henry R. Luard, 7 vols., Rolls Series 57 (London, 1872-1884), 3: 102.

[23] Rose Graham, "The Civic Position of Women at Common Law before 1800," in her *English Ecclesiastical Studies* (London, 1929), pp. 366-367; *CPR 1225-1232*, p. 431.

[24] *Curia regis Roles*, Vol. 15, *17-21 Henry III, 1233-1237* (London, 1972), No. 1070, pp. 240-241.

[25] Janet E. Burton, *The Yorkshire Nunneries in the Twelfth and Thirteenth Centuries*, Borthwick Papers 56 (York, 1979), pp. 18-27, illustrates for Yorkshire the family role in establishing nunneries.

who remained in Salisbury until 1233, the process of getting agreements and royal and episcopal permissions was set on foot in 1229. In 1230 the bishop of Salisbury confirmed Ela's own foundation charter, which had also been confirmed by her son as heir, and declared the house was to follow the Augustinian rule.[26] Although Countess Ela shared the general English preference for the Cistercians, their general chapter of 1228 had refused to accept convents of women. Despite this the house was dedicated to Blessed Mary and St. Bernard, and more than twenty years later Ela was successful in obtaining from Citeaux letters of confraternity for herself and her community.[27] The countess formally founded her abbey on 16 April 1232, on a twenty-acre meadow known as Snaylesmead, bordering the Avon in her manor of Lacock, although by this time the buildings were almost certainly underway. The first nuns were veiled at Lacock in the same year and the new community began to establish itself. A series of grants show Ela using her influence to acquire oaks from the nearby royal forests for building and lime for the mortar, as well as stones from a local quarry. The abbey's revenues were enhanced by grants of an annual three-day fair in July, a weekly market, and further acquisions of land.[28]

Sometime during these years there was further proof of her continuing friendship with Edmund Rich. The life by a monk of Pontigny tells how the countess ran a high fever and Edmund promised to send a doctor who would quickly heal her. He sent a relic of St. Thomas's blood, which indeed worked a rapid cure. The archbishop humbly ascribed Ela's recovery to the martyr's merits, but his biographer stoutly asserted that "no one of sane mind" denied it was due to Edmund's own virtues. The monk underlines his humility by reporting that the archbishop would hardly look at, much less accept, the gift of precious jewels that the countess wished to give him in thanks.[29] It has also been suggested that the Anglo-Norman version of Edmund's *Speculum ecclesie* can be connected with Lacock. Given the material on which it draws, it would appear to have been composed while Edmund was preaching in Salisbury, and might well have been written as a mark of friendship towards Ela's foundation, which he had encouraged.[30]

Probably at the end of 1237, certainly before April 1238, Ela surrendered her secular position – she had already given up custody of the

---

[26] *CPR 1225-1232*, p. 328; Dugdale, *Monasticon*, 6: 501-503.

[27] *Victorian County History, Wiltshire* (henceforth *VCH Wiltshire*), Vol. 2 (London, 1955), pp. 303-304.

[28] *CR 1237-1242*, pp. 39, 41; *CChR 1226-1257*, pp. 274, 225; *VCH Wiltshire*, 2: 304-305.

[29] Martène and Durand, *Thesaurus*, 3: 1798-1799.

[30] M. Dominica Legge, *Anglo-Norman in the Cloisters: The Influence of the Orders on Anglo-Norman Literature* (Edinburgh, 1950), pp. 91, 94-96.

county and castle by January 1237 –[31] and entered her nunnery at Lacock. By August 1239 it appears that she had already been chosen abbess, an office she held until 31 December 1257. During this time, according to the annals of Lacock, she "strenuously governed" her house and nuns and "served most devotedly ... in fasts, holy vigils, meditations, assiduously strict discipline, and in other good works of charity."[32] Nevertheless, her life does not seem to have been unrelievedly austere, for the rolls show frequent gifts of venison for the abbess and oaks for her hearth. Even after she retired as abbess the king continued to send his kinswoman such special gifts.[33]

A final personal glimpse of Ela as abbess comes late in her life, when her son, William Longespee II, led a group of English nobles to join Louis IX's ill-fated crusade in Egypt. Matthew Paris – always eager to taunt the French – blames William's death at Mansourah on the insolence of Robert of Artois, Louis' younger brother, who derided the English as cowards so that William joined in the rash expedition led by Robert. The impetuous group was overwhelmed by superior force and all killed. The night of the battle, Paris asserts, Ela had a vision of heaven opening to receive a knight with all his arms. Recognizing the escutcheon, she asked who the knight could be who was so gloriously received by the angels, and heard a voice telling her, "William thy son." She noted the night and, when she later heard news of the great disaster, prostrated herself in memory of her vision, praising God that she, an unworthy sinner, had been privileged to be the mother of a son thus given the crown of martyrdom. Paris ends his account with one of his typical flourishes: "praising the constancy of a non-womanish woman, astounded at the maternal piety of such a great lady, not breaking down into words of lugubrious complaint but rather more readily exulting with spiritual joy."[34]

According to the *Historia fundatorum* in the Register of Lacock, Ela had retired in 1257 when she felt the pressure of old age, and died 24 August 1261 in her seventies.[35] She was buried in the choir of the abbey church, where she was ultimately surrounded by the bones or the hearts of her other three sons. Lacock was very much of a family house. Two granddaughters (children of her daughter Ida) became nuns there, while the family concern and protection continued throughout the century. Ela, the daughter named after her mother, who married Thomas, earl of

[31] *CPR 1232-1247*, p. 172.

[32] Dugdale, *Monasticon*, 6: 502.

[33] *CR 1247-1251*, pp. 138, 315, 381, 479; *CR 1251-1253*, pp. 97, 118, 388, 402; *CR 1256-1259*, p. 247.

[34] Matthew Paris, *Chronica majora*, 5: 150-154, 173.

[35] " ... demum vero cernens se senio et nimia debilitate affectam, cum non potuit, ut voluit, religioni suae prodesse, renunciavit, et recusavit praeesse," Dugdale, *Monasticon*, 6: 502.

Warwick, and after his death Philip Basset, continued to interest herself in the affairs of Lacock almost until her death in 1297. She intervened at court to help them gain privileges and to maintain their claims.[36] The family connection, always on the female side, was carried on by the daughter and heiress of William Longespee III. Margaret was only an infant when her father died in 1257, and on Ela's death she inherited her great-grandmother's title, though the earldom had been in abeyance since the death of the original William Longespee. Nevertheless, after her marriage to Henry de Lacy, earl of Lincoln, Margaret acted as patron, friend, and protector of the family house. Her death in 1309 was recognized as depriving them of powerful aid and counsel in both internal and external affairs.[37] The tradition inaugurated by Ela in her years as abbess, when she safeguarded her abbey's interests as she had earlier protected her family's, was carried on by her descendants for almost a century. Ela, in erecting some of its buildings, improving its revenues, managing its properties, and working for further privileges, used her secular prestige and friendships to advance her well-run and prosperous house of some twenty nuns. Both she and her descendants who carried on her work would have seen as suitable to her dual position and social status that her nuns at Lacock should mark the anniversary of their foundress with the distribution to 100 poor of a wheaten loaf and two herrings each, while they themselves celebrated with simnel cakes, wine, three courses at dinner, and two at supper.[38]

Finally, in a less conventional form of religious life, there is St. Birgitta of Sweden, who had an extraordinary career of religious and political influence during her thirty years of widowhood. Her unusual importance in England has led to the description of her as "that most popular of Lancastrian saints."[39] Her *Revelations,* embodying frank and unpalatable advice to kings and popes as well as lesser individuals, and her semireligious life and conception of the new Brigittine order are well known. Two facets of her life are relevant here. One is her strong emphasis on widowhood as an estate pleasing to God, a conviction she felt had been divinely reinforced by Christ's revelation to her that "a humble widow is more pleasing to me than a proud virgin."[40] The other is her enormous popularity in contemporary England. Birgitta aroused considerable

---

[36] *CChR 1257-1300,* p. 29; *Calendarium genealogicum,* ed. Charles Roberts, 2 vols. (London, 1865), 1: 336, 351.

[37] *VCH Wiltshire,* 2: 308. *List of Ancient Correspondence of the Chancery and the Exchequer,* revised ed., *Lists and Indexes* 15 (London, 1969), 27/74, 27/75.

[38] Power, *Medieval English Nunneries,* p. 121.

[39] Joycelyne G. Dickinson, *The Congress of Arras, 1435: A Study in Medieval Diplomacy* (Oxford, 1955), p. 146.

[40] *Les Révélations célestes et devines de Sainte Brigitte de Suède,* trans. Jacques Ferraige, 4 vols. (Avignon, 1859), 3: 461.

controversy, but, like other mystics of her time, wielded substantial moral and political influence on a wide stage.

The main facts of her life can be quickly stated.[41] She was born in Finnsta, Sweden in 1302/1303 and related to the royal house of Sweden through both her parents. Her bent for mystical experience began early, for at the age of ten she had an always-remembered vision of Christ crucified. At fourteen she was married to an eighteen-year-old Swedish nobleman, and they had eight children. King Magnus called her to the Swedish court in 1335 to serve as mistress of the royal household for his young bride from Namur. Her hopes of influencing the royal pair towards a serious and pious life proved vain, so after two years she returned home to supervise the education of her children and share with her husband in a life of increasing piety and asceticism. In 1341 the couple went on a pilgrimage to Compostela. After an illness on their way home her husband died at the Cistercian monastery of Alvastra in 1344, soon after their return. Birgitta then turned wholeheartedly to a life of prayer and penance, and began receiving mystic revelations, many of which included warnings to be transmitted to kings and the pope. These were able to gain wider distribution and effectiveness through her social importance in Sweden and her ability to ensure their forwarding to the important people involved.

In 1349 Birgitta felt divinely impelled to go to Rome. She was accompanied by Prior Peter of Alvastra and the Augustinian Peter Skenninge, her spiritual advisers and the translators into Latin of the visions she had written down in Swedish. They were later assisted by Alphonse of Pecha, a Spanish bishop who had originally retired to a hermitage but became part of Birgitta's household, probably in 1368, and acted as prime editor of her *Revelations*.[42] She remained in Rome at the head of a devoted company, leading a quasi-monastic life, until her death in 1373, although she went on occasional pilgrimages to shrines in Italy and in 1371 made a trip to the Holy Land. Her canonization was pushed vigorously by her devoted followers, led by her daughter Catherine, and despite opposition, especially from the French, was achieved in 1391. The Scandinavians insisted on having it confirmed by John XXIII at the Council of Constance and again by Martin V in 1419. Despite the problems of the Schism and the competing popes, they wanted to be sure of their saint.

Birgitta's voluminous *Revelations,* usually in the form of dialogues with the Divine Persons, the Virgin, and assorted saints and devils, are

---

[41] P. Debongnie, "Brigitte de Suède," in *Dictionnaire d'histoire et de géographie ecclési-astiques*, Vol. 10 (Paris, 1938), pp. 719-727.

[42] Eric Colledge, "*Epistola solitarii ad reges:* Alphonse of Pecha as Organizer of Birgittine and Urbanist Propaganda," *Mediaeval Studies* 18 (1956) 19-49.

vivid and dramatic, with homely similes and lively conversations. They express her passion for the reform of both church and lay society and bear a strongly personal imprint. Much of the English enthusiasm for Birgitta and her visions came from her message to the English and French kings in Book IV, chapters 103-105.[43] In a discourse by the Blessed Virgin, the sad state of the kingdom of France is discussed, along with the argument over the rightful king. The final text, which emphasizes Christ's wish that the kings should proceed to peace by way of a royal marriage, is actually a heavily revised version, probably by Alphonse of Pecha, of the original revelation of 1348. Birgitta had persuaded King Magnus to send this to Edward III and Philip VI. The early version declared that the king of England was closer to the throne of France than Philip, but that, as Philip had not taken the throne by violence, he should keep it for his lifetime. However, he should consider Edward as his eldest son and take him as his successor. Although plausible in 1348, when the English victory at Crécy was fresh and Edward young and vigorous, it bore no relation to the situation after the deaths of Edward and the Black Prince.[44] The poet Thomas Hoccleve paraphrased the later version in *The Regement of Princes,* destined for the future Henry V,[45] and English negotiators used it as a tool in their negotiations with the French at Arras in 1435 and four years later at Oye. In an apparent battle of the mystics, the English use of Birgitta's visions encouraged the French to put forward a visionary hermit who prophesied the final destruction of the English. Cardinal Beaufort, whether in exasperation or with a rare ray of humour, suggested that a marriage between Birgitta and the hermit might be a good idea.[46]

When Henry V decided to found two monasteries at the beginning of his reign, one was confided to the double order conceived by Birgitta. The king had probably been influenced in their favour by his sister Philippa, wife of King Eric of Denmark, who had Birgitta's granddaughter as the mistress of her household. The queen herself also had close ties with the Brigittine motherhouse at Vadstena. An earlier English enthusiast was Adam Easton, Benedictine monk of Norwich and cardinal, who had come to know Birgitta during her last years in Rome. He became her devoted admirer and defender, writing a long refutation of criticisms against her rule for her proposed order when her canonization was being pursued. It is possible that he circulated some of Birgitta's

---

[43] *Révélations,* 2: 401-407.

[44] Colledge, *"Epistola,"* pp. 32-33.

[45] Thomas Hoccleve, *Works,* ed. Frederick J. Furnivall, EETS e.s. 72 (London, 1897), p. 194, stanza 771.

[46] Christopher T. Allmand, "Documents Relating to the Anglo-French Negotiations of 1439," in *Camden Miscellany 24,* Camden Fourth Series 9 (London, 1972), p. 116.

writings to his old monastery in Norwich, as he bequeathed them six barrels of his books.[47] In any case, they had become known in England by the beginning of the fifteenth century, for Margery Kempe had the *Revelations* read to her and went to visit St. Birgitta's chamber when she was in Rome in 1414.[48] English translations of some of the *Revelations* became fairly common, and retained their place among the spiritual reading of such devout fifteenth-century English laity as Cicely of York, mother of Edward IV and Richard III.[49]

These brief sketches of the second careers of three upper-class medieval widows remind us that not all aging medieval women can be regarded as poor or passive. The fortunate accidents of birth in a class accustomed to the exercise of power, some wealth, physical good health (including survival of childbirth), and individual ability and initiative provided some women with the ability to arrange for themselves a different but very satisfying life during the years of their widowhood. It can be presumed that these women were reluctant to consider remarriage, whether from religious conviction, fear of disparagement in a second marriage, or concern for the successful launching of the children of the first marriage. Remaining unmarried could be difficult – the rich widow has always been a prize – especially in the thirteenth century, but a widow's choice of one or another form of religious life was legitimate and plausible. It would be approved and respected by her peers and considered suitable for her social level. The women discussed here had all been born to power and influence. Widowhood freed them to act as individuals, and they had the ability to adapt to their own desires and requirements the form of religious life each found most suitable. In so doing they made a secure and respected path for themselves in their later years, slightly separated from but not completely alien to the world in which they had originally moved. They also retained a considerable amount of the influence and power to which they were accustomed. Even the Middle Ages, with its much shorter life expectancy, occasionally had to face the problems of the aged in its society. These women worked out their own individual solutions to deal with aging. In so doing, they suggest some of the possiblities that might also have been adopted by other contemporaries, whose lives, unlike these, are unknown.

---

[47] William A. Pantin, *The English Church in the Fourteenth Century* (Oxford, 1955), pp. 122, 181.

[48] *The Book of Margery Kempe, 1436: A Modern Version*, ed. and trans. William Butler-Bowdon (New York, 1944), pp. 215-216, 82.

[49] *Revelations of St. Birgitta*, ed. William P. Cumming, EETS o.s. 178 (Oxford, 1929); Pantin, *English Church*, p. 254.

13

Retirement and the Life Cycle
in Fifteenth-Century England*

Joel T. Rosenthal

State University of New York, Stony Brook

Modern historians and social scientists are voracious chauvinists. Not content with the overwhelming bulk of all the extant records and material remains of human society, they lay claim to most of our institutions and cultural substructures as well. We are now told that childhood is a modern invention or discovery, though admittedly children themselves do seem to go back a way. This declaration of historical imperialism is only doing for childhood what comparable landgrabs have done for adolescence and for old age. No wonder modernists find so few fruits in historical study before the industrial revolution: they have cut all the roots.[1]

But we know that such recent discoveries are bogus. To the medieval self-consciousness childhood, adolescence, and even old age were all familiar entities. All were recognized as occupying distinct segments of the life line. They were different from each other, and different from full adulthood. Each had its own dominion, characteristics, and attributes. And for those who managed to survive to become the elderly, the "elde" of poetic discourse, there was even the possibility of retirement. Yes,

* A fellowship from the National Endowment for the Humanities made possible the research on this paper.

[1] For childhood: Philippe Ariès, *Centuries of Childhood: A Social History of Family Life,* trans. Robert Baldick (New York, 1962). For adolescence: G. Stanley Hall, *Adolescence,* 2 vols. (New York, 1907). For old age: Peter N. Stearns, *Old Age in European Society: The Case of France* (London, 1977); Stearns, ed., *Old Age in Preindustrial Society,* (New York, 1982); W. Andrew Achenbaum, *Old Age in the New Land: The American Experience since 1790* (Baltimore, 1978). For retirement: William Graebner, *A History of Retirement: The Meaning and Function of an American Institution, 1885-1978* (New Haven, 1980); Tamara K. Hareven, "The Life Course and Aging in Historical Perspective," in *Aging and Life Course Transitions: An Interdisciplinary Perspective,* ed. Hareven and Kathleen J. Adams (New York, 1982), pp. 1-26.

Aging and the Aged in Medieval Europe, ed. Michael M. Sheehan, CSB. Papers in Mediaeval Studies 11 (Toronto: Pontifical Institute of Mediaeval Studies, 1990), pp. 173-188. © P.I.M.S., 1990.

retirement in the fifteenth century. If we peel off the modern baggage labels and hotel stickers, we find an ancient, if not always an honourable, pedigree behind this particular handshake of modernity. In this paper I shall examine some of the types and forms of medieval retirement, and I shall discuss why – beyond the obvious economic reasons – medieval society did not convert a sporadic practice into a general institution.

As a working and workable institution, retirement is born of the fruitful union of two social constructs, one conceptual, one practical. The conceptual is the idea of the life line – a term I use in preference to the more evocative but less accurate "life cycle" – with its presentation of old age as a specific segment of the whole, a segment defined chronologically and/or experientially and worthy of its own peculiar treatment. As the old were distinct from those of lesser age, so were their problems and the problems they posed to and for others. Almost all human societies recognize something special about their most aged – as they do about their least aged – whether the old happen to be a bit over 30 or just pushing 90. However, the conclusion that each society reaches about how to deal with the aged can range from veneration and idealization to desertion on an ice floe. But regardless of precise delineation and of the varieties of treatment or of ascribed role, the aged tend to be set apart.[2] This seems to be a social constant, running from such biblical laments as Jacob's "my grey hairs with sorrow to the grave" through current "senior citizen" privileges and discounts.

In the parentage of retirement the practical partner is the labour market and the work force, that combination of socio-economic and psychological parameters within which disengagement and withdrawal can operate. The latter phenomena can only flourish with encouragement and subsidization. In the modern industrial world, when we wish to let people retire or when we acknowledge that they no longer have much alternative in market-value terms, we can generally afford this decision, considerable though the costs may be. In the fifteenth century the concept of old age as a special segment of life was certainly present. But retirement, as we shall see, was not usually its logical extension or concomitant attribute. Furthermore, in economic terms, it was hardly a solution for the many. What could be offered to or imposed on the few was in no wise convertible into a universal solution for a universal problem. Fifteenth-century society contained neither the will nor the coinage for such a conversion.

*   *   *

[2] For a survey of various "other" cultures, Leo W. Simmons, *The Role of the Aged in Primitive Society* (New Haven, 1945).

But there was retirement, at least in limited quantity and quality, as an institutional approach and as a personal solution. This essay makes no claim to a complete examination of all the options. Corrodies, we know, had long been used as a form of old-age pension. Fortescue said in 1470, "than shall men off his howsold be rewarded with corodyes and have honeste sustenance in þer olde dayis .... Ffor such corodes and pencions were ffirst geuen to þe kyng."[3] But corrodies are not treated here, and it is possible that we are prone to exaggerate their popularity.[4] Neither are the various family arrangements: the stem-family exchange, the private charity or pension, the widow's life in the household of the married son or daughter, etc. This spectrum of interpersonal strategies, with its wide emotional range and varying degrees of support, is beyond our ken. Clearly, the impoverished field hand, with his "Hosen overhongen his hokschynes on everiche a dise,/ Al beslombred in fen as he the plow folwede,"[5] was not about to live very well or very long on his annuities or on an accumulated family surplus. If he fell, an old man but still in harness, familial grief was more than tempered by the knowledge of one less mouth to feed.

We do offer here four variations on the theme of retirement, four nibbles at the larger cheese of a societal approach. We present these in an ascending order of modernity, of comprehensiveness, and of nurture. We begin with a pedestrian example that is actually a policy of superannuation imposed because of age, rather than a mutually agreeable retirement scheme. Nevertheless, age is the explicit factor, and the examples offer some food for thought. The regular victims of such a policy were the coroners, those keepers of records who probed into both criminal and civil matters of concern to the king. In theory their appointments were for life. As minor officials of the crown they were mostly men of at least small property, often with other local administrative and legal experience. Consequently their enforced retirement says little about real disability, as it tells us little about their affluence and life-style after dismissal. Superannuation may really hide some political desire to phase out an older (but not especially aged) generation of petty officials: the records are too laconic to admit of much informed speculation. The policy of enforced

---

[3] John Fortescue, *The Governance of England*, ed. Charles Plummer (Oxford, 1885), pp. 153-154. For Plummer's discussion of corrodies, see pp. 337-339.

[4] Richard Harper, "A Note on Corrodies in the Fourteenth Century," *Albion* 15 (1983) 95-101. Harper suggests that they were not so commonly used, and this seems borne out by an examination of the index of Archbishop Chichele's registers, wherein only three entries are cited: *The Registers of Henry Chichele, Archbishop of Canterbury, 1414-1443*, Vol. 4, ed. Ernest F. Jacob, Canterbury and York Society 47 (1947).

[5] From Pierce the Ploughman's Crede, quoted in *England from Chaucer to Caxton*, ed. Henry S. Bennett (London, 1928), p. 69.

retirement was administered by means of royal instructions to the sheriffs, who might simply be told to elect a new coroner, "William Hales of
Kirketon being too sick and aged to travail in the exercise of that office."[6]
The king often alleged that he was spurred to act in this authoritarian
fashion after learning from "credible witnesses" that so many men were
unfit for service. Sometimes these blanket dismissals were the real order
of the day. Between 1422 and 1429 the *Calendars of the Close Rolls*
show over two dozen such instances of superannuation, covering all cor-
ners of the realm and even nipping the verderor of Buckinghamshire.
Between 1429 and 1435 some 25 coroners for the counties and their sub-
sections, for example the East and West Ridings of Yorkshire, were
adjudged to be too old or too ill. Between 1435 and 1441 new coroners
were to be "elected" in at least twenty counties because the incumbents
were "too sick and aged" or "too weak and too hampered with divers
infirmites" to continue serving. Can we take these writs at face value?
Such "retirements" were not peculiar to the fifteenth century: in the early
years of Edward III 21 percent of 275 coroners had been relieved because
of old age, sickness, blindness, or paralysis.[7] The tides of extensive turn-
over seemed to ebb and flow. However, whatever the "real" motives
behind the wide-scale replacements, "too sick and aged" was the guise in
which they were dressed before being sent out in public.

So the king's coroners suffered a form of retirement, certainly one that
speaks to the idea that "old" may mean too old to be useful. Similarly,
there was a "retirement policy" for some men who sought and received
medical excuses for absence from the House of Lords. These excuses
have been collected by Professor Roskell in his study of attendance in the
upper house.[8] Since the obligations of attendance and service could be
unwelcome ones, a medical excuse might mask privileged treatment as
well as or instead of a real instance of diminishing capability. But there
were relatively few such excuses, and even if some favouritism existed,
the form of rhetoric is still worthy of note. Between 1399 and 1483 some
twelve men were given permission to absent themselves, for reasons of
interest to us: age, sickness, years of service, debility. Such excuses were
a permission to withdraw from public life, to retire. Since all these men
had incomes in no way dependent upon parliamentary attendance, the
royal nod means little regarding support and comfort. Of the bishops,

---

[6] *Calendar of Close Rolls, Henry IV*, Vol. 1: *1399-1402* (London, 1927), p. 21.

[7] Helen M. Cam, "Shire Officials: Coroners, Constables, and Bailiffs," in *The English Government at Work, 1327-1336*, III: *Local Administration and Justice*, ed. James F. Willard et al. (Cambridge, Mass., 1950), pp. 143-165.

[8] John S. Roskell, "The Problem of Attendance of the Lords in Medieval Parliament," *Bulletin
of the Institute of Historical Research* 29 (1956) 153-204.

some were excused because of specific maladies, whether curable or not. There was sympathy for Bishop Edmund Lacy in 1435, "prevented from riding on horseback by long-standing disease of the shinbones."[9] But in some instances old age was clearly indicated as the prime factor, at least in the wording of the excuse. Bishop William Heyworth was excused in 1439 "by reason of his age and infirmities," and Bishop John Arundel in 1474 "on account of his debility and old age," as Bishop Thomas Beckington had been in 1452.[10] Illness and long service in tandem sufficed to get Bishop Adam Moleyns an excuse granted in response to a petition "shewing that he is weak in body and sight and constrained in conscience to oversee his cure and in consideration of his long labours and usefulness."[11] Bishop Walter Lyhart was allowed to send proctors to Parliament in 1461: personal service was henceforth waived, "in consideration of his age and long service in France and elsewhere and of his desire to follow things divine."[12]

Most of these excuses were meant to be more-or-less permanent. Though Bishop Lacy lived twenty years after the trouble with his shins, he only attended two or three more parliaments and then sank back to the regular use of proctors. Beckington and Lyhart seem to have cashed in on their exemptions and neither ever attended another session, though they survived by thirteen and twelve years respectively. Some of the men were more clearly at or nearing the end of the road when the permission to withdraw was registered. John Arundel was dead within two or three years of the session from which he had been allowed to absent himself. Moleyns, already acknowledged to be "weak in body and sight," was murdered within a year: the most final of all forms of retirement, the most ironclad of excuses. Bishop William Booth received a life exemption in August 1464: he was dead before the end of September. These data are few, given the number of bishops crossing the stage in eighty-four years, but they argue that some excuses were justified, some men really *seen to be* in need of relief because of the ravages of time and nature. Nor is the story much different for at least a few of the secular peers. Lord Vescy was exempted because of "age and infirmity" in 1456, when he was about 66 and had some thirteen more years to live. A second exemption, in 1462, was for life.[13] The earl of Oxford was allowed to absent himself,

    [9] *Calendar of Patent Rolls* (henceforth *CPR*), *Henry VI*, Vol. 2: *1429-1436* (London, 1907), p. 543.
    [10] *CPR 1436-1441*, p. 362; *CPR 1461-1467*, p. 358; *CPR 1446-1452*, p. 558, and Thomas Rymer, *Foedera*, 3rd ed., 10 vols. (The Hague, 1739-1745), 5.2: 41.
    [11] *CPR 1446-1452*, p. 297; Rymer, *Foedera*, 5.2: 20.
    [12] *CPR 1452-1461*, p. 642.
    [13] Ibid., p. 285; *CPR 1461-1467*, p. 115.

"for good service in France, Normandy, and England, and in consideration of his infirmities ... (and) if he should come of his free will he shall enjoy all privileges as other earls or barons."[14] He was about 52 in 1460, and his execution in 1462 made academic any further questions of health and longevity. Exemptions to Ralph Boteler, lord Sudeley, and to John, lord Beauchamp of Powick, spoke of "debility and age," and one even conceded that "he shall not be compelled to leave his dwelling for war."[15] Sudeley lived for twelve more years, Beauchamp for thirteen, after the permissions to withdraw. If health permitted, they may have had some "golden years" without the burden of service.

So far we have seen an example of imposed or enforced retirement, and of permitted or limited withdrawal. They offer us a quick trip across the uneven terrain of a working life, briefly summarized as "construction, culmination, and reduction." None of our examples so far even lurches towards a larger social policy or outlook regarding age and service. Excuses and exemptions to peers and bishops are too individualized, too much in the realm of ruling class and feudal relations to lead directly to a broader policy or outlook. Nor was turning the coroners out to pasture, ostensibly because of age and debility, a serious answer to the chronic problems of an aging labour force. We know far too little about what was behind the wording of a close letter. We can now turn, however, to some other and perhaps clearer models. It is in the cities of the realm that we can isolate further strains of our elusive species. Like the king's government, the cities needed a constant labour supply to lubricate their machinery of public life. Such labour was largely honourific, and many men of substance sought to rise into and through the municipal *cursus honorum*. But for various reasons – hard times, other obligations, real personal disability – citizens might seek to leave as well as enter this prestigious work force. In medieval York the burdens of public life could weigh only too heavily on aging shoulders:

> Most often, aldermen were allowed to resign without payment or fuss but others had to pay and one or two had quite a tussle with their colleagues. John Tong, mayor in 1477, had to ask the council several times "for God's sake", to be dismissed because he was "broken by great sickness" before his demand was granted in 1490.[16]

14   *CPR 1452-1461*, p. 645.
15   *CPR 1461-1467*, pp. 72, 213.
16   Jennifer I. Kermode, "Urban Decline? The Flight from Office in Late Medieval York," *Economic History Review* 2nd ser. 35 (1982) 192. Also, Charles Phythian-Adams, *The Desolation of a City: Coventry and the Urban Crisis of the Late Middle Ages* (Cambridge, 1979), pp. 125-127.

London data bespeak a milder climate of urban politics. Men of 70 were allowed to escape from service on the city's juries because of age, and others were eligible for relief if they could argue some compelling collection of ailments and disabilities. Nor, in these instances, are we in an anomalous backwater of exemption. *The Letter Books* of the City show that scores or even hundreds of such cases were accepted and recorded through the course of the fifteenth century. Perhaps the size of the city ensured an adequate labour force and may have allowed the liberal retirement and exemption policy to be honoured. It was but another ordinary occasion when a citizen was "discharged by William Walderne, the mayor, and the aldermen from serving on juries, etc, except on urgent occasions, owing to increasing old age."[17] When one citizen asked to be discharged from his duties, an investigation was held to determine "if he be found to be seventy years of age." The worthy old man was more than vindicated, "he having been found on inquiry to be over seventy years of age and afflicted with deafness."[18] The usual slide from health to decline to decrepitude and old age is not hard to follow, as we find exemptions for "deafness and other infirmities," for "failing sight and deafness," for "deafness and increasing old age," or "as he was afflicted with colic and old age," or "owing to his suffering from sciatica and other infirmities," or "owing to ill health," or "owing to his being afflicted with stone," or "on account of deafness."[19] But mainly it was just plain old age, hard and irremediable. The mayor and sheriffs were told not to place Ralph Hogman, grocer, on the assize or on juries if he was indeed 70, "that age having been prescribed by the Common Council as the limit for such service and (they) to restore any distress they may have taken on that account." Old Ralph "should be discharged," and there was no doubt or equivocation in this order.[20] The collective weight of such an entry, along with so many others, is to move us – in company with a lot of elderly Londoners – towards some glimmer of social policy. It probably was one that could only exist in artificial or cultivated conditions. There had to be the luxury of plentiful and unpaid labour, offered by a large pool of men of substance, and few other places or institutions could match London in this regard. But that the building has a deep foundation is hardly a telling indictment of its attractive facade. Modern welfare policies have often

---

[17] *Calendar of Letter-Books of the City of London: Letter-Book K,* ed. Reginald R. Sharpe (London, 1911), p. 6.

[18] Ibid., pp. 86-87.

[19] Ibid., pp. 349, 59, 94, 347, 307, 309, 396, 190.

[20] Ibid., p. 271. For material on statutory limits of service and on mandatory or permitted ages of withdrawal, see Keith Thomas, "Age and Authority in Early Modern England," *Proceedings of the British Academy* 62 (1976) 205-248.

begun as controlled experiments under laboratory conditions or as the result of trial and error in some sheltered environment.

For the fullest analogue to a modern retirement and pension policy, we must turn to the church. Here, finally, we seem to have a propitious combination of ingredients, though not quite in a critical or self-sustaining mass: manpower, resources to subsidize both the superannuated and their successors, and an ideology concerned with the social consequences of age and disability on those below as well as above. Furthermore, since clerical status was for life, and parochial responsibility at least to the end of this world, there could be no question of waiting out any particular fall into senility or decrepitude, no ignoring the embarrassing dotage of an Edward III or a Henry VIII. And in statistical or demographic terms, life status in the church meant a clerical age pyramid approximating that of the entire population above age 20 or 25. The king's civil service or the municipal labour pool might be tilted, for the bulk of its personnel, towards youth and young maturity. But in its clergy the church had to run the full gamut of life and to deal with all the woes of its staff from or before ordination through and beyond burial. It could neither simply dismiss its elders, as did the king to so many of his coroners, nor allow a mass exodus, as with the septuagenarians on the London rolls. The church had to cultivate some of the sensitivity to individual problems we saw for the elite few of the House of Lords, and it had simultaneously to cope with an army of labourers that ran to thousands rather than to several score.

Bishops, we know, could pass into honourable retirement, with handsome pensions, and so, presumably, could abbots, priors, and archdeacons. But it was among the lesser clergy that the problems of age, of chronic illness, and of declining mental and physical powers could be most in evidence, hardest to hide. It was such men, often working in a considerable degree of isolation and without the "backup" support of neighbours and associates, who posed the toughest problems. Though the church had a large reservoir of unbeneficed personnel and some economic resources with which to combat the constant erosion in its work force, it is obvious that there were finite limits to such resources, as well as to the administrative willingness to expend them for such purposes. Clergy could be in short supply, at least in rural and isolated areas, and ecclesiastical revenues at the parochial level not readily transferable from locale to locale. So while it was a giant step for the church to embrace the concept of retirement-cum-pension, let alone to try to implement it, aging clergy were but one of many dilemmas, their demand for resources but another competing claim in a world of a limited and probably a shrinking exchequer.

If the fifteenth-century church had approximately 8,100 secular, beneficed clergy, it seems reasonable to estimate that perhaps 1,000 were over age 50, and at least half that many around 70.[21] And of these numbers, we cannot know how many were able to go on without noticeably flagging, how many could still cope but at a slower pace, and how many were in real need of replacement. All we have are occasional references to individual cases, from which we generalize with due caution and trepidation. For a few clerics whom the records illuminate, at least, there could be something very close to real retirement as we define it. Priests who could no longer perform their duties could be turned out to pasture with relief from labour and with comfortable or even handsome pensions. An unfortunate priest who had to step down in 1414 was consoled by his bishop, an understanding superior who recognized that retirement was a necessity, not a sensual indulgence. Bishop Rede of Chichester admitted the wisdom of the move, "because you are broken down by age and weakened in sight by palsy of the eyes, and for many years incurably troubled with heavy sickness, as notoriously you are now troubled." The poor man was to receive 12 marks annually from his church's revenues.[22] Under the burdens of age monks could leave the cloister, canons their residential duties. Some men needed but a lesser dispensation, as the priest who "on account of his old age and bodily weakness" was allowed to eat meat during seasons of abstinence.[23] But there was no hiding from the fact that even the most dedicated could break down. A chantry priest who was "old and ailing" was allowed a deputy, "removable at will."[24] Does this mean that recovery was a possibility, or rather, that there was freedom to shift marginal personnel? Probably the latter. Certainly few parishioners at Abbot's Ripton expected to see the old rector resume his duties. He had been adjudged as broken with age, infirm, blind, and unfit to exercise his office, the parish considered to be without a cure of souls.[25] A combination of mental and physical infirmities and old age and blindness were more than sufficient to end the working life of the rector of St. Martin's by Loo in Cornwall.[26]

[21] Josiah C. Russell, "The Clerical Population of Medieval England," *Traditio* 2 (1944) 177-212.

[22] *The Episcopal Register of Robert Rede, ordinis predicatorum, Lord Bishop of Chichester, 1399-1415*, 2 vols., ed. Cecil Deedes, Sussex Record Society 8, 10 (1908-1910), 1: 164.

[23] *Calendar of Entries in the Papal Registers Relating to Great Britain and Ireland: Papal Letters* (henceforth *Calendar of Papal Letters*), Vol. 7: *A.D. 1417-1431* (London, 1906), p. 456.

[24] *Calendar of Papal Letters*, Vol. 15: *1484-1492* (Dublin, 1978), No. 905, pp. 497-498.

[25] *The Register of Bishop Philip Repingdon, 1405-1419*, 2 vols., ed. Margaret Archer, Lincoln Record Society 57, 58 (1963), 2: 297-298.

[26] *The Register of Edmund Lacy, Bishop of Exeter, 1420-1455*, 5 vols., ed. Gordon R. Dunstan, Canterbury and York Society 60-63, 66 (1963-1972), 2: 202-203.

The cases all sound legitimate. However, the percentage of such priests who were able to retire, especially those with adequate pensions, must have been but a fraction of those whose qualifications were obvious. Of the rest, few records other than an occasional complaint of parishioners or a petition for a pension in an episcopal register remain to tell us of the innumerable parishes served by the senile and the feeble, of the masses left unsung, the marriages and baptisms unperformed. Bishop Rede learned that the priest of Finden had been "afflicted through many years continually and incurably with severe and diverse infirmities and particularly with the complaint of deafness as he is now notoriously afflicted, so that he is now rendered altogether useless for the cure of souls entrusted to him." And how did the good and kindly bishop become aware of such a dreadful situation? Alas, it was "by public rumor and the notoriety of the fact which by no subterfuge can be concealed reporting it in many ways."[27] For those clerks fortunate enough to catch the enlightened interest of such a sympathetic superior, retirement could be a not uncomfortable chapter at the end of the longer tale. Men in the higher rungs of ecclesiastical careerism could draw lavish pensions. The prebendary of Oxton and Crophill in Southwell Minster was turned out to a green pasture: his annual settlement was for £16.[28] The canon of Osbaldwick's 40 marks in York cathedral was more than comfortable. The rector of Great Torrington's £20 was at least some compensation for the old age, weakness, and blindness that in 1453 forced his resignation and retirement.[29] To ensure payment, his successor was threatened with excommunication and sequestration if he defaulted. But can we determine, across the years, whether the rector of Norwold was being disingenuous? He was "almost a sexagenarian" and "constantly unwell ... on account of the unwholesomeness of the climate." He was now to be permitted to receive his church's revenues whilst residing "in an honest or religious place, or studying letters in an university or serving some ecclesiastical prelate."[30]

In a world where chantry chaplains often received but £5 *per annum*, and with beneficed clergy living on much less than the prescribed £10, a pension of £5-8 was quite passable. John Applebey's 5/6/8 from his vicarage was probably reasonable.[31] But other pensioners on £4 or 5 marks or 4 marks were getting dangerously near the poverty line, at best, with

---

[27] *Rede's Register*, 1: 24.
[28] *The Register of Thomas Rotherham, Archbishop of York, 1480-1500*, ed. Eric E. Barker, Canterbury and York Society 69 (1976), No. 907, p. 108.
[29] *Lacy's Register*, 3: 188-191.
[30] *Calendar of Papal Letters*, Vol. 13, pt. 1: *1471-1484* (London, 1955), p. 446.
[31] *The Register of Thomas Langley, Bishop of Durham, 1406-1437*, 5 vols., ed. Robin L. Storey, Surtees Society 164, 166, 169, 170, 177 (Durham, 1956-1966), 5: 115.

supplementary income or agricultural returns badly needed to ensure any degree of comfort. The vicar of Wath received but £2 as his pension. Presumably his church's limited resources were the reason he was so far beneath the vicar of Dewsebury's £10.[32] New priests appointed to parish churches could be saddled with the obligation to meet the pension of a predecessor. The payments were usually quarterly, badly needed by the previous incumbent, "by occasion of his bodily infirmity and senile age," and to be paid lest he be reduced to begging, "to the disgrace of the clergy." Shame and honour were motivating forces in northern Europe as well as in southern, it would seem, and sometimes the injunction specified that the pension was to be paid "lest he be seen begging."[33] The church could be badly embarrassed, as when it turned out that an aged prior of Bodmin, relieved of his duties because of "bodily weakness and blindness," had had his pension "maladministered" by lay executors.[34]

*   *   *

So it is not hard to argue that in some ways, to some degree, there were pension plans and retirement policies in fifteenth-century England. However, I have not worked to rescue fifteenth-century society from the idols of modernism and presentism to sacrifice it on the altar of sentimentality. Traditional society was as cruel as modern society. Our agenda now takes us from the question of what there was to a discussion of "why" and "why not." Why did the concept and institution of retirement not spread more widely, embrace more of the aging and impoverished work force in their comforting arms? Retirement and pensions not only sustain, in a material sense, they give some measure of dignity and reciprocity to the ultimate process of withdrawal and disengagement. They help counter the inevitability of alienation. If few people wish to be in a condition for which retirement is the only solution, many are nevertheless reduced to such a plight, while many more are in search of a halfway station on their long march.

Some of the reasons for the "half step but no further" are clearly economic. Only in a few leeward situations were resources forthcoming to carry those who had broken down. Most of the superannuated whom we have seen – the peers and bishops, the royal civil servants, and the citizen-burgesses – were left to their own devices. They were allowed (or forced) out of their normal obligations because of age and its attendant

<hr/>

[32] *Rotherham's Register*, passim.
[33] *Rede's Register*, 1: 25-26, 254.
[34] *Lacy's Register*, 2: 201-202.

woes, but they were hardly being thrown into the scrap heap. That their own resources were probably sufficient unto the need is comforting, given our itch for historical empathy. But the sources can be extended to argue, *ex silentio,* about the desperate plight of most others, not so protected. Furthermore, economic constraints were but part of the tale, and perhaps not the causal one. Societies – big or little, rich or poor, medieval or modern – somehow manage to pay for those items that are accorded high priorities. Then as now, war had more sex appeal than welfare, King's College Chapel and Eton more than almshouses and soup kitchens. Priorities are set by political and philosophical convictions, then justified through a rhetorical apparatus that can make much of economic "shortfall." In this sense there was no impetus for pensions and retirement simply because no one cared enough: they never achieved a high-priority status. The role Simone de Beauvoir has endeavoured to play, with her monumental *The Coming of Age,* is almost without western precedent.[35] In the fifteenth century, as through most of our history, the old and well-endowed took care of themselves, the old and poor suffered.

But in a larger explanatory framework the old were allowed to suffer, pension and retirement schemes to lie partially developed but dormant, because of a pronounced cultural dissonance between theories about life, age, and numbers on the one hand, and observed reality on the other. The society we have been examining knew about old age as a part of life, about the high incidence and survival rate of the elderly, about exact ages and vital statistics, and about the crying social needs of old men and women, prey as they were to hunger, poverty, disease, and anomie. That they chose not to translate awareness into social policy only puts them into a common pool with most other historical societies. To blame them is as pointless as to excuse them. I simply wish to show that it was ignorance neither of demography, nor of arithmetic exactitude, nor of social problems, that retarded the birth of policy-planning. We must assume that their world made sufficient sense with the pieces left in disjunction: neither sensibility nor conscience was offended.

From classical times through the Enlightenment there was a large body of literature that talked about the stages of life.[36] The seven-fold scheme of *As You Like It* is the most familiar to us, but other authors argued for almost every number of divisions between three and sixteen. The various

[35] Simone de Beauvoir, *The Coming of Age,* trans. Patrick O'Brian (New York, 1972).

[36] There is a large literature on this topic. For an introductory glimpse: Samuel C. Chew, *The Pilgrimage of Life* (New Haven, 1962); the two "Variorum" editions of *As You Like It,* that of Horace H. Furness (Philadelphia, 1890), pp. 121-129, and that of Richard Knowles (New York, 1977), pp. 130-138; John W. Jones, "Observations on the Origin of the Division of Man's Life into Stages," *Archaeologia* 35 (1853) 167-189.

partisans supported their cause through the use of mystical numerology, biblical parallels, and analogies from the heavens, the calendar, and the clock. I paid brief tribute to the weight of these writings in shaping the medieval consciousness when I said that youth, adolescence, and old age were all recognized as legitimate segments of a whole life. However, the exgetes of the "stages of life" metaphor wrote within the context of didactic and creative literature. None thought to move from theoretical exposition to a literary analysis of biographical and historical material, let alone to empirical studies. Each author presented old age as a natural and integral part of his scheme, and those whose tastes ran much beyond four or five divisions often made old age into a finely developed period, with gradations and internal subdivisions. But no moral was drawn, regarding our treatment of those in the most dependent and vulnerable segments of the life line. What was natural might be a source of pleasure, of moral edification, or of penitential reflection. It was not a social problem. The "senio ac debilitate nature" lay beyond the medieval sense of human engineering, just as the incurable and irremediable were of little interest to either physicians or philanthropists.

Cultural dissonance took many forms. One was manifested in the self-dramatizing tendency to emphasize the early approach of old age. Many saw its frosty touch by age 30 or 35, few argued to postpone it until 50 or much beyond. This view, from the wrong end of the telescope, was a commonplace through Europe, and it made individuals prone to adapt their self-perception to fit the external, literary scheme. We have before us a clear case of a cultural model shaping identity, of art telling nature how to define itself. Chaucer was only about 50 – an age attained by over half the late medieval peers and by most of the bishops – when he had Scogan say about him: "Wel I wot, thow wolt answere and saye: 'Lo, olde Grisel lyst to ryme and playe!'"[37] Caxton, who lived to be 70 or more and who worked to the very end, still said, around age 50, "age crepeth on me dayly and febleth all the bodye."[38] Lord Scrope was about 57 – far below the longevity of his father and grandfather – when he referred to himself as "senex aetate, debilis corpore."[39] Hoccleve was

[37] "Envoy de Chaucer a Scogan," lines 34-35; ed. Fred N. Robinson, *The Works of Chaucer*, 2nd ed. (Boston, 1957), p. 539.

[38] Caxton was just over 50 when he wrote these words, quoted in Sylvia L. Thrupp, *The Merchant Class of Medieval London* (Ann Arbor, 1948), p. 195.

[39] From Scrope's will, in *Testamenta Eboracensia*, Pt. 2, ed. James Raine, Jr., Surtees Society 30 (London, 1855), p. 184. This was John, fourth lord Scrope of Masham (ca. 1398-1455). His father Stephen, second lord, had lived from 1345 to 1406, and his grandfather Henry, first lord, ca. 1312-1392. Clearly, the stock was declining.

about 53 when he spoke of the imminent "ripeness of death": a little prematurely, given that he lived to somewhere between age 65 and 80. But literary conventions about the length of life and the onset of age weighed more in self-expression than did autobiographical experience. This is hardly the kind of conjunction of the conceptual and the practical that would lead us to general social policy regarding the needs of the elderly.

Nor should we explain away this dissonance on the grounds that medieval society, or the medieval mind, did not run towards precise thought, that it was more at home with allegory and symbolism. This is not so. When it suited their purposes, great precision (if not accuracy) was readily adduced. When there was the will, there was the mechanism, in both psychological and administrative terms. Inquisitions post mortem speak quite easily of heirs who were "fourteen on St. Lambert's day last," or "fifteen on St. George's day last," or "32 weeks," or "twenty and more on the day his father died."[40] A proof-of-age proceeding rested on the sworn statements of witnesses who identified themselves quite precisely, regarding age: 60, 60, 50, 50, 56, 70, 50, 80, 50, 51, 56, and 60, in a typical set of inquisitions.[41] In the Scrope and Grosvenor controversy, back in 1386, witnesses often had some chronological information incorporated into their testimony. Chaucer was identified as "Geffray Chaucere esquier del age de xl ans et plus armeez par xxvii ans." Nothing ethereal or allegorical about this. Nor was his precision unusual. Other men spoke of themselves, in an administrative-judicial hearing, in a similar fashion: "del age de sessantz ans et armez quarant anz et plus," or "del age de cynquant ans & armez trent et deux anz," etc.[42] When it was appropriate to the business at hand, men and women could be precise about their own age and that of their contemporaries. Data that argued for longevity and for the ubiquitous presence and needs of the aged were hardly beyond their reach. Large numbers of folk were in no doubt but that they were well-advanced into old age, into the sixth or seventh act of Shakespeare's drama. But they were conditioned not to move from such information to questions about themselves or the larger social order.

---

[40] *Inquisitions post mortem, Relating to Yorkshire, of the Reigns of Henry IV and Henry V*, ed. W. Paley Baildon and John W. Clay, Yorkshire Archaeological Society, Records Series 59 (1918), passim.

[41] Ibid., No. 28.

[42] *The Controversy between Sir Richard Scrope and Sir Robert Grosvenor in the Court of Chivalry A.D. MCCCLXXXV-MCCCXC*, 2 vols., ed. N. Harris Nicholas (London, 1832), 1: 51-66 passim. For Chaucer's entry, see *Chaucer Life-Records*, ed. Martin M. Crow and Clair C. Olson (Oxford, 1966), p. 370; and for instances of memory, at the hearings of 1386, reaching back to events of the 1330s, see Juliet Vale, *Edward III and Chivalry: Chivalric Society and Its Context, 1270-1350* (Woodbridge, Suffolk, 1982), pp. 61, 66.

If this is so for the intelligentsia and those atop the social pyramid, we can hardly wonder that others saw nothing in old age to necessitate any reassessment of priorities or resources. It comes as no surprise by now to learn that the aged were explicit recipients of but a fraction of the alms that went to such deserving beneficiaries as "presoners in the archebisshopis preson ... (and) to every pore man and woman ... (and) to xv pore madyns well disposed to mariage."[43] Many a hospital took, as part of its charge, the duty of "sustaining the pore and seck."[44] Few, by comparison, were explicitly instructed to look out for "fourteen poor men and women ... decrept with age, or (who) languished under incurable diseases."[45] If you outlived your quota of threescore and ten, it was "by reason of strength," as the Psalmist said. The extra years were not a negotiable social or economic commodity. There was no treasury of merit for the sweat of one's brow, for seniority *per se*.

Because age was part of the grand scheme, the aged of the fifteenth century were not deviants or interesting eccentrics whom society was pressed to treat. By rescuing them from the back-drawer of modern scholarly condescension, I have tried to show how a few – and how and why they remained a few – became flecks of light in the long dawn that prefigured modern social welfare. Gerontology speaks today in terms of four activity patterns for the aged: full engagement, full disengagement, gradual disengagement, and disengagement and reengagement. This seems reasonable, and I could easily produce details of medieval case studies that fit each permutation. But we should not berate the reluctant and wayward social conscience and social consciousness of fifteenth-century men and women, be they rulers, opinion-makers, or humble followers. Medieval institutions were not intended to be seedlings for their modern counterparts. Our great agenda is not to look for precedents out of context, but rather to assess the extent to which those people were like us, the extent to which they differed. In special or specific situations they met some of the problems posed by the aged with a quasi-modern institutional response. They phased some old people out of the work force, they let a fortunate few phase themselves out if they so chose, and they turned a few out to subsidized pasture. In most situations they displayed the universal human knack for rationalizing about the inescapability of other people's problems. Innocent III's *On the Misery of the Human Condition*,

---

[43] *Testamenta Eboracensia*, Pt. 4, ed. James Raine, Jr., Surtees Society 53 (London, 1869), p. 29.

[44] *Chartulary of the Hospital of St. Thomas the Martyr, Southwark, 1215-1525* (London, 1932), No. 11.

[45] Francis Blomefield and Charles Parkin, *An Essay Towards a Topographical History of the County of Norfolk,* 11 vols. (London, 1805-1810), 4: 432.

the most influential medieval treatise on age, is part of that genre of explanation that we now characterize as "blaming the victim." The aged were no doubt conditioned to blame themselves: isolation and hardship were but the natural returns for longevity. No one had promised them a garden of delights, whether young or old. De Beauvoir quotes Saint-Evremond, who wrote in 1680 that "nothing is more usual than the sight of old people who yearn for retirement: and nothing is so rare than those who have retired and do not regret it."[46] Clearly, the best solution to old age – God willing and strength lasting – was that of John Howard, sixth duke of Norfolk, dead in battle on the field at Bosworth, aged about 75.

[46] De Beauvoir, *Coming of Age*, p. 263.

14

The Quest for Security in Medieval England

Elaine Clark

University of Michigan, Dearborn

During the Middle Ages in England, as elsewhere, many men shared the view that the welfare of the old depended on the goodwill of the young.[1] Of course, the conduct of the younger generation was not easily overlooked at a time when few public agencies had either the means or the personnel to help the old and infirm. Plans for their welfare invariably took shape within the family as parents and children confronted hard questions about present and future needs, the allocation of labour, and the utilization of limited resources. This leads us to ask whether people without children and heirs experienced uncertainty during their final years. In other words, to what extent did a partnership between the generations actually afford the old and disabled a sense of security in past society?

One way to gain perspective on the problem is to examine the testimony of peasants in the courts of manorial lords. This testimony is notable for the detail it contains about the management and redistribution of resources among kin, about deathbed settlements of land, and about property arrangements for the old. In court, peasants had family agreements, pensions, and occasionally wills publicly read and entered into the official record. Widows testified about dower rights. The poor and disabled gave evidence about overdue rents and unpaid debts. For none was the threat of insecurity, or the need for support, an insignificant concern. As a result it would be an error to suggest that in the Middle Ages the things of most importance to people found little if any mention in the

---

[1] For specific references, see Simone de Beauvoir, *Old Age*, trans. Patrick O'Brian (Harmondsworth, 1977), pp. 144-165; George C. Homans, *English Villagers of the Thirteenth Century* (Cambridge, Mass., 1941), pp. 152-159.

Aging and the Aged in Medieval Europe, ed. Michael M. Sheehan, CSB. Papers in Mediaeval Studies 11 (Toronto: Pontifical Institute of Mediaeval Studies, 1990), pp. 189-200. © P.I.M.S., 1990.

courts of manorial lords.[2] It was, after all, in the manor court that peasants spoke about the problem of survival. In so doing they explained how the uncertainties of old age prompted them to plan for the future, to set priorities, and to voice what they valued.

Any number of court rolls can make this testimony clear. Of particular interest, however, are records that span the later Middle Ages and thus include the generations both before and after the Black Death (1349-1350). These years are well represented in the estate documents of lay and ecclesiastical lords throughout East Anglia and in the nearby counties of Berkshire, Buckingham, Hertford, and Middlesex.[3] Although these records are not perfectly matched over time, all bring into focus a region influenced by London's market and characterized by mixed farming, industry, and trade. All, too, suggest that the rural perception of security and social welfare was in itself decidedly complex.

To begin with, there was the problem of tenurial security in a world where peasants held customary land at the will of manorial lords. Certainly no lord would countenance his land being allowed to deteriorate in the hands of the infirm. Nor would a lord overlook the labour and services that customary tenants were liable to perform on his behalf. He not only derived a portion of his income from their rents but relied on tenants to cultivate his demesne, to plow, to seed, and to labour at harvest. It was hardly in a lord's interest, then, for his court to ignore the tenurial obligations of the old. Instead, what he required to facilitate the important business of manorial production was the assurance that customary land would be in the hands of productive workers. Consequently the disabled had to find caretakers to manage their tenements or, failing this, see the land revert to the lord. At law he had custody of the holdings of those tenants his court judged "impotent, incompetent or of unsound mind."[4] Simply put, the lord held their land in his own hands until a suitable caretaker was found. If no kinsman or neighbour came forward, the lord placed the burden of support on the jurors of his court, compelling them to find a tenant to help the old or to render the requisite rents and services them-

[2] For a discussion of this matter, see Michael Clanchy, "Law and Love in the Middle Ages," in *Disputes and Settlements: Law and Human Relations in the West,* ed. John Bossy (Cambridge, 1983), p. 65.

[3] See Appendix 1 for archival references. The following sigla will be used: BL, for British Library, London; BRO, for Berkshire Record Office, Shire Hall, Reading; CUL, for Cambridge University Library, Cambridge; ERO, for Essex Record Office, County Hall, Chelmsford; GLRO, for Greater London Record Office, London; NRO, for Norfolk Record Office, Central Library, Norwich; PRO, for Public Record Office, London; SRO, for Suffolk Record Office, County Hall, Ipswich.

[4] BL, Add. MS. 40625 (18 October 1336); CUL, MS. Dd 7 22 aa (6 May 1435); also note that enfeebled tenants could petition the lord directly for help, e.g. BL, Add. MS. 40625 (13 December 1317). This matter is discussed by Michael M. Postan, "The Charters of the Villeins," in his *Essays on Medieval Agriculture and General Problems of the Medieval Economy* (Cambridge, 1973), p. 116.

selves.[5] This is not to say that peasants retired from farming only at the lord's command. Nor is it to imply that a concern for family and the needs of the young failed to influence the decisions of the old.

All households confronted the problem of economic uncertainty whenever members lost the capacity to support themselves through farming or by-employment in a craft or a trade. It was at this time that property accorded the old an unmistakable asset. Land generated income. And when peasants possessed land, income could accrue to them whether they farmed or not. In other words, rights in property gave householders the necessary leverage to obtain labour and support from children, and thus to bargain for income maintenance in old age. Similarly, the plans made by parents and children took into account the social security to be derived from arranging for the continuity of the family estate. Such plans invariably included provisions for the use of land during and beyond the tenancy of parents. A final but equally important issue involved security in the afterlife and drew attention to requests that children honour parental debts and pray for the souls of the dead.

This combination of concerns ultimately informed the strategies that peasants devised to cope with the spectre of insecurity in old age. Admittedly the strategies reflected individual needs and preferences, particularly about how to settle problems that ranged from the onset of infirmity to the coming of age of children wanting land in order to marry, to a man's acute weariness after years of hard labour. Yet in every case the older generation recognized the importance of retaining sufficient authority within the household to minimize risk and ensure survival. To this end maintenance strategies brought into correspondence issues of tenure and contract, yet remained flexible enough to accommodate the needs of the old to the long-term interests of the young. Such an accommodation involved a partnership between the generations and also entailed the surrender of property rights, a transfer that in itself took one of two forms.[6] The first prescribed the delayed devolution of land on the young. The second facilitated conditional devolution.

Delayed devolution was the more commonplace practice. It derived from the parental promise that adult children could claim a specific portion of land at some future time, that is, when parents died.[7] This promise often coincided with the decision of the young to marry, and as such, the settlement of land remained a matter of familial negotiation. Nevertheless, a parent's intention to allocate property was publicized in court,

---

[5] BL, Add. MS. 40625 (18 October 1340, 19 May 1341).

[6] For a detailed discussion of both forms of devolution, see Michel Verdon, "The Stem Family: Toward a General Theory," in *The American Family in Social-Historical Perspective,* ed. Michael Gordon, 3rd ed. (New York, 1983), pp. 24-37.

[7] See Appendix 2, case 1.

subjected to the lord's approval, and made a matter of official record. The court's record rendered the promise of land legally binding and afforded children the written assurance of a share in the parental estate even though the father retained the use and control of his land until he died or suffered senility. As a result of the bargain, neither a son's subsequent marriage nor residence in a separate household necessarily diminished his father's authority over him. Instead, the practice of delayed devolution brought old and young into a partnership the very nature of which postponed the full independence of sons. Although they had rights in the land settled on them, the young had neither its management nor profits as long as their fathers remained alive.

In much the same way conditional devolution reflected the reluctance of the older generation to relinquish its control of production. What men and women did instead was to surrender the use, albeit not the control, of land to the young in return for lifelong payments in cash or in kind.[8] In this way the old and infirm made the use of their property contingent on support. And they went further: they arranged to have such bargains enrolled in the manor court, to which they would appeal if the payments due them fell in arrears. Thus any dereliction of duty to the old became subject to communal review, to possible censure and even intervention. The principal penalty comprised reversion of the land in question to the elderly. At their request courts ousted remiss tenants and, if necessary, disinherited children indifferent to parental care.

Admittedly, this is a formal view of the partnership between the generations. To be sure, it was not just a legal matter. Yet the transmission of resources from one generation to the next did involve the law in many ways. Given the older generation's quest for security, issues of property and tenure were hardly unimportant. Nor were the constraints of lordship and custom without practical consequence in the private lives of the old. They understood that their future well-being required planning and cooperative effort rather than reliance on providence or the good intentions of disinterested men. Of course, the collaboration of young and old did not remain everywhere the same. Much depended on the actual demands the old made on the young, whether for help with farming, for pensions, for companionship, or simply for masses and prayers when they died. Insofar as the requests differed in complexity and substance, so too did relations between the generations.

Nowhere was this more apparent than in the property settlements reached by fathers and sons. For example, there were settlements that

---

[8] For a fuller discussion, see Elaine Clark, "Some Aspects of Social Security in Medieval England," *Journal of Family History* 7 (1982) 307-320.

simply reflected a father's need for labour and a son's fear of disinheritance. In these situations fathers came into court and promised that they would never alienate the lands and property their sons expected to inherit.[9] The sons, in turn, agreed to serve their fathers "day and night," thus assuring the older men that they could rely on the labour of adult sons for life. Although no property changed hands, it invariably did when fathers decided to withdraw wholly or in part from farming. By any measure the decisions underscored the problem of financing consumption during retirement. To meet this need, the old both leased and sold land on credit to the young. The practice was of long standing and involved little more than the exchange of land for the payment of annuities in cash or in crops. At Ingatestone in Essex, during 1359, a father let all his land to his son in return for half of its yearly harvest.[10] The old man offered to pay part of the annual rents due to the manor's lady if his son performed all the labour services and also agreed not to use or even enter the barn where his father's crops were stored. When cash annuities were at issue, fathers generally expected payments to be made in quarterly installments throughout the year.

A different problem arose when fathers required day-to-day care. To secure help of this sort, the men settled land on sons in return for an adequate home and proper provision of food and clothing for themselves and their wives. A good example is provided by William Swift of Walsham-le-Willows (Suff.), who in 1411 surrendered twenty acres of land, meadow, and pasture to John his son.[11] The older man established the following conditions for the future. He and his wife were to have their lodging, food, and clothing for life; also an annual livery of four bushels of wheat and four of malt. On the day each parent died John was to disburse 2s. 6d. for thirty requiem masses, then within eight days to pay each parent's executor 7s. more. These requests linked the welfare of both parents to the labour of their son. Widows and widowers (see Table 1) made identical demands on the young. Indeed, it appears that the involvement of the younger generation in the lives of the old derived as much from economic need as from familial expectations about the duty of children to honour both father and mother. This duty remained in force even after parents died. Men and women believed that God allowed souls to linger in purgatory if no prayers were said on their behalf. As a result deathbed

---

[9] NRO 19499 (date illegible, probably 1276): "... filius predictus suus deserviret patri suo die et nocte prout decet in omnibus necessariis ejus et ad istam observandam tenementum suum obligat et quod non tenementum suum de domibus nec de arboribus deteriorat vel alienat infraude hereditatem."

[10] ERO, D/DP M 19 (20 June 1359).

[11] SRO, HA 504/1/10 (21 March 1411).

settlements of property often admonished the living to remember the dead by having masses celebrated for their souls.[12] What is more, peasants expected courts to expel sons from the land in question should they fail to honour a father's last wishes.[13]

Table 1				
Marital Status of Pensioners and Caretakers, 1258-1460				
	Pensioners		Caretakers	
Status	Pre-1350	Post-1350	Pre-1350	Post-1350
	%	%	%	%
Living with spouse	33.7	54.6	37.6	62.8
Men without spouses	33.7	24.7	58.8	34.7
Women without spouses	32.5	21.1	3.5	2.4
Number of persons	83	194	85	207

Of course, pensioners remained just as concerned about the future when they made plans with daughters. At law the young women did not automatically become the heads of households; their husbands did.[14] On this account the old sometimes feared family quarrels, should a daughter predecease them and her husband misappropriate property or neglect their support. To forestall conflict, parents defined the exact nature of a son-in-law's tenancy. In some cases he was to inherit his wife's holding; in others, simply to manage the land at the pleasure of the old.[15] In any event, parents kept the prerogatives of authority and decision-making in their own hands. They did so by limiting the discretionary control of the young over the disposition of the resources they had acquired at the retirement of the old. In sum, parents established the conditions on which children along with their spouses were to manage land in the present and hold it in the future.

There was, however, another side to this partnership between young and old. It involved the needs of childless peasants and the support strategies they planned with brothers, nephews, and nieces, with servants and parish priests. In fact, the evidence we have shows that the old would share houses and resources with a neighbour or friend in much the same

[12] NRO 5074 (8 July 1377), 4824 (29 September 1390); BL, Add. MS. 40167 (23 June 1393, 22 June 1413); NRO 19509 (10 November 1431).

[13] BL, Add. MS. 40167 (May 1390).

[14] NRO 4814 (2 February 1263).

[15] NRO 19505 (30 November 1312); BL, Add. MS. 40625 (9 October 1294), MS. Stowe 849 (18 October 1333). See also Appendix 2, cases 4-5.

way as they did with kin.[16] In so doing they had the sanction of courts as well as lords. Neither remained indifferent to the needs and expectations of pensioners. As long as they were legally competent and secured the lord's license they had the option of settling land on whomsoever they chose.[17] Their choices indicate the extent to which contract along with kinship afforded peasants the means to extend cooperative activity into old age.

Yet it must not be supposed that this cooperation invariably put childless pensioners at an advantage. Peasants understood only too well that a cottage and a few acres of land gave the aged poor little bargaining power. Indeed, the very paucity of their resources forced smallholders to hard choices. In 1425 at Winslow (Bucks.) a widower surrendered his messuage and a shop to a married couple in return for shelter, food, clothing, and the promise that, if he fell ill, they would put to his use the forty shillings he otherwise wanted to have distributed for the sake of his soul when he died.[18] This request, although unusual, was hardly unique. Smallholders often had to make concessions in order to secure the support they needed. When a widow at Norton (Suff.) bargained for her maintenance in 1456, she surrendered four and a half acres of land along with her house to a married couple, then offered to remember them in her will.[19] In much the same way childless couples offered caretakers small parcels of land and also household utensils, pots, pans, bedding, and used clothes.[20] If necessary, pensioners agreed to labour for the tenants of their land, at least for as long as it was physically possible.[21]

Needless to say, whenever substantial holdings were at issue, the old had the upper hand. They made demands of their own on the young and carefully planned the maximum use of available resources. We consequently see some caretakers compelled to follow the express instructions of the old in planting and harvesting land, in sharing its yield and storing its crops.[22] Pensioners claimed parcels of the "best land" for their own

---

[16] In 69 contracts, made between 1258 and 1349, 50 percent involved parents and children. In 142 contracts, made between 1350 and 1450, only 19 percent were made with children. Yet, as Dr. Hanawalt suggests, manorial records may overrepresent nonkin arrangements, since well-to-do peasants might make pension arrangements by will, and "wills usually entrusted the care of the old person to close kin rather than strangers." See Barbara A. Hanawalt, *The Ties That Bound: Peasant Families in Medieval England* (New York, 1986), pp. 232-234.

[17] For an example of parents at Codicote (Herts.) deciding to arrange a pension with neighbours rather than children living in the village, see BL, MS. Stowe 849 (27 March 1334, 18 October 1338).

[18] CUL, MS. Dd 7 22 aa (25 July 1425).

[19] SRO 553/60 (21 March 1457).

[20] NRO 10049 (14 September 1393).

[21] NRO 4871 (11 July 1397); BL, Add. MS. 40167 (6 December 1322).

[22] NRO 19498 (date illégible, 1275); PRO, SC 2 153/68 (23 November 1324); NRO, ING 74 (13 January 1355).

use and also requested gardens for vegetables, orchards for fruit, ponds for fish.[23] When the farmstead had livestock, the old expected to have milk, meat, and wool.[24] They wanted poultry kept for eggs, bees tended for honey, pigs fed to provide "bacon at Christmas."[25] And this was not all. The old demanded fuel, clothing, shoes, bedding, and food that was "pleasing." If so inclined, they requested vats for brewing and ovens for baking.[26] In addition, caretakers discharged debts for the elderly, arranged for burials, or found priests to celebrate requiem masses.[27]

Although not all pensioners were equally attentive to details of indebtedness or the welfare of their souls, all took an interest in how they would live with the young. Co-residence was the norm in the households of the aged poor. Some simply required a "small place for a bed," or a "garyte" in an attic and a place by the fire.[28] Others wanted a room to themselves, whether it was above the stables or adjacent to a barn.[29] Still others preferred rooms overlooking the garden or by the "stretedore."[30] The well-to-do wanted more. When houses had two floors as well as several rooms, the owners claimed specific areas for themselves and demanded access to kitchens, to pantries, to "latrines," to barns for storing fuel, to wells for drawing water and washing clothes.[31] The old also valued visits from friends, and so ordered caretakers to allow neighbours free entry to "bedchaumbres" and rooms called the "spence."[32] When pensioners wanted a dwelling entirely of their own, they reserved to themselves the use of a detached house variously styled the "besthous," the "newhous," or the "oldhous."[33] In every case pensioners assigned the upkeep

---

[23] SRO, HA 504/1/9 (21 February 1396); BL, Add. MS. 40167 (6 May 1356); CUL, MS. A 1.1. (1 May 1349); BL, Add. MS. 40625 (4 May 1323); GLRO, Acc 76/2413 (25 July 1390); NRO 4871 (10 November 1378); ERO D/D es M2 (7 July 1404).

[24] NRO, ING 70 (10 August 1355); ERO, D/DE s M3 (20 July 1415); SRO 533/60 (19 May 1435); NRO 19509 (25 January 1439).

[25] CUL, MS. A 1.1. (1 May 1449); NRO 19508 (1 November 1410), 19509 (25 January 1439), 19509 (30 June 1456); BL, Add. MS. 40625 (6 April 1393).

[26] NRO 19509 (25 January 1439), 8861 (12 March 1452), Hare 6330 (8 December 1452).

[27] SRO, HA 504/1/9 (7 July 1392), HA 12/C2/22 (18 October 1407); NRO 18484 (13 January 1413), DC 1 (14 September 1401), 18484 (13 January 1413).

[28] NRO 19599 (8 July 1454); BL, Add. MS. 40167 (17 June 1336).

[29] NRO 19509 (25 November 1443); BL, Add. MS. 40626 (17 May 1384).

[30] NRO 11262 (1 August 1434); ERO, D/DF y M1 (25 November 1396); CUL, MS. A 1.1. (6 May 1343); SRO, HA 504/1/9 (7 July 1392); NRO 11262 (19 May 1436).

[31] NRO 4871 (10 November 1398); ERO 19508 (21 September 1410); NRO 19508 (1 November 1410), ING 119 (1 August 1415); CUL, MS. Dd 7 22 aa (9 May 1458); NRO 8861 (25 April 1452), 18500 (1 August 1438), 11253 (19 May 1389), 11262 (1 August 1459).

[32] NRO 10049 (12 March 1391); ERO, D/DF y M1 (25 November 1396); NRO, DC 1 (30 November 1427), 8861 (1 August 1455); SRO, HA 12/C2/22 (18 October 1407).

[33] NRO 19509 (25 January 1439); Holkham Hall, Norf., Holkham Papers: Billingford (7 July 1402); SRO, HA 30 312/94 (4 April 1428); BL, Add. MS. 40167 (6 May 1356); NRO 11286 (18 October 1379).

of property to the young. At the same time the old threatened to oust caretakers if they were quarrelsome or failed to provide proper support.

Pensioners were no less cautious on those occasions when they made loans available to the young. The transactions entailed mortgages whereby children or neighbours "put land in gage" to the old so as to secure outstanding debts. As part of the bargain borrowers had to agree not only to repay the loan but also to maintain lenders in food, clothing, and lodging for life. In this way a pension easily served to cover the interest on the initial loan. At Gymingham (Norf.) in 1422 John Pylter resurrendered a messuage and twenty acres of land "in the name of mortgage" to Joan Talyour, a widow, while agreeing to pay her 13s. 4d. every Christmas for the following six years.[34] He promised, too, to feed, clothe, and shelter Joan for the remainder of her natural life. During 1442 Thomas Stonnard, also of Gymingham, stood party to the mortgage of ten acres of land whereby he secured the unspecified loans he owed his mother, then agreed to visit her when she fell ill, comfort her when she grew old, and bury her when she died.[35] Should he neglect the support of his mother in any way, Thomas was told that he would forfeit the land. In this case, and others like it, only the pensioner's death extinguished the borrower's debt.

All of this is to suggest that the elderly left little to chance when property was at issue. Whether they had cash on hand or not, all pensioners meant to offset economic uncertainty in the future. To this end they wanted the assurance of knowing that, even if a caretaker predeceased them, support would be forthcoming. Pension arrangements thus included one of two provisions. The first subjected the tenure of land to recall. In other words, if the new tenant died the holding reverted to the old; then he negotiated a pension with a partner of his choice. The second qualification, and the more usual one, made support encumbent on "whomsoever held the tenement," that is, on any tenant who, during the pensioner's lifetime, derived title from the surrender in question. Simply put, a caretaker held land on condition that he, his children, and the heirs maintain or arrange for the maintenance of the old. In this way pensioners encumbered land with a personal obligation but, at the same time, afforded caretakers the prospect of someday inheriting land. The exchange allowed the younger generation to "buy" an inheritance simply by pledging to maintain pensioners until they died. Put another way, the propertied old represented a potential source of credit for the young.

---

[34] NRO 5781 (14 September 1422).
[35] NRO 5794 (28 January 1442).

By now it should be clear that mutual self-interest, along with negotiation and careful compromise, characterized partnerships between young and old in rural society. Indeed, it appears that all maintenance strategies were contractual in nature and essentially pragmatic in purpose. They reflected the resource constraints facing any given household and, as such, required peasants to achieve a balance between the use of limited resources and the claims of successive generations. In this context mutual needs for security made it practical to link the welfare of the old to the devolution of property on the young. Delayed devolution enabled a household to sustain reciprocal services between the generations. Conditional devolution both supplemented and ensured familial support and, when necessary, allowed the aged to arrange a substitute for it. As a result, the task of caring for the old fell not only to their children but also to unrelated neighbours and friends. Since the role of caretaker was available for sharing with kin and nonkin alike, maintenance strategies remained inherently complex. At one level they corresponded to the relationships that developed in the family to carry out mutual support functions. At another they reflected the need to match productive resources with productive workers so as to ensure the welfare of the old and disabled.

In any event, a strong argument can be made that peasants were not without choices when planning for the future. Insofar as they had property, the aged had status and the means to bargain for support. To be sure, their plans remained subject to practical limitations, particularly in the decades after the Black Death when epidemic disease and recurrent plague occasioned high mortality. The premature death of children or spouses, the subsistence needs of the infirm, as well as the constraints of lordship and custom, variously affected the options that rural households had. It was with good reason, then, that the old and disabled chose to keep the control of property in their own hands until they died.

Appendix 1. Manor Courts

The records cited in this essay include the courts of thirty-five East Anglian manors in Essex, Norfolk, and Suffolk. These records are described in Clark, "Some Aspects of Social Security," pp. 317-319. Additional material has been drawn from courts in Middlesex and Berkshire as well as from the court books of the abbots of St. Albans for manors in the counties of Hertford and Buckingham. See the following: BL: Barnet, Cashio, Codicote, Park; BRO: Cookham; CUL: Abbots Langley, Winslow; GLRO: Harrow, Iselworth; PRO: Brightwalton.

Appendix 2. Family Agreements

Case 1.   NRO 19498 (6 October 1276): Horsham St. Faith (Norf.)

Walterus Heryng in plena curia reddit sursum in manu domini, de se et heredibus suis, unam peciam terre sue continentem unam dimidiam acram terre sive plus sive minus in eadem habeat, jacentem in Westfeld et occidens capud abuttat super le Wayngate, ad opus Stepheni filii sui et heredum suorum de corpore suo legitime provenientium ad faciendum servicia etc. salvo etc. Et si predictus Stephenus obierit sine herede de se legitime procreato predicta pecia terre revertatur Roberto Hering fratri suo et heredibus suis ad facienda etc. Et predictus Stephenus concedit in plena curia quod predictus Walterus pater suus habeat et teneat predictam terram in tota vita sua cum omnibus pertinenciis suis capiendo explecia etc. Et predictus Stephenus dat domino xviij denarios de fine pro ingressu et seysina habenda post decessum Walteri tenenda etc. facienda etc.

Case 2.   CUL, MS. Dd 7 22 aa (26 May 1339): Winslow (Bucks.)

Henricus Ailwyne per licenciam domini dimisit Hamoni filio suo j messuagium et unam virgatam terre cum pertinenciis tenenda eidem Hamoni et suis in villenagio et ad voluntatem domini ad terminum ejusdem Hamonis et post terminum ejusdem Hamonis predicta terra cum pertinenciis ad rectos heredes ipsius Henrici revertatur. Et dat pro termino habendo et pro licencia se maritandi xvj solidos. Et predictus Henricus dabit herietum precii v solidorum cum obierit per plegium predicti Hamonis, nisi predictus Henricus habeat aliquod animalium melioris precii de catallo suo proprio. Et predictus Hamo dabit herietum cum obierit. Et predictus Hamo sustinebit predictum patrem suum sicut decet competenter.

Case 3.   NRO 19505 (10 May 1317): Horsham St. Faith (Norf.)

Willelmus Bercarius in plena curia reddit sursum in manu domini quatuor acras terre sue arabilis et unam dimidiam acram prati et quicquid juris et clami in eisdem habuit ad opus Willelmi filii sui habenda et tenenda predicto Willelmo filio suo et heredibus suis ad facienda domino servicia et consuetudines etc. salvo etc. Et idem Willelmus dat domino dimidiam marcam de fine pro ingressu et seysina in predictis tenementis. Plegius de fine Johannes Messor. Pro predicto, ante redditionem, predictus Willelmus filius suus solvet predicto Willelmo patri suo iiij libras argenti, videlicet a festo Nativitatis Johannis Baptiste proximo post istam curiam futuro citra aliud festum Nativitatis ejusdem proximo sequens sine ulteriore dilatione. Et tenetur invenire predicto Willelmo patri suo dum vixerit esculenta et potum prout sibi et uxori sue et prout predicta tenementa exigent. Et solvet etiam predicto patri suo dum vixerit quolibet anno duo paria pannorum lineorum et duo paria sotularum videlicet quodlibet cum uno knoppe et unum par caligarum scilicet unum collarium vel unam supertunicam et unum pannum de blueto (?). Et idem Willelmus pater suus dum vixerit habebit in hospicio filii sui predicti unam vaccam suam propriam quam nunc habet et sex bidentes quos insupra habet, capiendo de eisdem vacca et bidentibus predictis commodationem et profectum et de eisdem disponendo prout sibi placuerit sine contradictione filii sui seu alicujus alterius.

Case 4.   BL, Add. MS. 40625 (9 October 1294): Park (Herts.)
Adam de Hukelford reddit sursum in manu domini totam terram suam. Et dominus seisivit inde Chelestriam filiam suam et Ricardum Ailward maritum dicte Chelestrie sibi et heredibus suis et si dicta Chelestria sine herede de se decedat dictus Ricardus terram teneat quoad vivat; post mortem dicti Ricardi terra revertatur ad veros heredes dicti Ade. Et est conventio inter Adam et Ricardum quod dictus Ricardus inveniet dicto Ade et uxori sui quamdiu vivent in cibis et potibus ut ipsi et uxori sui. Et si dictus Adam non sit contentus de vita et victu eorum Ricardus ei hospicium inveniet et qualibet septimana j buscelum duri bladi sicut in terra crescit, et preter qualibet die dominica unum oblum argenti, et preter quolibet anno dabit dicto Ade unum pannum precii ij solidorum vel ij solidos. Et Ricardus faciet servicia debita et consueta et dat pro gersuma et herieto dicti Ade decem solidos. Plegii Walterus le Hunte, Thomas de Smaleford, Rogerus Herlewyn, Gregorius Hildemar.

Case 5.   NRO 19505 (30 November 1312): Horsham St. Faith (Norf.)
Hubertus ad Portam reddit sursum in manu domini de se et heredibus suis unum messagium cum vj acris terre et iij rodis terre de tenemento ad opus Willelmi Heryng et Beatrice filie predicti Huberti et heredibus de se legitime procreatis. Et si contingat quod Beatrix filia predicti Huberti obiit sine herede de se et predicto Willelmo legitime procreato, tunc liceat predicto Willelmo desponsare aliam ad voluntatem domini optentam. Et si habeant heredem legitime procreatum ex tunc habeant et teneant predicta tenementa sibi et heredibus ut predictum est. Et si contingat quod predictus Willelmus obierit sine herede de se et predicta Beatrice legitime procreato et dicta Beatrix ipsum Willelmum supervixerit, tunc liceat predicte Beatrice capere alium maritum secundum voluntatem domini. Et si habeat heredem de se legitime procreatum, tunc dicti habeant et teneant predicta tenementa cum pertinenciis suis illis et heredibus suis ut predictum est. Et si omnes predicti obierint sine herede de se legitime procreato ut supradictum est, tunc omnia predicta tenementa remaneant cum pertinenciis suis omnibus Rogero filio predicti Huberti et heredibus sui inperpetuum. Et predicti Willelmus et Beatrix concedunt pro se et heredibus suis ad inveniendum omnia necessaria secundum posse illorum ut in victu et vestitu, sustentatione, domorum etc. predicto Huberto et Emme uxori sue in tota vita illorum. Et predicti Willelmus et Beatrix pro se et heredibus suis concedunt et cognoscunt se teneri predicto Rogero filio predicti Huberti et Margarete uxori sue in tota vita illorum in j quarterio et dimidio ordei, solvendis eisdem vel alteri illorum qui vel que supervixerit ad festum Omnium Sanctorum proximo sequens post obitum predicti Huberti et Emme uxoris sue. Et si contingat quod predictus Hubertus obierit ante Emmam uxorem suam aliter Emma ante Hubertum, tunc cognoscunt se teneri predicto Rogero et Margarete uxori sue vel alteri illorum qui vel que supervixerit alium in vj buscellis ordei solvendis, ut predictum est etc. Et predicti Willelmus et Beatrix dant domino ij marcas de fine pro ingressu et seysina habenda in predicta tenementa ut supradictum est etc. salvo etc. Plegii de fine Willelmus Bercarius et Walterus ....

Afterword

Michael M. Sheehan, CSB

Pontifical Institute of Mediaeval Studies

A set of essays such as that presented in this volume is at once an indication of the magnitude of the problem that is being investigated and of the work that remains to be done. It is true that to speak of Medieval Europe is to speak of a millenium in which many races, drawn from different cultural traditions, took on sufficient community of outlook and societal structure to be studied as a unit. None the less, such a complex set of traditions and the changes to be expected during such a long period necessarily imposed considerable variety on all aspects of human endeavour. Thus the study of aging and the aged can be expected to reveal a variety of understandings and usages even though the decline of powers associated with aging was a common experience and mankind might be expected to respond to that experience with some degree of consistency. Before any common patterns can be established – if they are to be established – it will be necessary to carry out many detailed studies of the various aspects of aging in medieval society. The results of several enquiries of this sort are presented here; from them it is already possible to draw a few conclusions, and to suggest other patterns of understanding and activity that future study may vindicate.

However varied the response to the aging process and to those who were old may have been during the Middle Ages, it is clear that the considerations of the philosophers and physicians of classical antiquity provided the essential structure of ideas for those medievals in the universities and schools – philosophers, theologians, physicians – who reflected on these matters. Medieval society as a whole may have been slow to recognize the elderly as a group, let alone as a class, or, in its efforts to provide for its weaker members, to see the senescent as a distinct set

Aging and the Aged in Medieval Europe, ed. Michael M. Sheehan, CSB. Papers in Mediaeval Studies 11 (Toronto: Pontifical Institute of Mediaeval Studies, 1990), pp. 201-207. © P.I.M.S., 1990.

within the population for whom special care was needed, but those who were familiar with Greek science and philosophy – and the philosophers of the faculties of arts were of significant number – were well aware that such was the case (Demaitre, Lewry). They understood that, where accident or disease had not ended life earlier, the senescent would increasingly suffer illness and the other *accidentia senectutis* (Demaitre, Dutton, Wortley), a process that would eventually lead to death, and that the process was normal. Its cause was seen to lie in a developing imbalance of the humours, an explanation that was to remain the standard until the nineteenth century (Demaitre). Thus, in a development that was the reverse of the experience of Western society during the past generation, senescence was approached as a scientific question before it was identified as a social problem or as a subject of analysis by the social scientist. It is important, however, not to overstress the abstract quality of medieval gerontology: the fact that the scholars under discussion reflected much on how to delay the onset of old age is evidence enough of the trials they knew it to bring (Demaitre, Lewry). Their theories and regimes of medical practice were intended to alleviate physical pain and the mental and emotional debilities of those who already suffered from its onset.

Classical authors had tended to divide the life course into ages or periods characterized by different physical, mental, and emotional qualities. There might be four, six, seven, or many more periods. (Some authors tended to divide either the stage of growth or that of decline into smaller units.) Though the different ages were functionally specified and that specification can sometimes be shown to have been socially constructed (Rosenthal, Signer, Talmage), each age was also assigned a set of years to which it applied. As was the case in the choice of terms to characterize the ages of man, so the years allotted to each period varied considerably. This usage remained a commonplace among medieval thinkers (Demaitre, Lewry, Signer, Talmage). Furthermore, the chronological definition of old age was not entirely without practical significance: in various parts of Europe, those who were sixty or seventy might be excused from military or other civic duty and from the payment of taxes (Demaitre, Herlihy, Rosenthal). Furthermore, there seemed a general agreement that the portion of life to which one or other term derived from the word for "old" applied was divided between one period, when the aging person might be expected to be wise and humanly fulfilled whatever his physical disability, and another, when he was simply old and decrepit. (They would correspond respectively to the "elderly" and the "aged" in Laslett's terminology.)

Philosophers and theologians were moved to pursue the matter further, to consider whether there were a purpose in the process of aging, whether the activity of those years, when higher powers functioned somewhat more freely than was the case in youth, when "this tent of clay weighs down the teeming mind," were of special value. All through the Middle Ages, as before and since, there was the notion that the elderly are wise, that to be wise is to be old or at least to possess a quality that is often associated with the elderly. The discussion of precedence between the elder who was not especially wise and the young man who was learned found in Jewish Responsa literature is evidence of that attitude (Signer). More basic evidence is to be observed in the rich content of the English word "old" and its cognates in other languages: whatever negative connotation – the worn out, the useless, the decrepit – the word may carry, there is always the notion of wisdom, trustworthiness, even of comfort (Amos, Signer, Wortley). Medieval philosophers reflecting on the ages of the life course saw a period variously named, associated with maturity, when a special development of mind could and should occur, a development that was good in itself and that more than compensated for the shrinking of physical competences. Man's spiritual powers, after all, were what distinguished him from the lower animals, so it was to be expected that special importance should be attached to the period of life in which intellectual powers were thought to reach their highest achievement, whatever the pain of arthritic joints might have been.

Furthermore, in the religious traditions of that world, be they Christian, Jewish, or Muslim, man had a destiny after his life in this world, a destiny to which his later years were specially related. Since the life after death was seen as a time of unimaginable fulfilment, it was a problem for some whether old age, which delayed the enjoyment of that life, were desirable. But here, again, the value of those years of comparative calm and growth of the mind was placed in context, for that development – it might be the growth of the active intellect, in a Jewish tradition, or the generative process of assuming those childlike qualities of which Christ spoke, in the Eastern monastic tradition – decided the quality of life after death and, as such, was potentially of great value (Nitecki, Talmage, Wortley). On the other hand, it was possible to see old age as a time of spiritual corruption, when the worst qualities of a person might assert themselves, qualities that might reach beyond death as well (Nitecki). This whole area is rich in possibility for further research: the tension between a long life and the desire for the vision of God to which St. Paul referred, and the degree of recognition of the value of a long life as preparation for that vision, are but two of the many problems that present themselves to the historian.

From all of this it becomes evident that many medieval thinkers made an important and, on the whole, essentially consistent distinction between the old and the very old (*senectus* and *senex*), between those, on the one hand, whose physical powers had ceased to augment, or had begun to decline, who found it agreeable to withdraw somewhat from ordinary activity, but who enjoyed a period of mental growth, of specifically human activity, and those, on the other hand, whose powers were generally in decline and whose days were marked by depression and confusion of the mind. Thus the aging process was seen to pass through two final steps, one in which the balance of disability and increased mental powers was often, though not always, struck in favour of the latter (Talmage), and one of inevitable and inexorable decline.

The notion that the life course was divided into different periods and that those periods could be described in both functional and chronological terms is also to be found in the belles-lettres of the period. These authors also wrestled with the problem of what is good and what is bad in being old. As mentioned above, the very words that were used speak of an attitude to old age; the unravelling of this very complex tale is likely to prove a difficult but rewarding task. Thus a study of the corpus of Old English literature reveals a neutral, often positive, but rarely negative attitude to the old (Amos), one that seems to have shifted in English usage by the sixteenth century. On the other hand, vernacular literature of fourteenth-century England showed a very negative attitude both to the process of growing old and to the elderly, a burden, often a disgusting burden, to others as to themselves. Yet a notable change of attitude occurred in the century that followed (Nitecki). In both cases the reader is aware of reflection on the behavioural aspect of aging, and one is led to ask whether these patterns were simply usages that were literary commonplaces currently in vogue or there were some deeper social cause, related perhaps to political, economic, or demographic developments (Dutton). Many further studies in detail must be made, however, before the complex evolution of attitudes in these regards can be fully described, or any explanation of its causes attempted.

It does seem reasonable, however, to suggest that the size of the proportion of population perceived to be elderly played some role in the formation of attitudes. Thus it is to be desired that the modern scholar have information on this matter that is as exact as possible. But, since the age at which medievals were seen to be old was functional rather than chronological (Clark, Dutton, Rosenthal, Signer), and since it is virtually impossible to estimate the numbers of those whose disabilities (or wisdom) were such that they were considered to have entered the elderly class, it is unlikely that the matter will have a successful issue if the problem is posed in strictly medieval terms. Abandoning the functional measurement in favour of the chronological seems necessary, if some idea is to be obtained of the proportion of adults in society that can be considered elderly in modern terms. Here much work will have to be done and considerable ingenuity applied in the detailed studies that are needed. In an example provided here, data derived from four different kinds of evidence, relating to four geographical areas and periods, yield important though limited results, some of which might provide the basis for an hypothesis on medieval longevity: areas of dry, temperate climate seem to have been conducive to a considerably longer life than those that, whatever their economic advantage, provided inferior health conditions; periods of plague seemed to create a situation in which the proportion of elderly increased, an indication of stronger resistance to infection by that part of the population, whether it is to be explained by their medical condition or by the less exposed position in which they lived (Russell). In another, more sharply focused study, that of the Knights Templar, the brutal light of evidence from the trials that destroyed them (1307-1311) reveals much of the age pattern of the community: a small sample, skewed by the fact that the order had recruited many young members after the disaster of 1294, shows that within this rather special group a higher proportion than was to be expected lived to be sixty or more (Gilmour-Bryson).

These Templar records have a special advantage in that they make it possible to shift perspective from conclusions on medieval attitudes to aging and the aged, discussed thus far, to an examination of the positions the elderly held or assumed in medieval society. Here, too, it is possible to suggest several conclusions and hypotheses for future research. In the case of the Templars, the responsible role of older members becomes evident: highest authority was usually exercised by those who were fifty or over. Perhaps even more interesting: decisions as to suitability for responsible positions seem to have overridden the claims of status: older members of the *servientes* class often held high office (Gilmour-Bryson). In both the age and the comparative ease of assumption of high office by members of inferior classes this pattern may well be found to have been common in the medieval Church, though detailed studies of ecclesiastical institution, region, and period will be necessary before conclusions touching this matter are made.

The significance in broad societal terms of the contribution of monasteries and other ecclesiastical institutions in receiving those who wished to retire from the world partly or with complete dedication to religious life remains to be investigated, but enough has been seen to show that some aristocratic women were able to use them, rather than their families, as the social base for lives remarkable for both length and vigour (Dutton, Labarge).

The old age of officeholders produced varied responses. Kings by and large were allowed to remain heads of state until the end of their lives. Withdrawal from active campaigning and, to a greater or lesser extent, from government was often the case, and the example of the elderly king in the hands of old and ineffective counsellors or dominated by the unscrupulous was not unknown (Dutton). Other officeholders experienced partial or complete retirement at their request or as demanded of them. Thus late medieval English bishops, pleading old age, obtained permission to withdraw from some of their civil obligations. Others, like parish rectors, were required to work with an assistant or to withdraw completely as their ability to render proper services diminished. In the case of these ecclesiastical retirements, be they partial or complete, income was maintained. Such does not seem to have been the case with the English coroner who, by the fifteenth century, was simply forced to retire when age was judged to limit effectiveness (Rosenthal). The elderly citizen was sometimes excused from obligations of office, military service, or even taxes – and this specifically in terms of age rather than disability (Demaitre, Herlihy, Rosenthal), a usage redolent of several contemporary ones, the generality of which remains to be examined.

In the private sector, the role of the elderly and the solution of the problems that flowed from their limitations are mainly to be seen within the family circle. (It will be remembered that medieval religious teaching on respect and support of parents was extended to all the elderly, but that it was seen to be most binding in the case of older members of the family.) Here, in the case of males, the degree to which a patriarchal regime was realized in the society in which they lived was of major importance. Thus, in the study of the exercise of authority by older men in Florence and its region in the fourteenth century, it becomes clear that they continued to exercise control of family fortunes, though different economic conditions implied differences in financial stability. In the countryside, where fortunes were based on land, heads of families were able to maintain a unified estate and to direct it with financial success until the end of their lives. In the city, on the other hand, the responsible employment of younger members in family enterprises involved a sharing of wealth, with the result that members of the older generation often found themselves in financial difficulties. In both cases, however, the elders were ordinarily expected to remain in complete or partial control until death (Herlihy).

North European family structures were somewhat different from those of Italy, and the position of the elderly might be expected to assume different forms there. In this region as in all parts of Europe, studies in detail will be needed. A very interesting example is provided by a local study of English peasants, where a position for the elderly radically different from the Florentine model obtained, one with significant parallels to some of the arrangements currently employed in Western society. In principle, it involved short- or medium-term planning for the problems that would develop as capacity for work and self-care diminished with age. Solutions were invented that involved a nice example of intergenerational cooperation buttressed by contract (Clark). The question was usually posed in terms of the tenant whose failing powers made it impossible for him to fulfill his obligations to his lord; loss of land and of livelihood was the likely consequence. Various solutions were invented. They extended through partial to complete retirement with regularly assured housing (usually though not always co-residential), nourishment, and care during the remainder of life; they also occasionally guaranteed the free disposal of some property by testament, and made provision for the soul in the life after death. Usually family members of the next generation were principals to the agreement, and their effective desire to honour their parents was reinforced by the fact that the likelihood of their succession to family property was enhanced. On the other hand, the detail with which the rights of the older generation were stipulated and the seriousness of failure to honour the agreement (heirs might well see their customary right of inheritance defeated) leaves little doubt that the elderly saw the wisdom of exploiting their position as landholders to coax the younger members of their family into the *pietas* that, in a more perfect world, might have been expected. Furthermore, an extrafamilial authority, the lord of the manor or a local court, enforced the terms of the contract. Thus the elderly who had this institution at their disposition were in a position to arrange for their future with dignity and with some hope of reasonable comfort. In many ways, these systems of self-help for those facing the loss of strength that we, if not they, associate with aging, are among the most interesting that have been presented in this volume. This development marks a significant medieval example of planning for old age.

Did intergenerational contract to ensure the position of the elderly survive the radical economic changes at the end of the Middle Ages? This is but one of the many questions that remain.

A Preliminary Bibliography on
Aging and the Aged in Medieval Europe

Treatises from Antiquity and the Middle Ages

Albert the Great. *De aetate sive De juventute et senectute liber.* In *B. Alberti Magni Opera omnia.* Vol. 9. Ed. Auguste Borgnet. Paris, 1890. Pp. 305-321.

————. *Liber de morte et vita.* Ibid., pp. 345-373.

Averroes. *Compendium libri Aristotelis De causis longitudinis et brevitatis vite.* In *Averrois Cordubensis Compendia librorum Aristotelis qui Parva naturalia vocantur.* Ed. Emily Ledyard Shields and Harry Blumberg. Corpus philosophorum medii aevi. Corpus commentariorum Averrois in Aristotelem. Versionum latinarum vol. 7. Cambridge, Mass. 1949. Pp. 129-149.

————. "Book Three: Length and Shortness of Life." In *Epitome of Parva naturalia.* Trans. Harry Blumberg. Corpus philosophorum medii aevi. Corpus commentariorum Averrois in Aristotelem. Versio anglica vol. 7. Cambridge, Mass., 1961. Pp. 54-61.

Bacon, Roger. *De balneis senum et seniorum.* In *Opera hactenus inedita Rogeri Baconi.* Fasc. 9. Ed. Andrew G. Little and Edward Withington. Oxford, 1928. Pp. 96-97.

————. *De retardatione accidentium senectutis.* Ibid., pp. 1-89.

————. *De universali regimine senum et seniorum.* Ibid., pp. 90-95.

Boncompagno da Signa. *De malo senectutis et senii.* "Il *De malo senectutis et senii* di Boncompagno da Signa," ed. Francesco Novati. *Rendiconti della Reale accademia dei Lincei,* Classe di scienze morali, storiche, e filologiche, 5th ser. 1 (1892) 49-67.

Cicero, Marcus T. *Cato maior De senectute.* Ed. and trans. J. G. F. Powell. Cambridge, 1988.

Aging and the Aged in Medieval Europe, ed. Michael M. Sheehan, CSB. Papers in Mediaeval Studies 11 (Toronto: Pontifical Institute of Mediaeval Studies, 1990), pp. 209-214. © P.I.M.S., 1990.

Ficino, Marsilio. *Liber de vita longa.* In *De vita libri tres.* Venice, 1498; repr. with critical apparatus by Martin Plessner, Hildesheim, 1978. Fols. 21-41.

Henryson, Robert. "The Praise of Age." In *The Poems of Robert Henryson.* Ed. Denton Fox. Oxford, 1981. Pp. 165-167, 449-452.

Innocent III. *Lothario cardinalis (Innocentii III) De miseria humane conditionis.* Ed. Michele Maccarrone. Lugano, 1955.

––––––. *De miseria condicionis humane.* Ed. and trans. Robert E. Lewis. The Chaucer Library. Athens, Ga., 1978.

Maimonides, Moses. *The Preservation of Youth.* Trans. (from the original Arabic of the "Essays on Health") Hirsch L. Gordon. New York, 1958.

Maximianus. *The Elegies of Maximianus.* Ed. Richard Webster. Princeton, 1900.

Peter of Spain. *Translatio vetus libri "De longitudine et brevitate vitae" (vocatus "De morte et vita" in corpore vetustiori) cum expositione Petri Hispani.* In *Obras filosóficas.* Vol. 3. Ed. Manuel Alonso. Consejo superior de investigaciones cientificas, Istituto de filosofia "Luis Vives." Ser. A, núm. 4. Madrid, 1952. Pp. 413-490.

Sedulius Scottus. *Senex et adolescens.* Ed. Siegmund Hellmann in his *Sedulius Scottus.* Quellen und Untersuchungen zur lateinischen Philologie des Mittelalters 1.1. Munich, 1906; repr. Frankfurt, 1966. P. 120.

Villanova, Arnaldus de. *De conservanda iuventute et retardanda senectute.* In *Opera omnia.* Lyons, 1509. Fols. 86r-90v.

––––––. *Epistola de accidentibus senectutis et senii.* Ed. Magninus Mediolanensis in his *Regimen sanitatis.* Strasbourg, 1503. Fols. 114r-128r.

Zerbi, Gabriele. *G. Zerbi Veronensis ad Innocentium VIII Pon. Max. Gerontocomia feliciter incipit.* Rome, 1489.

––––––. *Gabriele Zerbi, Gerontocomia: On the Care of the Aged, and Maximianus, Elegies on Old Age and Love.* Trans. Levi R. Lind. Memoirs of the American Philosophical Society 182. Philadelphia, Pa. 1988.

Modern Studies

Ackerknecht, Erwin H. "Geriatriegeschichtliches." *Praxis* 65 (1976) 320-323.

Ariès, Philippe. "Une histoire de la vieillesse? Entretien avec Philippe Ariès." *Communications,* 37: *Le Continent gris* (1983) 47-54.

––––––. *The Hour of our Death.* Trans. Helen Weaver. New York, 1981.

––––––. *Western Attitudes towards Death.* Baltimore, 1974.

Acsádi, György T., and Janós Nemeskéri. *A History of the Human Life Span and Mortality.* Trans. K. Balás. Budapest, 1970.

Beauvoir, Simone de. *Old Age.* Trans. Patrick O'Brian. London, 1972. (See pp. 124-147 et passim.)

――――. *La Vieillesse.* Paris, 1970. (See pp. 135-159 et passim.)

Beitscher, Jan K. "The Aged in Medieval Limousin." *Proceedings of the Fourth Annual Meeting of the Western Society for French History, 11-13 November 1976, Reno, Nevada.* Ed. Joyce D. Falk. Santa Barbara, Ca., 1977. Pp. 45-52.

Berman, Lorna, and Irina Sobkowska-Ashcroft. *Images and Impressions of Old Age in the Great Works of Western Literature (700 B.C.-1900 A.D.): An Analytical Compendium.* Lewiston, N.Y., 1987.

Boll, Franz. "Die Lebensalter: Ein Beitrag zur antiken Ethologie und zur Geschichte der Zahlen." *Neue Jahrbücher für das klassische Altertum, Geschichte und deutsche Literatur und für Pädagogik* 16 (1913) 89-145.

Bullough, Vern, and Cameron Campbell. "Female Longevity and Diet in the Middle Ages." *Speculum* 55 (1980) 317-325.

Burstein, Sona R. "The 'Cure' of Old Age: Codes of Health." *Geriatrics* 10 (1955) 328-332.

――――. "Care of the Aged in England: From Mediaeval Times to the End of the 16th Century." *Bulletin of the History of Medicine* 22 (1948) 738-746.

Chew, Samuel C. *The Pilgrimage of Life.* New Haven, 1962. (See pp. 144-173 et passim.)

Clark, Elaine. "Some Aspects of Social Security in Medieval England." *Journal of Family History* 7 (1982) 307-320.

Coffman, George R. "Old Age from Horace to Chaucer: Some Literary Affinities and Adventures of an Idea." *Speculum* 9 (1934) 249-277.

Costa, Antonio. "Echi celsiani e spiriti nuovi in un libro quattrocentesco d'igiene dell'età senile (il *De vita producenda sive longa* de Marsilio Ficino)." *Archivio "De vecchi" per l'anatomia patologica* 62 (1977) 223-236.

Dutton, Paul E. "Awareness of Historical Decline in the Carolingian Empire, 800-887." Ph.D. Diss., University of Toronto, 1981.

Finley, Moses I. "Les Personnes âgées dans l'antiquité classique." *Communications,* 37: *Le Continent gris* (1983) 31-45.

――――. "The Venetian Republic as a Gerontocracy: Age and Politics in the Renaissance." *Journal of Medieval and Renaissance Studies* 8 (1978) 157-178.

Folts, James D. "Senescence and Renascence: Petrarch's Thoughts on Growing Old." *Journal of Medieval and Renaissance Notes* 10 (1980) 207-237.

Fowler, David H., et al. "Themes of Old Age in Preindustrial Western Literature." *Old Age in Preindustrial Society.* Ed. Peter N. Stearns. New York, 1982. Pp. 19-45.

Freeman, Joseph T. *Aging: Its History and Literature.* New York, 1979.

Gavazzi, Milovan. "The Tradition of Killing Old People: Prolegomena to a Revised Methodical Treatment of the Subject." *Folklore Today: A Festschrift for Richard M. Dorson.* Ed. Linda Degh et al. Bloomington, Ind., 1976. Pp. 175-180.

Ghellinck, Joseph de. "Iuventus, gravitas, senectus." *Studia mediaevalia in honorem admodum reverendi patris Raymundi Josephi Martin.* Bruges, [1948]. Pp. 39-59.

Gilbert, Creighton G. "When Did a Man in the Renaissance Grow Old?" *Studies in the Renaissance* 14 (1967) 7-32.

Grmek, Mirko D. *On Ageing and Old Age: Basic Problems and Historic Aspects of Gerontology and Geriatrics.* Monographiae biologicae 5.2. The Hague, 1958.

Gruman, Gerald J. *A History of Ideas about the Prolongation of Life: The Evolution of Prolongevity Hypotheses to 1800.* Philadelphia, 1966.

Hareven, Tamara K. "The Life Course and Aging in Historical Perspective." *Aging and Life Course Transitions: An Interdisciplinary Perspective.* Ed. Tamara K. Hareven and Kathleen J. Adams. London, 1982. Pp. 1-26.

Harper, Richard. "A Note on Corrodies in the Fourteenth Century." *Albion* 15 (1983) 95-101.

Henke, Winfried, and Karl-Heinz Nedder. "Zur Anthropologie der fränkischen Bevölkerung von Rubenach." *Bonner Jahrbuch* 181 (1981) 395-419.

Herlihy, David. "Growing Old in the Quattrocento." *Old Age in Preindustrial Society.* Ed. Peter N. Stearns. New York, 1982. Pp. 104-118.

———. "Vieillir au Quattrocento." *Annales E.S.C.* 24 (1969) 1338-1352.

Herlihy, David, and Christiane Klapisch-Zuber. *Les Toscans et leurs familles: Une étude du catasto florentin de 1427.* Paris, 1978. (See pp. 350-392, 606-611.)

Hofmeister, Adolf. "*Puer, iuvenis, senex.* Zum Verständnis der mittelalterlichen Altersbezeichnungen." *Papsttum und Kaisertum: Forschungen zur politischen Geschichte und Geisteskultur des Mittelalters Paul Kehr zum 65. Geburtstag dargebracht.* Ed. Albert Brackmann. Munich, 1926. Pp. 287-316.

Homans, George C. *English Villagers of the Thirteenth Century.* Cambridge, Mass., 1941. (See pp. 149-159.)

Howell, Trevor H. "Avicenna and the Care of the Aged." *The Gerontologist* 12 (1972) 424-426.

Jones, George F. "The 'Signs of Old Age' in Oswald von Wolkenstein's *Ich sieh und hör* (Klein No. 5)." *Modern Language Notes* 89 (1974) 767-787.

Jones, John W. "Observations on the Origin of the Divisions of Man's Life into Stages." *Archaeologia* 35 (1853) 167-189.

Kiszely, István. *The Anthropology of the Lombards.* 2 vols. Trans. Catherine Simán. B.A.R. International Series 61.1-2. Oxford, 1979.

Laslett, Peter. "The History of Aging and the Aged." *Family Life and Illicit Love in Earlier Generations.* Ed. Peter Laslett. Cambridge, 1977. Pp. 174-213.

―――. "Societal Development and Aging." *Handbook of Aging and the Social Sciences.* Ed. Robert H. Binstock and Ethel Shanas. New York, 1976. Pp. 87-116.

Lehr, John Robert. "The Old Man in Fourteenth and Fifteenth-Century English Literature." Ph.D. Diss., University of Toronto, 1979.

Lorcin, Marie-Thérèse. "Vieillesse et vieillissement vus par les médecins du moyen âge." *Bulletin du Centre d'histoire economique et sociale de la région lyonnaise* 4 (1983) 5-22.

Löw, Leopold. *Die Lebensalter in der jüdischen Literatur.* Szegedin, 1875. (See pp. 23-36.)

Lumbreras, Pedro. "*De senectute:* quid divus Thomas senserit." *Angelicum* 46 (1969) 318-329.

Menard, Philippe. "Le Coeur dans les poésies de Bernard de Ventadour." *Actes du 5ᵉ Congrès international de langue et littérature d'Oc et d'études franco-provençales, Nice, 6-12 septembre 1967.* Ed. Gérard Moignet and Roger Lassalle. Publications de la Faculté des lettres et des sciences humaines de Nice 13. Paris, 1974. Pp. 182-197.

Minois, Georges. *Histoire de la vieillesse de l'antiquité à la Renaissance.* Paris, 1987.

Niebyl, Peter H. "Old Age, Fever, and the Lamp Metaphor." *Journal of the History of Medicine and Allied Sciences* 26 (1971) 351-368.

Nitecki, Alicia K. "The Convention of the Old Man's Lament in *The Pardoner's Tale.*" *Chaucer Review* 16 (1981-1982) 76-84.

Old Age in Preindustrial Society. Ed. Peter N. Stearns. New York, 1982. (See pp. 1-18.)

Patlagean, Evelyne. *Pauvrété économique et pauvreté sociale à Byzance, 4ᵉ-7ᵉ siècles.* Paris, 1977. (See pp. 95-101: "Durées de vie.")

Planche, Alice. "Le Corps en vieillesse: Regards sur la poésie du moyen âge tardif." *Razo* 4 (1984) 39-57.

Roots of Modern Gerontology and Geriatrics. Ed. Gerald J. Gruman. New York, 1979.

Rosenthal, Joel T. "Aristocratic Widows in Fifteenth-Century England." *Women and the Structure of Society: Selected Research from the Fifth Berkshire Conference on the History of Women.* Ed. Barbara J. Harris and JoAnn K. McNamara. Durham, N.C., 1984. Pp. 36-47, 259-260.

―――. "Mediaeval Longevity: The Secular Peerage, 1350-1500." *Population Studies* 27 (1973) 287-293.

Sears, Elizabeth L. "The Ages of Man in Medieval Art." Ph.D. Diss., Yale University, 1982.

————. *The Seven Ages of Man.* Princeton, N.J., 1986.

Simmons, Leo W. *The Role of the Aged in Primitive Societies.* New Haven, 1945.

Sprandel, Rolf. *Altersschicksal und Altersmoral: Die Geschichte der Einstellungen zum Altern nach der Pariser Bibelexegese des 12.-16. Jahrhunderts.* Monographien zur Geschichte des Mittelalters 22. Stuttgart, 1981.

————. "Alter und Todesfurcht nach der spätmittelalterlichen Bibelexegese." *Death in the Middle Ages.* Ed. Herman Braet and Werner Verbeke. Mediaevalia Lovaniensia, Ser. 1, Studia 9. Louvain, 1983. Pp. 107-116.

Steadman, John M. "Old Age and *contemptus mundi* in The Pardoner's Tale." *Medium Ævum* 33 (1964) 121-130.

Thompson, John D., and Grace Golden. *The Hospital: A Social and Architectural History.* New Haven, 1975.

Tillotson, John H. "Pensions, Corrodies, and Religious Houses: An Aspect of the Relations of Crown and Church in Early Fourteenth-Century England." *Journal of Religious History* 8 (1974) 127-143.

Trexler, Richard C. "A Widows' Asylum of the Renaissance: The Orbatello of Florence." *Old Age in Preindustrial Society.* Ed. Peter N. Stearns. New York, 1982. Pp. 119-149.

Wackernagel, Wilhelm. *Die Lebensalter: Ein Beitrag zur vergleichenden Sitten- und Rechtsgeschichte.* Basel, 1862.

Zeman, Frederick D. "The *Gerontocomia* of Gabriele Zerbi: A Fifteenth-Century Manual of Hygiene for the Aged." *Journal of the Mount Sinai Hospital* [New York] 10 (1944) 710-716.

Index

References to footnotes take the form "84n46," i.e. "page 84, note 46." The following abbreviations are used: abp./Abp. for archbishop, bp./Bp. for bishop, St. for saint.

Aachen 78, 86
Abbot's Ripton 181
abbots, retirement of 180
Abingdon Chronicle 101
Abravanel, Isaac 51, 56-58, 60, 61n29
Abruzzi, trials in 137
accidentia senectutis 10, 202
Adalhard 83n43
Adam of Buckfield 26-28
Adalhaid, daughter of Charlemagne 94
adolescence 10, 29, 173n1, 185
Africa, Roman North 121
Aeneid: see Virgil
agaric 20
age 176; vices of 109
age and death 115
age reporting 145n6, 146
aged: alienation of 183; attitudes to 73, 81, 107-116 passim; burial of 196, 197; control of property by 143-158 passim, 191-198 passim; debilities of 202; debts of 150-153, 189, 191; as a figure of spiritual corruption 113; housing of 195-197: "besthous" 196, co-residence 196, 207, "newhous" 196, "oldhous" 196; insecurity of 191; isolation of 108, 110, 112; Jewish community and 39-48 passim; longing for death by 115; lustfulness of 113; maintenance strategies of 191-198; mental characteristics

of 108-109; medical treatment of 3-22 passim; obligation to visit 197; population 119-127 passim, 142; poverty of 143-158 passim, 184; provision of care for 44-48, 190, 193, 195-198, 207; provision of clothing and shoes for 195-197; provision of food and drink for 14, 193-199; provision of fuel for 196; respect due to 45-47; set apart 174; vulnerability of 108, 110, 112; wills of 189; wisdom of 32, 45-46, 61-62, 97, 102-103, 203
aging 143, 145; attitudes to 48, 49n1, 64, 72-73; fear of 116; medical treatment of 3-22 passim; physical ills of 108; significance of 9-10, 109; study of 23-38 passim; symptoms of 9n25
aging flesh 113
aging process 9, 41, 72; significance of 109
Agnellus of Pisa 164
Agobard of Lyons 90
Agus, Irving 40
Aha bar Jacob, Rabbi 61
Ailred of Rievaulx 163-165
Ailward, Richard 200
Ailwyne, Henry 199
aktēmonsunē 72
Albert the Great, St. 9n26, 16, 23, 31-36; *De aetate* 32
Albertus Magnus: *see* Albert the Great